Public Sector Reforms in India

Public Sector Reforms in India
New Role of the District Officer

CHANDAN SINHA

SAGE Publications
Los Angeles ▪ London ▪ New Delhi ▪ Singapore

First published in 2007 by

Sage Publications India Pvt Ltd
B1/I1, Mohan Cooperative Industrial Area
Mathura Road, New Delhi 110 044
www.sagepub.in

Sage Publications Inc
2455 Teller Road
Thousand Oaks, California 91320

Sage Publications Ltd
1 Oliver's Yard
55 City Road
London EC1Y 1SP

Sage Publications Asia-Pacific Pte Ltd
33 Pekin Street
#02-01 Far East Square
Singapore 048763

Published by Vivek Mehra for Sage Publications India Pvt Ltd, typeset in 11/16 pt Century Schoolbook by Star Compugraphics Private Limited, Delhi and printed at Chaman Enterprises, New Delhi.

Library of Congress Cataloging-in-Publication Data Available

ISBN: 978-0-7619-3639-8 (Pb)   978-81-7829-804-7 (India-Pb)

The Sage Team: Sugata Ghosh and Anita Kakar

A customer is the most important visitor on our premises. He is not dependent on us. We are dependent on him. He is not an interruption in our work. He is the purpose of it. He is not an outsider in our business. He is part of it. We are not doing him a favour by serving him. He is doing us a favour by giving us an opportunity to do so.

Mohandas Karamchand Gandhi

The two most engaging powers of an author are, to make new things familiar and familiar things new.

Samuel Johnson

to my parents
Ravi Shekhar and Sheela
with
love and gratitude

A House for Pramila Sabar

Early on 31 October 2004, while serving as district officer of Paschim Medinipur, I, along with a team of officers, visited Lohamelia, a Lodha village. This was an assessment visit to prepare a proposal for a special low-cost housing project for the Lodhas, a primitive tribe.

After visiting most of the houses in Lohamelia, as I was about to get into the vehicle, a determined looking middle-aged woman in a red sari stepped out of the small crowd and said, 'You will have to come and see the condition of my hut. You will have to give me a house.' I stopped, and Pramila Sabar went on. When she had heard that I was in Lohamelia she did not leave for work but had waited for me. A landless labourer, she had forsaken her day's wages so that she may request me for a house. I could not leave without visiting her homestead.

Pramila and her husband, Hari, lived in a thatched, polythene covered, windowless mud hut about 12 ft long and 10 ft wide. Around their tumbledown hut bloomed bright orange marigolds. In their tiny kitchen garden, enclosed by a few young jackfruit and mango trees, they had planted potatoes, peas and string beans. These were all signs of industry, perseverance and hope.

In mid-January 2005, the state government sanctioned the special project and provided Rs 4.53 crore to build 2000 low-cost houses for the Lodhas in Paschim Medinipur. On 27 February 2005, Shri Buddhadev Bhattacharya, the Chief Minister of West Bengal, inaugurated the first cluster of 40 houses in Lohamelia. The first set of house keys he handed over was to Pramila Sabar, for the house she not only demanded but also helped build.

Contents

Acknowledgements

I would like to thank several institutions and persons who have contributed to the writing of this book.

Lal Bahadur Shastri National Academy of Administration, Mussoorie, during my four-and-a-half years on its faculty, provided opportunities to study and observe at close quarters district administration in different parts of the country. To the Maxwell School of Citizenship and Public Affairs, Syracuse University, which I attended in 2005–06, and its faculty members, I owe a special word of thanks. Prof. Jeffery Strausmann unhesitatingly wrestled with my ideas about the evolution of the district officer in India and helped me beat them into shape. Prof. Alasdair Roberts provided invaluable guidance and insights into the processes of public sector reforms around the world, *and* advice for planning the book. Prof. Jeremy Shiffman's perspectives on the relationship between NGOs and government and his insistence upon conceptual rigour proved most useful. Ms Catherine Gerard gave freely of her time, knowledge and experience to our discussions, usually in the corridors, on various aspects of leadership in public administration. I benefited immensely from my interactions with them; to all of them, I owe heartfelt thanks.

Four persons took the trouble to read through the manuscript: Dr Suraj Kumar, Dr Suryakanta Mishra, Mr Prasad Ranjan Ray and Mr Samar Ghosh. I am grateful to them for their time and their valuable contributions. Thanks are due to several colleagues: to Dr Pradip Bhattacharya, senior cadre colleague, for his advice and encouragement, and for allowing use of the library of the Administrative Training Institute, Kolkata; to Mr S. Krishnan, Mr L.K. Ateeq, and Mr Onkar Singh Meena for acting intermittently as sounding boards; to Mr Shantanu Basu for his reactions to the initial draft; and to Mr Sanjay Mitra for his unflagging enthusiasm and encouragement for all my little projects. I would like to thank all my colleagues, from the Indian Administrative Service and the State Civil Services, working in districts in West Bengal and in other States that I visited, for their views and thoughts; they helped me test my ideas and firm up my convictions.

I am grateful to Mr Randhir Arora for his advice and suggestions regarding the preparation of the book.

To my children, Neilabh and Vedushi, I am thankful for their patience and love. I am deeply grateful to my wife, Nandita; without her relentless persuasion, fitful provocation, and untiring support this book may not have been written.

Introduction

THIS BOOK is about change, and leading it.

In India, the office of the district officer (DO)—known variously as Collector, District Magistrate and Deputy Commissioner—has evolved over more than two centuries from an area administrator with the limited agenda of revenue collection to a multifaceted functionary at the centre of district administration. Not only has this evolutionary process been mistaken for diminution of the office but also, since the beginning of the 1990s, the impact of diverse and accelerated processes of reform of the public sector on the DO and the district administration appears to have gone virtually unnoticed. This book invites notice to these developments that have within a short span of about 15 years quietly but firmly altered the way the state goes about providing goods and services to the citizen customer in the field.

A FEW CLARIFICATIONS

At the outset a few clarifications may be in order.

First, in this study, the term 'public sector' denotes the realm in which the state operates in conjunction with other agencies to provide public goods and services. It is not to be mistaken for the narrow area of the operation of 'public sector undertakings', which in India are commonly referred to as the public sector.

Second, this work does not distinguish between the terms 'public administration' and 'public management'. To the contrary, it proposes that in the context of India and most of the developing world, 'public administration' is more appropriate because the role of the state in the globalized world may have altered but does not appear to have diminished. Economic liberalization and growing democratization may have sounded the bell for the withdrawal of government from certain sectors. To that extent, the new public management movement that has swept most of the Anglo-Saxon world 1980s onwards has also left its imprint on reform of the public sector in India. Nevertheless, there has been a simultaneous intensification and expansion of the role of the state in other areas, especially the social sector, albeit with the assistance of a host of non-state actors. Hence, the two terms are used here interchangeably.

Third, we have used the term 'citizen customer' in an attempt to focus attention on the citizen as a customer and consumer of the public goods and services provided by the state. It may also help distinguish among different kinds of citizen customers based upon their different requirements and service providers.

Fourth, it may be noticeable that this work does not make a strong case for e-governance. For this we must admit of two reasons: (*a*) e-governance does not lack for champions and a number of attempts are being made around the country for its introduction and popularization; and (*b*) although e-governance needs to be promoted speedily and strenuously, the need of the moment is the review and redesign of the fundamental processes and structures of governance at the district level. Governance must precede e-governance.

Finally, this book has a bias. It is the poor and the weaker sections that are the main targets of services provided by the state, particularly in the rural areas and in the urban fringes; the energies of the DO and the administration must primarily be directed towards them. This is the overarching perspective through which the emergent imperatives and new role of the DO are viewed in this study.

WHAT THE BOOK IS NOT

Before proceeding to introduce the subject matter of this study it may be useful to identify what this study is not and does not claim to be.

This book is not a history of the office of the DO, although we have traversed historical ground to analyse the evolution of the office; neither is it a description of the structures and functions of the office of the DO nor of district administration. There are several excellent efforts that have plumbed the opalescent deeps of time to piece together the history of the DO and district administration. Similarly, comprehensive texts on the structure and functions of district administration are available. We have, however, touched upon both the history and the structural and functional elements of district administration in the first segment of the book so that readers new to the subject may get an idea of the machinery of government at the field level and are able to fully appreciate the discussion in the following chapters.

This book is also not a compendium of schemes and programmes that the DO is responsible for implementing at the district level. Nor is it a compilation of laws and rules that he/she administers or that impinge upon his/her work, even though we have referred to these as required. Although useful for understanding the functions of the DO, these areas are not the foci of the present volume.

This work is also not a 'How to ...' book or manual for DOs and district administration that offers ready-made solutions. It is doubtful if such a manual can be written, and if written may serve a DO. Suggestions made for improving the effectiveness of district administration have emerged from the analyses of facts and trends in the light of theoretical frameworks; their application would depend upon the convergence of factors also discussed.

Finally, this book does not attempt to resolve a host of controversies in the area of district administration such as—the generalist versus specialist debate, the relationship between the DO and the Superintendent of

Police, and many more. Such issues have not only been written about extensively, but are likely to continue to draw ink and provoke argument for some time to come.

WHAT IT IS ABOUT

The overriding objective of this book is to draw urgent attention to the new role of the DO, and the district administration that he/she leads, with reference to the impact and the implications of public sector reforms at the district level in India.

Although there are a number of books on district administration in India, most of them either concentrate on its historical evolution or describe the administrative structures and functions at the district level. There are also several collections of articles on the subject. Few books have also appeared in India on reforms in the public sector. However, there is no work that examines the impact of public sector reforms undertaken at the national level, or even of the more focused administrative reforms, upon the delivery of public goods and services at the district level, i.e., the cutting edge of governance. How have the 73rd and 74th Amendments affected the structure of the state and administration? What direct or indirect impact has the policy to privatize public services, or support services within government had on government institutions? Is down-sizing of importance to government machinery at the field level? How has the increasing tide of public interest litigation or the dramatic expansion of the media affected the accountability of the district-level civil servants? These are a few questions that have not been asked very often or loudly enough. They merit attention.

To the best of our knowledge, the existing books on district administration neither examine the emerging role of the DO and district administration in the light of ongoing reforms nor do they assess his/her new responsibilities— and the requisite capabilities for effectively discharging them. This study breaks new ground in terms of redefining the role of the DO in the context of rapid changes confronting the field operations of the state in the 21st century.

This study also highlights the lack of research in a number of areas in public administration in India. The bases for creation of new districts: the relationship of the DO with local government bodies (LGBs)—in the light of 73rd and 74th Amendments to the Constitution; the scope of market forces in providing basic services to the citizen consumer, especially in the remote and rural areas and to the weaker sections in urban areas; the role of non-state actors in providing services and enforcing accountability in the field; and many similar topics often generate discussion but appear to have escaped the eye of researchers. To that extent, a subsidiary objective of this book is to flag these issues with the hope that academics and practitioners in public administration will engage with them.

Another secondary objective of this book is to draw attention of the state to the need for redesigning district administration and supporting the new role of the DO. While this study delineates the new role of the DO with reference to the reforms in the public sector and while the resourceful DO reinvents himself/herself, the onus of change cannot lie solely upon the DO. In the interests of efficient and effective field administration, the state must also facilitate the change. In this regard, even though the central government may play a catalytic role, the primary responsibility for modifying the policy framework for changes in district administration rests with state governments. There is a critical need for revisiting issues such as redesigning the administrative machinery at the district level (including the Collectorate), re-engineering existing processes, and capacity building.

METHODOLOGY

Material for this work has been drawn mainly from secondary sources. Curiously enough, despite its importance, the subject has received only fitful attention from scholars and practitioners; in the modern context there are few systematic, let alone empirical, studies on topics related to our central subject. We have tried to make good the shortage of such analysis in two ways: first, by casting our net wide and drawing upon various types of writings related to district administration in India in particular and the components of public administration in general from around the world; and, second, particularly in the latter half of the book, by drawing upon the author's experiences as a DO in two districts, and at district and sub-district level positions, over several years in the state of West Bengal.

Thus, the literature reviewed for Chapter Three on the evolving role of the DO is based on writings emanating from research on the subject within India—by Indian and international scholars. However, the survey of literature on coordination is based mainly on the developments in this field of study in public administration practice and scholarship in the United States. We have little hesitation in studying them. For within the matrix of democracy, the principles and precepts of coordination that have emerged in the West remain, with occasional and minor modifications, equally relevant in the East. Similarly, the analysis of the feasibility of collaboration between NGOs and government draws upon international experience and scholarship. Due to the paucity of research on the impact of public sector reforms, the survey of literature in India includes articles from journals and newspapers/magazines.

Apart from historical analyses of district administration and analysis of available facts and trends, conceptual models and theoretical frameworks developed in the West have also been used as and when deemed suitable. However, we have attempted to underline both their utility and their constraints in the Indian context. Thus, in Chapter Six while we employ Gulick and Urwick's (1937) ancient but still relevant model, POSDCORB,[1] for analysing the tasks of DOs, fully recognizing its limitations, in Chapter Seven we also make the most of two recent frameworks for the development of managerial/ administrative leadership.

STRUCTURE

The book may be broadly divided into three main segments. The first segment describes the district as the
basic unit of administration in India and briefly discusses
the environment, institutions and agencies charged with
a variety of state responsibilities at this level. The first
chapter introduces the reader to the system of administration at the district level in India. It acquaints the
reader (new to the subject) with the notion of the 'district'
in Indian administration; the factors that may determine
its nature and size, and the implications of the popularly
used term 'district administration' (DA). Building upon
this, the second chapter provides some basic details about
the structure and functions of DA, the Collectorate and the
DO. The administrative units at different levels in the
district that constitute DA across various states are also
described in some detail.

The second segment of the book analyses the evolving role
of the DO, dwells upon the drivers of public sector reforms
in India, and, thereafter, in the light of these developments
assesses its impact upon district administration. The third
chapter argues that the office of the DO has never been
static. Rather, it has evolved continuously in response to
the changes in its environment and context. The fourth
chapter is the veritable heart of the book. It explores the
impact of four major processes of reform at the district
level: decentralization, market forces, administrative reforms and new forces of accountability. The implications

of these reforms in terms of new responsibilities and refurbished priorities of the DO are examined in the next chapter. These are: Social Sector Regulation and Development, System Maintenance through Regulation, and Development Promotion.

The third segment focuses upon the DO's role as an administrator and a leader, the existing and the new. The sixth chapter reviews the breadth of functions performed by the DO through the POSDCORB framework while the next chapter discusses the new roles and responsibilities of the DO as the administrator–leader. The seven components of the new role are identified as Knowledge Management, Vision, Strategic Planning, Design, Teambuilding, Monitoring, Coordination and Facilitation. The last two chapters deal in detail with certain ambiguities and controversies connected with the DO's re-emphasized role as Coordinator and new role as Facilitator, respectively.

DOs past and present, and their colleagues at the district and sub-district levels, may find many issues and observations in this book familiar; many may also agree with the theme of the book while some may dispute the inferences drawn and conclusions reached. Quite possibly other readers may feel that there are issues related to the subject that this study has not taken into account; some may find the elaborate handling of some issues excessive. However, within the tight boundaries that this study has set for itself, we hope it has achieved the objectives set out. If this book succeeds in generating debate and add impetus to the recognition of the impact of public sector reform on field administration in India and the consequent transformation of the role of the DO, it would have served its purpose.

Note

1. An acronym that stands for the tasks of administration, formulated by the authors—Planning, Organizing, Staffing, Directing, Coordinating, Reporting and Budgeting.

Chapter One

The District and District Administration

THE MACHINERY of government in a district, in India, is both elaborate and complex. To be able to appreciate the full import of the responsibilities of the district officer (DO) and district administration (DA), it is necessary to recognize the perimeters of the matrix within which he/she functions, its internal architecture and the functions that he/she performs. This chapter introduces the reader unfamiliar with the subject with some of the basic concepts in DA. A few questions that it tries to answer are: what is meant by the phrase 'district administration'—for long a part of common parlance? What are its areas of activities and through whom does it function? What are the levels at which it operates or the areas that it covers? And, how and under what influences it has changed and is changing?

THE DISTRICT

For the federal and the state governments in India, the district is the cutting edge of administration. S.S. Khera

(1960: 3), a former civil servant, described the district as 'a practical, sound and viable unit of administration that has stood the test of time'. A territorial unit, the district is widely understood to be the unit for planning, implementation and evaluation of a variety of federal and state programmes in regulatory and developmental administration. In India, such is the importance of district in the popular mind that it also defines people's identities (Chopra 1978; Nawani 2005); whether from a town or a village, each individual belongs to a district.

Inaccurately described as a British legacy, the system of territorial administration at the district level may be traced back to Mauryan times. Certainly many of its features were developed by the Mughals; many of these, including the single administrator-based administration, was consciously retained, first, by the East India Company and, then, by the British government.[1] Yet, there is no such thing as a typical district in India. Districts vary in size from state to state and within states. The population of a district may vary from as low as 150,000 to as high as 8 million. Similarly, in terms of area, a district may encompass a few kilometres or more than 40,000 sq km. Neither is it uncommon to find more than 10 dialects and a half-a-dozen languages being spoken in one district. Yet if districts in India have one thing in common it is the machinery of administration.

During the 1971 Census there were 360 districts in India; at the time of writing, the figure has risen to 604 districts, an increase of almost 70 per cent. In each of these districts the number of state and central government offices may vary between 25–35 and 5–10, respectively.[2] In every district one would find a system of administration headed by the office of Collector and District Magistrate/Deputy Commissioner as the representative of government and the integrating force in district administration.

DISTRICT ADMINISTRATION AND ADMINISTRATION AT THE DISTRICT LEVEL

District Administration and the District Officer

The term 'district administration' as referred to in day-to-day use by people, public representatives and the media, normally connotes the district magistrate and collector and the administrative machinery that he/she heads in the district. In this sense, 'district administration' is also often referred to as 'general administration'. Although they may vary in number and nomenclature from one state to another, numerous functions of government are performed by the DO's office (Appendix 1). These may cover the activities of well over 25 departments of the state government, not including those that are not based in the office of the DO (Appendix 2).

'District administration includes all agencies of government, the individual officials and functionaries, public servants, including a public servant who is a government servant and equally one who is not' (Khera 1979: 79). Khera's above definition of 'district administration' includes all kinds of functionaries and institutions set up by the government and includes institutions such as Panchayats, but does not include non-state actors, private individuals or even legislators. In today's context, however, the emphasis is not as much on a top-down system of government but on a more wide-ranging and participative model of 'governance' that perforce seeks to encompass non-state entities engaged in the provision of public service.

By statute and government notification,[3] the district magistrate is the representative of the governor and government in the district; he/she is also 'officer in charge of the district'. The office of the DO works as the lynchpin or the key stone of the administrative edifice in the district. He/she is engaged with the entire gamut of regulatory, development and crisis management functions. As the representative of the Governor, the DO is essentially the representative of the state government, 'its eyes and ears'. As Collector, he/she is the head of the revenue and regulatory functions that comprise the many duties of state government. As District Magistrate, he/she is the head of the executive magistracy and responsible for the maintenance of the rule of law in the district. Moreover, the DO is often called upon to take responsibility of various government activities which are departmentally not part of the statutory or specified functions; these may range from projects for general welfare, industrial development, to even the sale of lottery tickets (Dayal et al. 1976).

Until very recently, DOs in almost all the states were drawn from the Indian Administrative Service (IAS), since all the posts of Collector/DM/DC were cadre posts.

Yet, from the mid-1990s officers belonging to the State Civil Service (SCS) have also been posted as DOs in several states, starting with Orissa. The main reasons for this development are: rapid increase in the number of districts in some states such as Orissa (where, at one go, the number went up from 13 to 30); reduction in the recruitment of IAS officers; poor cadre management and late promotion of SCS officers; growing strength of the SCS associations; and, even parochialism combined with politicization. Noticeably, directly-recruited IAS officers are posted as DOs by their late 20s or early 30s. However, in states where promotion to the IAS is late, such as Uttar Pradesh, Bihar and West Bengal, promoted officers and SCS officers posted as DOs are usually in their middle or late 50s. In states like Kerala, Tamil Nadu and Andhra Pradesh, where promotion of SCS officers to the IAS takes place after 8–12 years of service, the DOs are neither aged nor is there much demand for posting of SCS officers as collectors.

ADMINISTRATION AT THE DISTRICT LEVEL

Administration at the district level, however, is a wider concept than district administration. The former term covers the entire sphere of government activities being carried out in the form of different programmes and schemes by various departments in the district either directly by government machinery or by associated organizations and public sector undertakings (for example, the public sector banking institutions or the State Transport Corporation). It is true that district administration and administration at the district level are often deemed to be coterminous. However, beginning in the 1920s and accelerating in the post-Independence period, the transformation of line departments into almost independent entities—ranging from the state headquarters to the district and sub-district levels, the two terms are no longer coterminous. This development has destroyed the principle of unity of command and broken up administration at the district level into a number of tunnel-visioned agencies often working in isolation and sometimes at cross purposes with each other. The most prominent reason for this is not administrative but political—the existence in government of fractious parties, or coalitions of parties. Each department is headed by a minister—a legislator of the ruling party/coalition. Wary of each other, coalition partners or faction-ridden parties are often more interested in carving out their separate empires rather than worrying about the principles of administration or the implications of violating them.

A number of ministries of the central government, that provide diverse public services, also have offices at the district and sometimes at sub-district levels (Appendix 3). Prominent amongst these are the Postal Department, Telecom Department, Railways, Income Tax Department, the Customs and Central Excise Department, and Military and Para-military organizations. All these organizations also form a segment of administration at the district level that provides a set of exclusive goods and services to the population.

Further, the establishment of Panchayati Raj Institutions (PRIs) in the 1960s and then their Constitutional institutionalization by the 73rd Amendment in 1993–94 has added new dimensions to administration at the district level. Effectively, this has led to the restructuring of the state. The setting up of local self-government bodies at three levels—the district, block and village, has created new politico-administrative structures empowered to carry out a range of governance responsibilities at local levels. Although in real terms, initially the thrust has been upon the devolution of developmental responsibilities, the aim of the 73rd Amendment is wider. It includes basic elements of regulatory administration at all three levels, thus envisaging vastly expanded administrative machinery in each district.

Apart from the three levels of PRI at work in the district, other organizations and entities also participate in the process of delivery of public services, and some would argue, governance. These may be well organized, legal and permanent entities, or loosely held, unrecognized and temporary ones; from large international public organizations (IPOs) to small, local citizens' groups formed all of a sudden to protest the death of a pedestrian on a national highway—the range is enormous. The role played by many of the groups is not new but it is a rapidly expanding one; therefore, district administration cannot ignore them. It must involve these groups in such a way that they are able to contribute to the public interest.

Depending upon the region under scrutiny in India, some examples of IPOs involved are WHO, UNICEF and UNDP. Foreign government organizations (FGOs) with a presence in state capitals and in districts are: DFID, GTZ and SIDA. The variety of NGOs in the field is immense. Some international NGOs like ActionAid and CARE work through local NGOs; national and state-level NGOs like PRADAN, Bharat Sevashram Sangha and Ram Krishna Mission having branches at the district and sub-district levels; while local NGOs may have a district or a sub-district level area of operation. Since most of the time the functions of these bodies fall within the programmes pursued by the government, they are found to be working on parallel schemes as the government agencies.

Therefore, we find that a combination of state government, local self-government and central government machineries working together with a variety of non-government organizations at the district and sub-district levels comprise in totality at administration or governance at the district level. All these government organizations implement state and central government programmes through their different functionaries; non-government organizations engage and interact with the work of these government bodies in matters of governance or with implementation of development programmes. Although in some cases local NGOs funded by certain central government agencies (for example, CAPART, Ministry of Rural Development) may implement projects without the involvement of the state government/district administration agencies, international NGOs and IPOs inevitably pursue programmes through the state government departments and local government bodies.

At this juncture it is necessary to take note of the development of the private sector and its role in providing services to its customers that earlier only the state provided to its citizens. For a long time a number of services at the district levels were the monopoly of the central or the state governments: postal, telegraph and telecommunications are three such services. In many areas, especially in the remote parts of the country, other services such as health, education and transport were largely provided by state-run agencies although in urban areas the private sector has had a presence for a long time. Further, sparked by the acute shortages during the Second World War, several essential commodities were also supplied solely by the state.

Economic liberalization initiated in the 1990s has altered the above situation considerably. The telecommunications revolution in the country and the entry of private courier services in the market in the middle and late 1990s, ended the monopoly of the state on postal and telecom services, first in the urban and semi-urban areas, and then even in the distant parts of the country. The 1990s also saw the weakening of state-run transport corporations around the country and the expansion of motor transport facilities by small and large private investors. In the health and the education sectors also private investment has considerably altered the scenario, especially in the technical and professional fields. Finally, the 1990s also saw the demise of controls on some essential commodities such as sugar and cement.

Undoubtedly, over the years there has been a reduction of the role of the state in providing certain basic goods and services that were earlier provided by the state and central government organizations. However, while appreciating the role of the private sector in this regard three issues need to be kept in mind: first, that investments made by the private sector in supply of such goods and services as noted earlier are still largely in the urban areas; second, adequate purchasing power among the people is a prerequisite for access to such goods and services; and third, state action through regulation of these privately provided facilities becomes necessary to ensure their equitable distribution.

Thus, with the proliferation of departments and directorates at state headquarters and their extension in the field, the administrative machinery in the districts has become denser than it was a quarter of a century ago.[4] This expansion of state and non-state actors engaged in provision of a variety of products and services to the citizen customer, has amplified and altered both the functions and the role of the DO and DA. In the later chapters we shall explore the new dimensions of his/her role as the chief administrator and representative of the government in the district.

LEVELS OF ADMINISTRATION

As noted earlier, most functions of government and its instruments are found at the district level. This is because traditionally the district has been perceived and treated as the basic unit of administration. It is the unit for planning;

development programmes are designed on the bases of district-level data on demography, productivity and other indicators. Financial allocation for plan and non-plan, or routine, activities of the central and state governments are made for districts. Implementation of programmes as well as evaluation of all activities of government—including those funded by government but not directly administered by it—are carried out with the districts as units. Table 1.1 illustrates the different levels at which some district level departments have offices or service facilities in a district in West Bengal.

As Table 1.1 shows, in terms of reach the traditional departments—Revenue and Police—have the greatest reach along with the Rural Development and Health departments that have also grown vertically after Independence. These departments all have a direct public interface unlike technical departments such as the Public Works Department (PWD) and Irrigation and Waterways departments. The latter, responsible for developing physical infrastructure in the district, have offices only at divisional headquarters at the district level or sub-district offices at the subdivisional level. In some states newly formed departments, like Horticulture, are yet to develop their infrastructure.

Thus, although almost all departments of government have their offices at district headquarters, the substantive work of almost all these departments and wings of government is performed not at headquarters but by their sub-offices at different levels within the district. Therefore,

TABLE 1.1 Levels of Offices* of Some District-Level Departments of District Administration, Cooch Behar District, West Bengal – 2004

Revenue and Development	Police	Rural Dev.	Forest	ARD	Health	Horticulture	Irrigation	PHE	PWD
District	District	District		District	District	District		District	District
Subdivision	Sub-division Circle	Sub-division	Division		Sub-division		Division Circle	Sub-division	Sub-division
			Range						
Block	Thana	Block		Block	Block PHC PHC			Block	
GP	Outpost	GP	Beat	GP	Sub health centre				
Village		Village							

Notes: GP: Gram Panchayat; PWD: Public Works Department; PHE: Public Health Engineering; PHC: Primary Health Centre; ARD: Animal Resource Development.

* Not all departmental levels are coterminous at all or even some levels. A perfect example is the Forest Department whose offices fall between the additional tiers of regulatory administration.

even though from the points of view of the central and the state governments the district may be the basic unit of administration, it is not always where most citizen customers access services of the state. In this regards, the trend in the progress of administration is the gradual decentralization of executive machinery of development and public service delivery from the district level to the subdivision, the block, and then to the village levels. Therefore, for most government programmes, the district is no longer the cutting edge—the block and the village are. However, the district has grown in significance for planning, supervision of implementation, conflict resolution, reporting and evaluation.

A large number of the government functions are performed at the sub-district levels by sub-offices of the district level officers. However, not all departments are represented at all levels within the district. Traditionally, in keeping with the emphasis on revenue, and law and order administration, the subordinate levels of administration within the district are the subdivision—the *thana*s (police stations) and village. The Community Development Block—with which the Panchayat Samity is now coterminous, and the Gram Panchayat were later additions to the district set up. The Community Development Blocks came into existence in 1952–53 and were made coterminous with the *thana*s. The Panchayat Samity and the Gram Panchayat came into existence after the tentative introduction by a few states of Panchayati Raj in the 1960s, and mandatory establishment after the 93rd Constitutional Amendment in 1993.

DETERMINANTS OF JURISDICTION

As Table 1.1 illustrates, not all departments of government are represented at all or only at these levels. Within one district, depending upon a number of factors, there may be several levels of operation for different departments. Some of the factors affecting the choice of the level at which departments operate are:

Nature of functions of the departments   Agencies that provide a good or service to people on an individual basis usually, within the constraints of resources, maintain a presence at the lowest levels. Traditional departments such as those related to land revenue, police and education provide services or function at the lowest level of the administrative structure. Therefore, they have a presence at various levels of the district ranging from the district headquarters to the subdivisions to the *thana*/block to the Gram Panchayat and sometimes even at the village level. The Health Department has also increased its levels of operation considerably after Independence and its presence can be felt even at the village or the sub-block level.

Size and shape of the district   Depending upon whether the district is very large and spread out or elongated or whether it is small and compact, different departments of government often create sub-district level offices to cater to the different areas within a district. For instance, the undivided Midnapore district in West Bengal was divided into two zones/districts for the purposes of land administration with two District Land and Land Reforms Officers and Additional District Magistrates reporting to the Collector and District Magistrate of Midnapore.

Geographical features and the terrain of the district Peculiarities of geography such as forests, rivers and mountains may lead to the development of different jurisdictions for departments whose work is determined by these features. For example, although its headquarters are located in Cooch Behar district, West Bengal, most of the forest areas of Cooch Behar Forest (Wildlife) Division fall under the Jalpaiguri district. Similarly, instead of following the existing district-based boundaries, other agencies such as the irrigation department have delineated their areas of operation on the basis of river basin and irrigation systems.

Demographic factors The concentration of certain population types in certain parts of a district may also lead to different levels of offices of a particular department. For instance, the presence of large indigenous populations in certain blocks may lead to the designation of these blocks as Integrated Tribal Development (ITD) blocks under the ITD Programme. Likewise, the incidence of certain diseases like leprosy or tuberculosis may also lead to the creation of treatment centres in certain parts of a district, services that may be available only in a few districts of a state. Accordingly these departments establish facilities for service provision at sub-district levels such as the sub-division, the block or the Village Panchayat or the village.

Level and nature of economic development of the area The type of economic activities and their elaboration may lead to the presence of certain departments in a given district. The Regulated Market Committees located in areas with surplus agricultural production are a case in point. Similarly, the extent and type of fishery activities or the absence thereof may determine the concentration or absence of the offices and functionaries of the Fishery Department in a particular district.

Historical factors and traditions of the district   Historical factors may also determine the levels and units of administration in a particular district. For instance, although Cooch Behar is a relatively small district comprising 12 blocks it has retained five subdivisions because of historical reasons harking back to the merger of the princely state of Cooch Behar into the Indian Union.

Political factors   The political clout of the district and the ministers at the state level also may result in creation of new levels of administration in certain departments from time to time. Division of districts and creation of new ones has taken place in almost all the states. Although the plea made for creation of new districts is usually administrative efficiency, political factors, rather than administrative ones, appear to have been responsible for the multiplication of districts in several states. Ostensibly, the logic for subdividing and bifurcating districts has been the need to bring administration closer to the people. However, often this has been aimed at creating new areas of influence for specific political parties and leaders.

Starting in the 1990s, a number of new districts were created in states such as Orissa, Uttar Pradesh, Haryana, Bihar and Madhya Pradesh. Creation of a new district even became one of the campaign promises in some states; often, new districts were created to consolidate a party's position. Therefore, several districts came into existence that consisted of a single subdivision or even a single block. The upgradation of a village from which the Chief Minister of the state hails, to a block and then to tehsil and subdivisional headquarters is also not unknown.

Intra-departmental specialization   From the earlier, it would be clear that the jurisdictions of different departments represented at the district level are coterminous only for a few departments. The jurisdiction of a particular department is often affected by the same factors influencing the levels of administration enumerated above. Further, jurisdiction may also vary because within a particular department there may be a number of functionally differentiated wings. For instance, within the police directorate, apart from the territory and level-based police organization, the Intelligence Branch (IB) and Enforcement Branch (EB) are also included.

The proliferation of specialized wings in some departments may be such that the offices of all the wings may not all be located in one district. This is particularly true for technical, line departments formed after Independence such as various divisions of the PWD, Public Health Engineering (PHE) department, and the Forest Departments. Specialized divisions of the PWD such as PWD Roads, PWD Construction Board and PWD Bridges are often found to be spread over traditional units of district administration such as *thana*s, blocks, subdivisions—and even across districts. For instance, in the Forest Department, the jurisdiction of Territorial, Wildlife and the Social Forestry, and Working Plan Division may be entirely discrete or may overlap. However, in the same department, the Forest Corporation, Parks and Gardens Wing may be spread over two or more districts. One reason for the jurisdictions of line departments not being coterminous with traditional administrative units, even districts, is the nature of specialization of the division and the quantum of work; while another reason for the mismatch also may be due to the multiplication of districts. Thus, the jurisdiction of different wings of the one department may be restricted to a district, may cut across two districts, or may run across several districts.

Finally, different levels of sub-offices may be located in a district depending upon the intensity of the operation of the department in a particular area, upon the social infrastructure available, and upon the importance of the district and its distance from the capital of the state.

Notes

1. For an extensive treatment of the legacy of Mauryan and Mughal administrative systems reference may be made to the extensive treatment of these periods in Arora and Goyal (1996) and Ramachandran (1996). Nawani's (2005) discussion of the contribution of Sher Shah in shaping territorial administration in India may also be seen.

2. An illustrative list of state and central government offices in Paschim Midnapore district, West Bengal is included as Appendix 1.

3. Executive order issued by government.

4. This has drawn criticism from many, like Jalan (2005), who say that this density has resulted in wasteful duplication of activities and structures among government agencies.

Chapter Two

District Administration: Structure and Functions

THE ADMINISTRATIVE structure of the district has been shaped and reshaped over the last 150 years. These changes also reflect the change in the nature of the state and its orientation towards its people. Three to four major shifts are perceptible: the move from a predatory mercantile rule to an imperial rent-seeking regime to an aspiring welfare state to participatory self-governance. These changes are reflected in the structure of field administration that was gradually modified to adjust to them. As we shall see in Chapter Four, public sector reforms in India are acutely influencing the priorities of the state and its functions.

As it has transpired in several developing countries, like New Zealand, UK and the US, in India economic liberalization, a major component of these reforms, has not effected a move to a market-based system. However, its impact is evident in the gradual withdrawal of the state from certain types of service provision and in encouragement to non-state actors to take over their delivery. Before moving on to the impacts of reforms and its consequences for the role of the district officer (DO), in this section we shall examine the administrative structure of a district, the main constituents of district administration and the DO's foremost areas of responsibility. The aim is to familiarize the reader with the administrative infrastructure of district administration.

ADMINISTRATIVE UNITS OF A DISTRICT

Village—The Basis

The village is the smallest unit of administration in India. Like districts, there is wide variation in the size of villages, again, among states and even within districts. The population of a village may vary from 15,000 to 25,000 people in Kerala to less than 50 in remoter regions of the north-east. Even within a state like West Bengal the strength of a village may vary from upwards of 5,000 to less than 50. Villages may consist of small clusters of habitations or (tolas)/hamlets, normally organized on caste lines, around a large one, or they may encompass a set of houses scattered over an area; the former is common in most parts of the country, whereas the latter may be found in areas populated by certain tribes in central, eastern and north-eastern India. Whatever is the size, population mix or structure of the village, its boundaries have been demarcated from ancient times by revenue laws except in some of the tribal areas noted above where traditional demarcations exist. For all administrative purposes the 'revenue village' is the atomic administrative unit.

Until Independence, and into the decade of the 1950s, administration from the viewpoint of a village was concerned chiefly with two things: revenue collection and maintenance of law and order. These two functions were usually shared by two government officials, the patwari (known as Lekhpal in Uttar Pradesh, Karnum in Tamil Nadu, Talati in Maharashtra) and the Chowkidar, in states like Madhya Pradesh, Punjab, Bihar, West Bengal and Orissa. Village headmen were also appointed in some regions. In the north-eastern states the traditional heads of villages, called *Gaon Burras* in Arunachal Pradesh and Nagaland and *Narkun* in Meghalaya, have been long recognized; the traditional councils in these regions have also been given a special place by a special provision after the 73rd Amendment to the Constitution.

Levels of Regulatory Administration

A group of revenue villages form the next tier of regulatory administration: the *Pargana/Fikra/*Circle as known in the states of Uttar Pradesh, Tamil Nadu and Maharashtra, respectively (Chopra 1978). The main task of the official located at this level is to supervise revenue administration and maintenance of land records by the village-level revenue functionaries. He/she is called Kanungo in Uttar Pradesh and Revenue Inspector in Tamil Nadu and West Bengal.

The Tehsil is the next level of revenue and regulatory administration in a number of states; it includes five to eight *pargana*s or *fikra*s. In Maharashtra, it is known as taluka or mahal and in Tamil Nadu as taluka. In West Bengal, Orissa, Jharkhand and the north-eastern states this level is missing. The Tehsildar is not only the supervisor for land revenue functions of the lower tiers, but also has magisterial powers in some states and plays an important role in the maintenance of law and order, the electoral process and other similar activities of district administration.

In the southern states of Tamil Nadu, Karnataka, Andhra Pradesh and Kerala, districts are divided into revenue divisions, which are equivalent to the subdivisions in the northern states. Revenue divisions are headed by IAS officers or SCS officers—the former are called Sub-Collectors and the latter Revenue Division Officers. In the northern states like Uttar Pradesh, Punjab, Haryana and Rajasthan these officials are called Sub Divisional Magistrates (SDMs) whereas, in the eastern states of Bihar, Jharkhand and West Bengal they are addressed as Sub Divisional Officers (SDOs). The SDO is an executive magistrate in charge of the subdivision who exercises authority not only under revenue laws but also under the provisions of the Criminal Procedure Code (CrPC). In Bihar, West Bengal and Orissa, the SDO functions as a 'mini-Collector' in his/her jurisdiction. Most of the offices of regulatory administration at the district Collectorate are replicated in the SDO's office, including in many places an Additional Regional Transport Officer. In these states, the SDO is also being gradually involved with the implementation of development programmes. However, in most other states, the SDM is primarily a Revenue Officer and a Magistrate.

Levels of Development Administration

Development became the priority of the new Indian state after Independence. Its immediate consequence was the Community Development Programme (CDP) and the National Extension Scheme (NES) introduced on a pilot basis in 1952–53 in a few districts across the country, and extended to the entire country within a decade. It introduced a new administrative unit—the Community Development Block covering a population of 15,000 to 20,000. The Block comprises a group of villages and in some states it is coterminous with tehsils or talukas. The aim of the CDP and NES was comprehensive socio-economic development of the community through its active involvement. Although the initial emphasis was on improvement of agricultural production, officials from other line departments were also posted in the block as Extension Officers to work under the overall supervision and direction of the Block Development Officer (BDO).

The Block has for long been the unit for planning and rural development. Over time, with the increase in population, existing Blocks have been divided to form new ones. Thus the population of a Block ranges from about 15,000 in sparsely populated states of the north-east to more than 150,000 in states like Uttar Pradesh, Tamil Nadu, Bihar and West Bengal. The administrative machinery in the office of the BDO has also been strengthened considerably in most states. In a number of states, such as Bihar, Orrisa and West Bengal, the BDO is also an executive magistrate and plays the same role as the SDO in his/her jurisdiction. After the establishment of the PRIs in the 1960s, the Block became the jurisdiction of the intermediate Panchayat body known variously as the Taluka Panchayat, Panchayat Samity and Kshetra Panchayat. This process was further crystallized after the 73rd Amendment and led to further consolidation of the Block infrastructure. The BDO functions as the executive officer of the Block Panchayats in most states.

For the purposes of development administration, no office was set up at the village level. However, the Village Level Worker (VLW)—a multipurpose worker—was introduced at the village level as the lower-most functionary of the Community Development Programme in 1952. He was meant to be the principal change agent on the spot to help advise farmers on various aspects of agriculture (Khera 1964, 1979). Later, Additional VLWs were also introduced in some states as specialists in different areas of farming. However, over the years with the extension of some of the departments down to the village level, and the growth of the PRIs in most states, the VLWs have been edged out. The growth of PRIs and the extension of police machinery have also led to the phasing out of the village Chowkidar in states like Bihar and West Bengal.[1]

Levels of Local Self-Government
Local Government Bodies (LGBs), that form the third level of governance, if not administration, comprise the three-tier Panchayat system: the District Panchayat at the district level, the Block Panchayat and the Gram Panchayat at the village level. The jurisdiction of Panchayat bodies is limited to rural areas. PRIs are meant to be units of

local self-government. However, due to the incomplete devolution of authority and funds in most states, currently they are mainly deliberative and executive bodies. Except in Karnataka and Kerala, and to a lesser extent in West Bengal, the services of the district and sub-district level functionaries of development-related line departments have not been placed at the disposal of the District or Block Panchayats. Members to the three-tiers are directly elected; however, depending upon the state, the heads of PRIs are either directly elected or they are elected from among the elected members of the Panchayat body.

The Village Panchayat does not have uniform characteristics in different states of the country. In states like Bihar, Uttar Pradesh, Haryana and Kerala, each village has a Panchayat body. In other states like Orissa and West Bengal, a group of villages with a population of about 15,000 to 20,000 make a Gram Panchayat. The head of the Village Panchayat is known as the Sarpanch or Gram Pradhan. The executive personnel placed at the disposal of the Village Panchayat also vary in number and quality among states. Village Panchayats in Uttar Pradesh have only one permanent executive, the Secretary; and, it is common for the lone secretary to be 'shared' between more than one Village Panchayat. On the other hand, in Gujarat, Kerala, Karnataka and West Bengal, the Village Panchayat has a complement of five to eight personnel to assist the Pradhan and the Panchayat. In West Bengal, junior engineers have also been placed in Village Panchayats. In view of the enormous increase in direct funding of the Village Panchayats under various rural development programmes, it is vital to equip them with an adequate number of competent personnel if service delivery is to be effective.

As noted earlier, the Block was adopted as the juris-diction for the intermediate Panchayat body. The Block Panchayat is presided over by a directly or indirectly elected president. Due to the amalgamation of the existing development wings of the Block with the Block Panchayat, the personnel situation is better than at the Village Panchayat level and most Blocks have a complement of professional and technical staff on their rolls.

The District Panchayat is the highest tier of the Pan-chayat system. In most states, the President of the District Panchayat is also a designated Minister of State. In states where PRIs have struck roots, such as Karnataka, Maharashtra and West Bengal, the District Panchayat functions through a number of standing committees on subjects such as public works, land and forestry, backward classes welfare, animal husbandry and fisheries, women and child welfare, education, health and finance. Standing committees are composed of elected members of the District Panchayat, one of whom is elected to chair it, and the officials of the related line departments at the district level. The District Panchayat has an executive officer and several other officers such as the secretary and deputy secretary. In view of the enhanced allocation of funds to the PRIs for rural development since the early 1990s, and especially after the establishment of the State Finance Commissions, the District Panchayats in the larger states often have annual budgets exceeding Rs 1 billion which are usually much larger than the budgets of many state government departments.

In urban areas there are Municipalities and Municipal Corporations and in certain regions, Development Authorities also exist. The Panchayat and municipal bodies are institutions of the local self-government and are charged with the delivery of basic services such as construction and maintenance of Panchayat/municipal roads, water supply and rural markets. Development authorities are created for planned development of specially identified areas adjacent to urban centres. The rural and urban LGBs have a clear-cut jurisdiction but the jurisdiction of development authorities may include both urban and rural areas.

The DOs role in relation to the PRIs varies from state to state. In states like Maharashtra and Karnataka, the DOs have not been given a major role in the PRI set up, although they have some supervisory and coordinating functions. In other states, like West Bengal, they have been made the executive officer of the District Panchayat. However, in most states, they are responsible for election to Panchayat bodies and supervising the training of Panchayat representatives. The inspection of Block and Village Panchayats and the audit of expenditures made by them are two important responsibilities of a regulatory nature that is carried out under the supervision of the DO. The District Panchayat Officer also carries out recruitment of officials to different Panchayat bodies under the supervision of the DO. The DO is also responsible for conducting municipal elections, formation of municipal bodies and their general supervision.

Components of District Administration

The Collectorate and a large number of state government offices in the district (Appendix 2) together comprise district administration. To appreciate the range of line departments that the DO interacts with on a regular basis and the variety of activities, which constitute the DO's many responsibilities, it may be useful to briefly survey them.

Law and Order—District Police

As the strong arm of the state, the District Police is responsible for maintaining law and order, and the prevention, detection and investigation of crime. The Superintendent of Police (SP), also known in some states as the Senior Superintendent of Police (SSP), heads it. Towards the second half of 19th century with the revamping of the police under the new imperial dispensation, the army provided many officers to staff the district police. The popular name 'Captain' (or Kaptaan) 'Saheb' of the SP in states like Uttar Pradesh and Madhya Pradesh, points at the former connection of the police force with the army (Khera 1979). The District Police functions under the general supervision and direction of the DO.

The District Police Headquarters is a large establishment. The creation of certain specialized divisions, like District Intelligence Bureau and the Enforcement wing, and increase in law enforcement activities have resulted in the expansion of the police force. The SP is assisted at the district headquarters by Additional Superintendents of Police, or in some states SP City, and by Deputy

Superintendents of Police (Dy. SP). The territorial units of the district police set up are the sub-division, circle and the police station (or *thana*). The Subdivisional Police Officer (SDPO) is the head of the police force at the subdivisional level. The subdivision is divided into Circles headed by Circle Inspectors. The *thana* is the lowest territorial unit of police administration; the efficiency of the police force depends as much upon the effectiveness of the *thana* today, as it did a century ago. Headed by the Officer-in-charge (OC) or Station House Officer (SHO), the *thana* is also the first point of point of contact for the citizen customer. All complaints related to crime are lodged at the *thana* and are taken up for inquiry or investigation subsequently.

Revenue Collection

Land revenue has for long ceased to be the major contributor to state government revenues. However, it is one of the important sources of revenue. The DO is assisted in this fundamental task by an officer of the rank of Additional District Magistrate (ADM) in most states; in Tamil Nadu it is the District Revenue Officer, in Bihar it is the ADM (LR), and in West Bengal it is the District Land and Land Reforms Officer. The major sources of revenue are commercial taxes, registration and stamp duties, motor vehicles and excise. The District Commercial Tax Officer, also known as the Deputy Commissioner of Commercial Tax in some states, heads the Commercial Tax department in the district. The District Registrar's office, in concert with the Sub-Registrar's offices at the sub-divisional level, collects stamp duty, under the supervision of the DO. The District Transport Officer and the Superintendent of Excise are a part of the Collectorate, as is the collection of entertainment tax. Most of these departments which also qualify as regulatory agencies are located in the Collectorate.

Regulatory Departments
Most regulatory functions at the district level are carried out directly from the concerned sections of the Collectorate. These include: issue of Arms and Explosive License, Cinema License, and Citizenship Registration and Passport. The DO is also the chairperson of the Regional or District Transport authority and supervises implementation of all laws and regulations pertaining to motor vehicles. The District Controller of Food and Supplies manages the Public Distribution System (PDS) executed by the Food and Supplies Department under the direct supervision of the DO. The same is true for the correctional centres in the district and probation of convicts.

Technical Departments—Physical Infrastructure
At the district level, there are several technical departments that are responsible for implementing various schemes planned by the government. Most of these are entrusted with the development and upkeep of physical infrastructure in the district. The Public Works Department (PWD) is the original such department created during the pre-Independence period. Its scope, however, has expanded

considerably and several new divisions of a specialized nature have been fashioned for provision of specific services. Thus, in one district PWD, PWD Construction Board, PWD Bridges and PWD Highways divisions may be found. Other important technical departments at the district level are: Public Health Engineering, Minor Irrigation, and Irrigation and Waterways departments. In the district, an Executive Engineer usually heads these organizations. Below the Executive Engineer, is placed the Assistant Engineer, and below are Junior or Sub-assistant Engineers. However, as discussed in the previous chapter, due to various factors, the jurisdictions of these departments may not always correspond to that of the traditional district.

The Forest Department is another agency that may be included in this category. Responsible originally only for the management and development of areas under forest and afforestation in a district, its role has also swelled considerably since Independence. The Forest Department has also been divided into specialized wings. To the original Territorial divisions have been added, based upon the local conditions, divisions for Wildlife Conservation, Social Forestry, Parks and Gardens, Soil Conservation, and Silviculture. Many states have also established Forest Development Corporations for carrying out the commercial affairs of the department and for the creation and management of physical infrastructure for eco-tourism. Divisional Forest Officers head Forest Divisions, which are divided into Ranges, which are further subdivided into a set of Beats.

Technical Departments—Social Infrastructure

Government agencies for development of social infrastructure have also grown in the scope of their activities and spread. The Health Department, headed by the Chief Medical Officer of Health, now has facilities for providing health services up to the grassroots. Although states where the average population of villages is generally small, do not have a Sub Health Centre in each village, according to the national norm there is one such Sub-centre, operated by the para-medical staff, for each population group of five thousand. There are usually two or three Primary Health Centres in each block with a Block Primary Health Centre or Community Health Centre at the Block headquarters. An Assistant Chief Medical Officer of Health is in charge, supervising and monitoring health programmes at the subdivisional level. Each subdivisional headquarters has a subdivisional hospital, whereas at the district headquarters is located the district hospital.

The District Education Officer or the District Inspector of Schools represents the School Education Department. In some states, the respective district level councils carry out the supervision of the primary and secondary schools. A good number of departments tasked with the development of social infrastructure form part of the Collectorate, which we shall examine in the next section.

Departments for Development of Livelihoods

The departments that are basically responsible for the development, support and promotion of livelihoods, combine the tasks of service provision, extension and improvement of physical infrastructure. They are meant to play a catalytic role in the economic development of the district, especially in the rural areas. Some of these are: Agriculture, Animal Husbandry, Horticulture, Fisheries, Handloom Development, Khadi and Village Industries, and Agricultural Marketing and Industries departments. Not all of them are equally well elaborated. For instance, the Agriculture or the Animal Husbandry departments headed by the District or Principal Agriculture Officer and the Assistant Director of Animal Husbandry, in most states, have administrative and service facilities at the district, block and village Panchayat levels with some extension staff who reach the villages also. Other departments, such as Horticulture or Food Processing, that have appeared on the scene relatively recently, may have offices and facilities only at the district level. The District Industries Centre has no branches at the sub-district levels. Yet, an industries extension officer of the department is placed in the Block Development office.

Collectorate: Office of the District Officer

Organizational structure not only demonstrates where authority resides, but also how the energy of the organization is channelized (Goold and Campbell 2002). It is equally true that the structure of an organization depends upon the functions performed by it. In this section, we review the structure of an organization that has not changed much in almost 150 years—the Collectorate, the office of the DO in India.

Although the structure of Collectorates in different states, and sometimes within the same state, is not identical, there is an overall uniformity due to similarity in origins and functions. Thus, the size and the contours of the Collectorate may change across the country, but its basic structure and essential functions do not. We shall examine how various departments/sections are usually grouped in Collectorates and their work processes organized. The Collectorate is a large organization that includes many departments (Appendix 1).

Configuration   In structural terms, the Collectorate may be seen as a classical pyramidal organization or a prime example of a 'machine bureaucracy' as developed by Henry Mintzberg (1983). At the head of the Collectorate, the DO is assisted in his/her work by one or more ADMs, also known as the Additional Deputy Commissioner or Additional Collector. In states such as Tamil Nadu and Andhra Pradesh, where there is only one position of the ADM in a Collectorate, although the officer in charge of development programmes is also of the same rank, other district level officers assist the DO. In Bihar, West Bengal and Orissa there are usually three to five officers either designated as ADMs or of the same rank. Each ADM has five to eight departments/sections in his/her charge (please see organogram in Appendix 4).

Each section in the Collectorate is headed by a Deputy Magistrate (Dy. M) or an officer of the department concerned and includes a head clerk, a senior clerk, two or three junior clerks and a peon. In some states such as Punjab, Uttar Pradesh and Uttaranchal, where fewer Dy. Ms and other officers are posted, a section may be headed by a section officer, or head clerk, who may directly report to the ADM, the SDM sadar (headquarters) or the City Magistrate. Normally, a section is responsible for looking after only one type of work; however, in some instances one section may be given the responsibility of several departments for example, issue of licenses for arms, permits for explosives and cinema licenses. It is possible to distinguish three types of departments in the Collectorate: system maintenance, regulatory and developmental. System maintenance sections such as Establishment and Nezarath provide support to the other sections in the office that provide services to external stakeholders.

Lines of Authority   As Chart 1 (Appendix 4) illustrates, lines of authority and division of responsibility are clearly demarcated in the Collectorate. The DO is the source of all authority and all actions in the organization are taken in his/her name. At present there is considerable centralization of authority in the hands of the DO in most states. As Chart 1 shows, authority flows down from the DO to the ADMs to the Dy. Ms down to the section. DOs may delegate authority to the ADMs or even down to the Dy. Ms but the final responsibility for all decisions and actions in a Collectorate is theirs. The first decision-making level is that of the officer in charge of a section.

Technology   The operating core of the Collectorate works on the basis of standardized procedures. Like most government organizations, the Collectorate implements laws and rules and delivers services and goods which are in the nature of sanctions—positive or negative. Depending on the department concerned, it may deliver a permit, a license, an amount of money, a certificate, and so on.

In the absence of a strategic plan, the Collectorate is normally a reactive organization. Usually, directions from above or applications from below prompt it into action. Citizen-customers seek services by: personally meeting and submitting an application to the DO, ADM, or the officer-in-charge of the section or even one of the clerks, or by mail. All applications, howsoever received, are put up before the DO on the same date as part of the *dak* (mail). The DO forwards the applications to the relevant sections via the ADM; he/she may also direct a certain type of action, usually with a deadline for its completion. In the section, the application is scrutinized with reference to the rules and in the light of the rules/law, a note is put up either granting or rejecting the request before the file starts its climb upwards. After scrutiny, decision may be taken on many files at the level of the officer-in-charge. However, depending upon the complexity of a matter several decisions are taken at the level of the ADM or even by the DO.

The system follows what Herbert Simon (in Pomerol and Adam 2004) calls 'programmed decision-making': standardized, predetermined responses are available for a set of predictable applications/situations. If no standardized response to the application exists and interpretation of law or exercise of discretion is required, the level of decision-making goes up. As mentioned earlier, delegation may lower the level at which a number of decisions are taken and is necessary for quick disposal of applications or cases. Certain standards for measuring performance exist but the use and implementation varies from state to state and from one district to another. Monitoring of work may also vary similarly and instruments such as Work Diaries have also known to be abandoned. Even though use of computers has grown in various sections of the Collectorate, in most states most of the work is done manually.

Environment   All organizations need to respond to their environment because they depend upon it for their survival; they receive their 'raw materials' from the environment and deliver their products to customers in it (Bolman and Deal 2003). The Collectorate is no exception. However, it is different from most other private and even public organizations, because it provides services to citizen-customers that are unique. In other words, it has a monopoly on the provision of goods and services that the state delivers through it. Absence of competition and inexorability of its functions make for a stable and predictable environment. Since the Collectorate is a creature of the state, legal and policy frameworks fashioned by statutes and rules demarcate its environment. It includes a multitude of stakeholders—individuals, interest groups, political parties, non-governmental organizations, private firms, media and other non-state actors. These stakeholders interact with the Collectorate, sometimes as customers demanding services and sometimes as pressure groups demanding change in the way it functions and what it provides. An illustrative list of stakeholders of a Collectorate is presented in Appendix 5.

Apart from the external environment of the Collectorate, the elements of its internal work environment also influences the way in which it performs its functions. Most prominent among the internal stakeholders are the employees of the Collectorate. Not all have many opportunities for self-development, but since all government employees are covered by the civil service rules, they are assured of job security. Employees of the Collectorate take pride in being a part of it but instead of translating pride into work, it is a common complaint that, it often finds expression in arrogant behaviour towards citizen-customers. Hierarchy and severe formalism puts up barriers between different levels of employees creating problems of communication. When this happens between different sections, it results in problems of coordination. Camaraderie usually exists among employees at the same level but not across the hierarchy.

The DO's Areas of Responsibility

The functions of the DO 'change in relative importance as well as in scale from state to state, even from season to season in the same state or district' (Maheshwari 1979: 99). This section introduces the major areas of responsibilities of the DO in most districts.

Regulatory Administration

Traditionally, the maintenance of law and order has been perceived as the main regulatory function at the

district level. It is an umbrella phrase that includes not
only administrative and police action in times of public
disturbance, but the maintenance of peace and conditions
for peace at normal times. The separation of the judiciary
from the executive put into effect by the amended Criminal
Procedure Code of 1973 circumscribed the judicial role
of the DO. It distinguished between two types of magistrates, judicial and metropolitan magistrates, and executive magistrates. The former try all kinds of criminal
cases and the latter deal with issues that are primarily
administrative. In this respect, the DO and subordinate
executive magistrates in the district carry out a variety of
functions. These include prevention of crimes (S. 108–10),
maintenance of public order and tranquility (S. 129–32),
prevention of public nuisance (S. 133–43), prevention of
nuisance or 'apprehended danger' (S. 144) and disputes
pertaining to immovable property that threaten public
peace (S. 145–48). It is significant that the role of Executive magistrates relates to the provisions of the CrPC
and not the Indian Penal Code (IPC); that is, to the
preventive sections of the law that require executive
action, rather than the punitive sections that require
judicial decision-making. Maintenance of law and order
includes within its ambit, regulation of observance of
different religious festivals that spill out into public space,
major local social events such as fairs (for example, the
Kumbh Mela at Allahabad or the Ganga Sagar Mela in
South 24 Parganas), and other occasions such as sports,
games or contests which need coordination of a variety of
agencies. The prosecution of criminal cases in courts of law

at the district headquarters and the subdivisions through a panel of pleaders is another important responsibility of the DO. On a regular basis he/she must review the disposal of cases, the service of warrants of arrest and orders for attachment of property.

The DO's regulatory responsibilities include revenue generation activities of the state government that may be of two types: first, the collection of taxes and cess from land, minor minerals, forest produce and so on; and second, from issuance of a variety of licenses and permits such as motor vehicles, arms, explosives and cinema. As the District Election Officer, the DO is responsible to the Election Commission of India for all stages of the election process: preparation of electoral rolls and Election Photo Identity Cards, selection of polling stations, and the complete process of conducting elections to the lower House of Parliament and the State Legislative Assemblies. Similarly during Census Operations, the DO takes on the role of the District Census Officer. The DO is also responsible for the management of Correctional Centres in the district, their inspection and the welfare of the inmates. SDOs are responsible for this function for the subdivisional Correctional Centres.

Another set of law enforcement activities that has grown and that requires the district magistrate's constant attention, is in the area of social justice. These constitute statutory, active protection of vulnerable groups such as scheduled castes and scheduled tribes, bonded labour, children and child labour, the disabled, and women. We shall examine this development more closely later in this book.

Developmental Administration

As noted earlier, the central and state governments implement a large number of development programmes in both rural and urban areas. The DO, in most states, is actively involved at almost all the stages of the programme, and especially during implementation and review. These programmes may be classified as: income generation, self-employment, asset creation and social security schemes. Often there may be an overlap between income generation and asset creation programmes. All four types of programmes envisage the involvement of several agencies. For instance, the National Employment Guarantee Act envisages the provision of work in the form of manual labour to the unemployed and the simultaneous creation of assets. Items of earth work such as excavation of wells or water harvesting structures, land development, and social forestry may be taken up with the help of line departments such as minor irrigation, soil conservation, or forest, the three-tier PRIs and local people. In such programmes, need for coordination by the DO is felt at every stage. In the asset creation, self-employment and social security schemes, other than government departments and PRIs, governmental financial institutions, banks and NGOs are also involved. Industrial development is another thrust area in which numerous actors are engaged and where more and more DOs are being involved as coordinators and facilitators.

Social Sector

The number of programmes in the social sector has increased rapidly—particularly in the fields of education,

health and social welfare. Specifically, the target groups
are children, women, the physically and the mentally challenged, or people suffering from diseases such as leprosy,
tuberculosis or blindness. Programmes aimed at providing
social security to certain classes of people among the poor
have also grown in number. The Annapurna and the
Antodaya programmes aim at ensuring food security for
the poorest of the poor by providing free rations and grains
at subsidized rates, respectively. The central and the state
governments provide pensions to widows, the disabled
and the aged.

Social welfare programmes include the running of
orphanages, short stay homes for women and child
labour schools. It is notable that government investment
and initiative in these areas are being complemented by
investment and technical support by foreign government
organizations, international public organizations, NGOs
and even private actors. Apart from the central and state
government schemes, several externally aided projects are
being undertaken.

The DO has direct responsibility for the proper implementation of these programmes by regularly supervising
and monitoring them.

Crisis Management
Disasters, natural or man-made, absorb administrative
time, effort and resources on a periodic or episodic basis.
In some districts, floods, cyclones, droughts are annual
affairs and dealt with as such leading to a routine system of
response. Close personal attention and involvement of the

DO is vital in disaster-preparedness; in provision of relief; and arrangement of short- and long-term rehabilitation; and the coordination of government departments, Panchayats, NGOs, international public organizations, private actors and local people. Other types of disasters that strike without warning such as earthquakes and thunderstorms also require preparedness—for which the DO is responsible overall.

Residuary Functions

'Residuary functions' may be those functions that do not fall into any one of the categories used to classify them, or includes aspects of all. The term does not reflect upon the importance of the function. It refers to a number of functions of government that either come up occasionally; that are not clearly defined; or for which there is no separate execution mechanism. The DO's residuary functions also include enforcement of special Acts, small savings collection, public relations and protocol duties (Chopra 1978).

Public Grievance Redressal (PGR) is a crucial but residuary function of the DO that cuts across all areas of his/her responsibilities identified above. The DO serves as a single window to the government for complaints of citizen customers dissatisfied with some aspects of district administration. The DO is often called upon to take up the responsibility for an emergent government action in the field. He/she may be asked: to serve as the administrator of a temple trust; as the vice chancellor, or president of a university; as the president of the governing body of a college or school; to mediate disputes between labour and industry or between labour and agriculturists; to make arrangements for the visits of a head of state or other important visitors to the district; or to organize meetings and conferences for government. The list is unending.

Committees

As part of his/her responsibilities the DO is also involved with a variety of government and quasi-government organizations in the district. He/she may be the Chairman, Executive Vice-chairman, Vice Chairman, Secretary or member of numerous committees. Table 2.1, showing the number of district-level committees department-wise in Midnapore district, West Bengal may give an idea of the number of committees in which the DO is involved to a greater or lesser degree.

Although the number of such bodies has changed since the aforementioned information was compiled, the total, and the DOs involvement in them is likely to have increased rather than decreased.

The District Officer and NGOs

Apart from the committees established by the government, the DO is also associated with a variety of institutions and NGOs, some with government sanction, others due to local convention and tradition, and yet others by local initiative. The DO is the Chairman of such government-sponsored institutions such as the District Red Cross Society, Debuttar/Temple Trusts and the District Sports Association. He/she is often the Chairperson of long established educational institutions, recreational clubs such as

TABLE 2.1   Number of District-level Committees Department-wise in Midnapore

Sl. No.	Department	No. of Committees
1.	Agriculture	2
2.	Animal Husbandry and Veterinary	1
3.	Civil Military Liason	2
4.	Commerce and Industries	6
5.	Development and Planning	11
6.	Education	9
7.	Fisheries	2
8.	Forest and Environment	2
9.	Health and Family Welfare	5
10.	Information and Culture	1
11.	Judicial Services	3
12.	Labour and Employment	4
13.	Miscellaneous	15
14.	PWD and Housing	2
15.	Scheduled Castes and Scheduled Tribes Welfare	2
16.	Sericulture	1
17.	Sports and Youth Services	2
18.	Social Welfare	6
19.	Urban Development	3
	Total	79

Source: Collectorate Manual, Midnapore, 1992.

film societies, and centres of art and music. Often times, the DO also is associated with the working of various NGOs operating in the areas of social welfare, health and rural development. Although the DO's role in these institutions is often ceremonial, there are institutions that call upon his active involvement and support for resource generation or programme implementation. Effective DOs are usually able to utilize these organizations—their manpower and their resources—for implementing a variety of government programmes, especially during natural or man-made crises. In view of the increasing role of NGOs, in the process of governance, greater facilitation by the DOs of their activities and their integration with government programmes is desirable. This subject is treated at length in a later chapter.

'The position of the Collector has remained a classic example of unclassified, unconsolidated, diffused responsibility that seems to be one of the marked features of the Indian administrative system' (Das 1958: 54). This view may have held good in the 19th century but, as we shall see in Chapter Three, with every change of leadership—from that of the Company Bahadur to the Crown to Independence and thereafter—there has been a steady clarification of the DO's role and responsibility.

Note

1. In West Bengal although the post of Chowkidar has not been officially abolished, no new appointment to the post has been made since 1982.

Evolving Role of the District Officer

THE DISTRICT Officer (DO) has been frequently and widely described as the 'kingpin,' the 'lynchpin' or the 'keystone' of district level administration in India.[1] From the days of the East India Company, or 'Company Bahadur,' until the present day he, and now also 'she,' has been seen as the pre-eminent administrative functionary of the sub-state territorial unit of administration. Nevertheless, at every stage, in describing the officer and his/her functions, scholars and practitioners alike have assessed the changing role of the office, either wistfully or accusingly, as a constant process of diminution of authority and stature. At the outset, this chapter contends that this line of examination of the DO's office does justice neither to the office nor to the politico-administrative system. For such a viewpoint assumes that apart from the DO, the environment and the context of administration in India have remained a constant; an assumption borne out neither by facts nor by common sense.

This chapter posits that the role of the DO has never remained static, but has continuously evolved in response to the changing nature of the state and its administrative requirements. What has remained unchanged and is unlikely to change as long as the federal, multiple-layered system of territorial administration continues, is the centrality of the DO. The question that needs to be addressed at each stage of this evolutionary process is not merely how the office of the DO changed but why. This chapter, therefore, attempts to explore the factors that have shaped the office in the past and those that are transforming it at this juncture in history. In the above context, the primary objective of this section is to depict the forces of change and the key characteristics of district administration in the past, especially in the 20th century.

To this end, we propose to pursue the evolution of the office of the DO from its inception in the days of the East India Company, and identify the growing demands on the DO and attendant alterations in his/her role through the pre-Independence and post-Independence era. In the following chapter we shall continue with this exploration by examining the impact of public sector reforms at the district level, originating from the priorities of the Indian state and the needs of its citizen customers in the late 20th and early 21st centuries.

Pre-Independence India

The DO, variously referred to as the Collector, District Magistrate and Deputy Commissioner, is by designation and in effect, the chief administrator of a district. As the nomenclature used for the office indicates, in the pre-Independence era, the collection of revenue and the maintenance of law and order were perceived to be his main responsibilities (Rai 1965: 238). Such has been the centrality of the DO's office that Ramsay Macdonald is known to have described the District Magistrate as 'the tortoise, which supports the elephant upon which rests the Government of India' (in Mukhopadhyay 1997: 697). It is noteworthy that the British later transplanted this pattern of district administration in their colonies in South-East Asia and Africa.

As noted in an earlier chapter, both structurally and functionally, the origins of the DO may be traced back to the Mauryan administrative system. The territorial system of administration in India flourished 2500 years ago with the revenue village as its smallest—atomic—unit, and the district (*janapada/ahara*) as the main unit of administration within a province (*janapada*) (Sadasivan 1985). This administrative system survived the ages and can be seen to be in operation in the pre-British days under the Mughals. The roots of the present system and the office of the DO, however, go back to the establishment of the Collector under the British East India Company.

In 1765, when the East India Company received the Diwani of Bengal, Bihar and Orissa, it appointed Supervisors with specific territory-based responsibilities to supervise the collection of revenues for the Company. The 'district' was the designated area of operation assigned to a representative of the Company Bahadur to carry out his commercial activities (Mishra 1965). On 11 May 1772, the Supervisor was renamed as 'Collector' by Warren Hastings who created the office of the Collector through a regulation stating, 'The Company having determined to stand forth as the Dewan, the supervisors should now be designated Collectors' (Mukhopadhyay 1997: 696). Thus, began the saga of the DO.

According to Philip Woodruff, the 'first essentials' that the DO was responsible for were: 'public order, the swift administration of justice, the prompt payment of taxes moderately assessed, the maintenance of accurate and up-to-date land records which would prevent disputes' (1954: 303). Macaulay described the DO under the British Raj as the sole consul of a great province, the district assigned to him being about the size of the four provinces in Ireland. Undoubtedly, the DO was the keeper of the land, for in 'a predominantly agricultural country where land was the primary source of wealth and possession, he was intended to be the chief land revenue official and, therefore, concurrently the law enforcing agency of the provincial executive...' (Sadasivan 1968: 117). Little surprise, therefore, that the system of taxation followed by the East India Company greatly enhanced its resources. The full extent of the flow of revenues from India may be estimated from the fact that in 1765, Bengal by itself generated revenue amounting to 50 per cent of the British public revenue; 'in the 1830s to the 1850s, the 20 million to 25 million pounds collected by the East India Company was about half the revenue of the domestic British state' (Marshall 1997: 91). Understandably, to ensure the regular and full collection of revenues from the depths of the trading hinterland, it was essential to set up a dependable system manned by the best available personnel.

The consolidation and expansion of the Company Bahadur's grip over the vast territories of India witnessed the development cf two models of district administration. In the provinces of Bombay, Madras, North-Western-Provinces and the United Provinces, the Munro school of district administration was followed in contrast to the Cornwallis model. The former carried forward the Mughal legacy of a strong area administrator in whose office was concentrated the role of the revenue collector, civil judge and magistrate; the latter was inspired more by the system of English political tradition and the separation of revenue and judicial functions. Indeed, in Madras Presidency, the absence of a Commissioner between the Collector and the Board of Revenue was a conscious choice intended to maintain 'the power, prestige and position of the Collector ... in the interest of effective administration in the district....' (Sadasivan 1968: 118).

In Bengal, where the foundations of the British Raj were laid, under the Cornwallis model of district administration, the DO was positioned 'as a coordinator of the activities of other district level officials' (Eames and Saran 1989: 192). Under the presumption of the democratic context in 1780, Civil Judges were established in districts. In 1787, to enable the collector to collect rent effectively, he was also made the civil judge and magistrate. Gradually, he became the representative of the governing power and the head of the general administration. In 1790, the Company

went a step further and took over the administration of
criminal justice from the nawab and made the district
collector the District Magistrate as well (Mishra 1965).

In 1793, Cornwallis, in a bid to separate the powers of
the Magistrate-Collector in Bengal, bifurcated the two
functions and bestowed magisterial functions upon the
Judge Magistrate of the district (Mukhopadhyay 1997:
696). Also in 1793, Cornwallis not only permanently
settled the land revenue in perpetuity, he also divested
the Collector of the remnants of judicial authority related
to revenue matters; these were transferred to the Civil
Judge of the district. The latter 'thus became the chief
executive officer of the district' (Mishra 1965: 352).
Yet, the shortcomings of this system and of permanent
settlement led to a gradual restoration of judicial and
investigative authority to the Collector. By the late 1820s,
need was felt to unify in the Collector the responsibilities
of magistracy, revenue collection, some judicial functions
and general administration. By 1831, this process had
advanced considerably even in Bengal. Yet the shift from
the Cornwallis school of district administration, based
on checks and balances, to the more centralized Munro
school in the vast areas of Bengal was completed after the
transfer of the government of India from the East India
Company to the British Crown in the wake of the mutiny
of 1857 (Rai 1965). It led to a concentration of power in
the hands of the DO.

The second half of the 19th century saw the emergence
of two seemingly opposite trends: progressive functional
differentiation of state activities on one hand, and their

coordination and control through the office of the DO on the other. The thrust for specialization resulted in the creation of the office of the Superintendent of Police (SP), the Public Works Department (PWD), and the Health Department. Almost concurrently Sir George Campbell, Lieutenant-Governor of West Bengal, strengthened the collector's office as the General Controlling Officer. While the direct, executive administration of these separate departments was withdrawn from the collector, he continued to be responsible for general control and supervision. Campbell was quite clear that as the head of the district, the collector 'was to control the local departments, not as the drudges of so many departments and master of none, but as the general controlling authority over all the departments in each district' (Mishra 1970: 495). The sentiment was iterated by the Famine Commission of 1880 (Mishra 1970) and the Royal Commission Upon Decentralization in India in 1909 (Rai 1965).[2]

Rai (1965: 239) calls the period stretching from 1859 to 1919 the 'Era of Triumphant Bureaucracy.' This was also the period that saw the crystallization of the British rule in India, through the passage of land revenue and tenancy laws on one hand and three comprehensive codes governing criminal and civil matters in 1861—the Indian Penal Code, the Criminal Procedure Code, and the Civil Procedure Code (Rai 1965), on the other. The Police Regulations of different provinces were also promulgated at this time. Although enactment of these laws curtailed the discretionary authority of the DO, they also recognized him as the principal agent of the government by assigning to him a central role in each case. Over the last 150 years, a pattern may be discerned in the nature of the changing role of the DO: at every stage as discretion has been reduced, the DO's responsibility and role have been defined more sharply.

Democratic administration—aimed at social and economic uplift of the people—was not unknown, but it did not flow from the policies of the colonial state. As Pai notes, development was an uncommon concern among the DOs and likely to be '... secondary and sporadic or extra-curricular. It might have been a personal fad or a hobby to ease boredom' (Pai 1962: 481). Woodruff records that most DOs had a personal preference which they nurtured as a pastime; these ranged from construction of embankments, to planting trees along roads, and building hospitals (Woodruff 1954: 96). Not a planned activity of the rulers, welfare activity initially depended upon the predilections of individual DOs and was often a source of amusement among colleagues.[3]

Thus, developmental duties were a largely unspecified part of the responsibilities of the Collector, but were 'of importance even in the Company days, though the weight and sense of proportion were different' (Pai 1962: 482). The Godavari and Krishna *ayacut*s (the command area of an irrigation scheme, particularly in the Deccan states), the Godavari dam, thousands of tanks, wells, roads, schools, hospitals and dispensaries were created by the DO's efforts in almost all the provinces of the Raj—with or without government prompting. Yet the stress was clearly not on development. Indeed, the Rowlands' report noted that

that at best, an energetic DO strenuously carried out his regulatory functions while paying some attention to the larger issues of welfare of the people of the district; at worst, he paid no attention to development. 'To remedy this, the committee recommended an extension of the duties of the DO, so that he combines the functions of a policeman and a tax gatherer with the beneficent activities of promoting the welfare of the people' (Bailey 1946: 91).

The period between 1919 and 1947 was a particularly trying one for the DO especially in his role as district magistrate. For this was a turbulent political period—of India's struggle for independence and also of the establishment of provincial legislatures and governments. In maintaining law and order, the DO had an independent role but was buffeted by the provincial government, agitating political parties and the central government (Sadasivan 1968). According to Rai, the creation of legislative bodies in the provinces led to the 'contraction of the influence of the DO both in relation to government and in local affairs and a reduction of the scope of his initiative' (Rai 1965: 241).

Thus, during the Indian struggle for independence, from the late 1920s onwards, the DO was under conflicting pressures and received contradictory signals from the provincial and central governments. For instance, Lord Irwin's fluctuating policy of harshness and leniency with the agitating Congress was not always comprehensible at the field level. To be sure, development of self-governing institutions as visualized by the Montague Chelmsford reforms of 1919 appeared to be a simple matter as far as its politics was concerned; the difficulty laid in the move from an authoritarian to a representative government and the transfer of power from administrators to politicians (Beaglehole 1977: 237). More than in the secretariats of the provinces, this may have been true in the districts. However, the district boards were nascent bodies and the DO was expected to help and advise its leaders and members. Yet to most people it was wonderful that within five years the same DOs were working under the Congress government in the provinces as efficiently and loyally as before (Beaglehole 1977). Difficult as the transition was, that it was achieved smoothly enough indicated the ability of the institution of the DO to adapt to changing times and new demands upon it.

Recruiting, Propaganda and Press Committee, and rationing were three responsibilities added to the DO's plate during the Second World War (WW II). In the straitened times and squeezed resources of the Great War, these activities at the ground level were necessary to sustain both, the British war effort and the people. Recruitment of soldiers for the expanding front was as important as keeping the people informed and fed; and chronic shortages of essential commodities needed skilled management and the institution of a control system—of supply and monitoring. These three activities 'symbolized the entry of government agencies into regulation of supply of daily needs of the common man and greater association of the officers with the media to mould public opinion' (Mishra 1998: 51). This accretion of responsibilities also resulted in the expansion of the office establishment of the DO. Prior to the WW II, the DO had little help in terms of gazetted officers posted at headquarters. As Sadasivan (1968) notes, it was at the peak of the WW II that the DO got his first gazetted assistant who was later joined by other officers like the District Revenue Officer in Madras and the Additional District Magistrate (Land Reforms) in Bengal and Bihar.

Thus, the history of the DO in pre-independent India, is a history of the gradual evolution of the principal officer in field administration. From a supervisor of revenue collection under the East India Company to Collector, and then to Collector and District Magistrate with the responsibility of overall administration under the British Raj was not a simple step up a ladder. The office of the DO changed at every stage to adjust to the changing demands of the political and administrative stimuli. During the independence struggle, we again notice the adaptability of the office, while WW II saw it grow in responsibility and stature. In the following section, we shall examine the influences that worked upon the office of the DO after independence and to what effect.

INDEPENDENT INDIA

Independence brought about the most dramatic changes in the environment of public administration in India. In the words of Dayal et al. (1976: 2), 'The real problems of district administration started with the changes in its ecology'. From a colony under an imperial regime,

India became an unfettered democratic state. Although the Minto Morley Reforms of 1909 and the Montague Chelmsford Reforms of 1919 had laid the foundations of democracy and set up elected provincial councils, they had been weak, even half-hearted attempts at representative governance. The Government of India Act, 1935 marked important developments in this regard. However, it was independence that brought with it universal adult suffrage and democratic governance at the central and the state levels with fundamental implications for the role of DOs. The civil service in India 'ceased to play the pre-Independence role of actually governing this country on 15 August, 1947. Prior to this date, the civil service was responsible for both, deliberation and policy formulation as also for implementation of the policy' (Buch, 1982: 41); after Independence, India's political administrators, as David Potter (1986) calls them, were called upon to function not as rulers but to serve the people and the government.

Little wonder then that, after Independence the question frequently asked was: 'Can the administrative structure established by the British for the maintenance of colonial rule be converted to the goals of social and economic development' (Eames and Saran 1989: 191). For, with change in the political framework there had also been a change in the orientation of the Indian state: from regulation to development and welfare. As Sivaraman (1965: 634) puts it, 'Welfare state was the pattern and planned economy the means identified to achieve it.' After studying and deliberating upon the appropriateness of the district administration machinery independent India inherited, the Administrative Reforms Commission (ARC) held that, 'The system has stood the test of time and even though it was basically designed to meet the colonial needs of the British, it can continue to serve the needs of a welfare state also' (ARC Report 1966: 209).

Thus after Independence, along with the alteration in the role of the state, there was a significant course correction in the role of the DO. Rai voices the concerns of the 1960s when he states, 'The institution of the DO has a long history behind it. From time to time there have been changes, additions and subtractions in the duties of the DO. But on the whole his duties have expanded while his powers have diminished' (Rai 1965: 382). However, in the eyes of the people and the government, the DO remained, as he/she does today, at the centre of district administration. He/she continued to be considered the chief representative of government in the district as well as the head of regulatory administration. His/her chief role, however, came to be the supervision and coordination 'of the work of sub-divisional officers, revenue officials, and all other departments in the district' (Saigal 1977: 209).

Apart from the downward spread of democracy and multiplication of departments, the separation of the judiciary from the executive modified the role of the DO (Dave 1965). Dayal et al. (1976) note two other significant developments challenging the pre-Independence DO-based system: the rapid elaboration of specialized line departments and the establishment of local government bodies. Therefore, from an 'integrated' stage, district administration passed into a 'differentiated stage'. However, they ignore a host of other influences that affected and altered the role of the DO in the new India that is Bharat. In this context it is noteworthy that even as the state sought to take on the responsibilities of a welfare state, the DO's primary role as a regulator maintaining law and order and a collector of revenue, underwent alterations but did not necessarily diminish.

The immediate post-Independence era beginning from the mid-1950s and the early 1960s witnessed the transformation of some of the principal regulatory functions of the DO. With the separation of the judiciary from the executive—that started in the early 1950s, the DO ceased to be in administrative charge of all magistrates in the jurisdiction, or to serve as a court of criminal appeal and a criminal court. This paring of judicial responsibilities, however, did not divest him/her of the responsibility for maintaining law and order in the district nor for overall supervision and control of the district police (Fletcher 1965). Even in the field of maintenance of law and order, we find changes in core issues and the nature of the DO's response to them. For instance, the state witnessed post-Independence violence in the late 1940s and communal tensions in the early 1950s and 1960s; the late 1960s and the 1970s were dominated by student violence and agitation against the emergency; while the 1980s saw the emergence of terrorism in a number of states such as Punjab, and Jammu and Kashmir; and, the 1990s have seen the rise of ultra-left inspired militancy. The district level response to these different types of violation of order has demanded differing responses for conflict resolution by the DOs in which negotiation and consultation have come to figure prominently.

In Revenue or Land Administration also, a key function of DOs under the Raj, the passage of Zamindary Abolition Acts and Land Reforms Acts shifted the emphasis from the collection of land revenue to the redistribution of ceiling surplus land and the formulation and enforcement of intermediary rights. It is noteworthy that although in the initial years, land reforms in most states proceeded haltingly at best and at worst not at all, they slowly gained importance in almost every state. Hence, within land administration itself a number of changes occurred. These ranged from new activities after the enactment of land ceiling laws, levy on land improvement, agricultural income tax, and expansion of old activities such as consolidation of land holdings and land acquisition (Rai 1965). For a variety of reasons that are beyond the pale of this study, the agenda of land reforms is a simmering issue even today in many states.

Further, the DO has continued as the head of revenue administration to supervise the collection of a wide variety of government dues—which include taxes, government loans, cooperative loans, excise revenue, motor vehicles revenues, mining cess and royalties, land revenue and water rates and other user charges (Singh 1994). A number of these sources of revenue, especially the user charges, belong to the post-Independence era.

Therefore, even in the regulatory sphere the DO's role has remained far from static. Although land revenue may have declined as the main source of government income, the importance of revenue collection has not.

At the same time, the changing nature of the state from a colonial rent-seeking regime to an independent, aspiring welfare state was reflected in the changes in the nature of territorial administration at the sub-district level. There was considerable variation in the sub-district level territorial units in pre-Independence India with the police station (*thana*), consisting of a large group of villages, occupying the level below the subdivision. However, 1952 onwards, with the introduction of the community development programme, the Community Development Block— comprising a population of about 15,000 to 20,000—became the intermediate level of developmental administration. In many states like Uttar Pradesh, Tamil Nadu, Andhra Pradesh and Bihar, revenue circles or tehsils also continued to exist. On the other hand, the creation of new districts has not followed any particular pattern. Political considerations have often predominated the formation of new districts; in some states like Kerala, Maharashtra and Jammu and Kashmir, communal considerations are allegedly responsible for creation of new districts with a concentration of minority population (Sadasivan 1985). Yet generally, the two justifications for the creation of new districts are:

(a) to take government closer to the people; and
(b) to make implementation of development programmes more manageable.

Thus, starting with 360 in 1947 the number of districts at the time of writing, stands at 604.

Instead of reducing the burden of the DO, the shift in the state's emphasis on development increased his/her functional responsibilities by making 'him the main instrumentality of the development programme' (Sadasivan 1968: 119). As Dayal et al. (1976) put it, 'the state has changed from being reactive to proactive. Although today there is great emphasis on planning, in pre-Independence India, planned development of rural areas was not known'. As Rajan observes, at the time 'of the First FYP, the district administration was totally unaccustomed to planned activity extending into the rural area' (1990: 211). However, planning became a key element of India's development strategy immediately after Independence. At the topmost policy making level, it led to the establishment of the Planning Commission of India in 1951 while at the field level it resulted in focus upon the district as the unit of planning and administration of development programmes with a further expansion of the DO's assignment.

The stress upon agricultural development by government may be noted from 1963 onwards. It began with the Intensive Agricultural District Programme (IIDP), followed by the Intensive Agricultural Areas Programme (IAAP), and culminated 'in the New Strategy of Agricultural Development in 1967 with the introduction of high yielding varieties, etc.' (Sudan 1985: 756). The context for this stress on agriculture and the DO's involvement in it, were the food shortages of the late 1950s and mid-1960s that egged the state towards self-sufficiency in food production and the extension of the public distribution system. While the former added developmental responsibilities to the DO's charges, the latter—with the passage of the Essential Commodities Act in 1955 and orders issued under it, added a new dimension to his/her regulatory duties.

After the first two decades of Independence, it is possible to distinguish attempts by states to experiment and change the structural arrangements at the district level. The creation of 'diarchy' in the form of a Deputy Development Commissioner (DDC) equal in rank and seniority to the DO in Bihar is a case in point. This step was taken in June 1973 with the aim of effective implementation of the development programmes. As Rai and Prasad (1983) note, it was a short-lived experiment. The new system fractured the unity of command at the district level and threw into confusion the chain of command and communication. The most important reason for restoring the traditional authority of the DO was: problems with interdepartmental coordination. It was widely felt that 'the coordination at the district level had become weak and nominal. The creation of the vertical hierarchies by various departmental agencies had left the DO out of reasoning from various activities pertaining to the respective departments' (Rai and Prasad 1983). The declaration of emergency and the urgency of implementing the 20-point programme, strengthened the course of restoring the authority of the DO in Bihar.

The experiment in Madras State, now Tamil Nadu took a different form. The Madras District Councils Act 1958 created district development councils with the DO as its chairman. This kind of body was created in other states as well to accelerate planned development and decentralization. As Sadasivan remarks, this step combined in the office of the DO 'two types of leadership namely, the bureaucratic and the democratic' (1968: 120). In neighbouring Andhra Pradesh, in 1968, the DO was appointed the head of the developmental departments in the district in the interest of speedy implementation of development programmes (Rao 1981).

The success of the Green Revolution also illuminated the problems of making the rural poor shareholders in development! To build upon the success of the Green Revolution and to expand it to include the rural poor—particularly the marginal farmers and the landless—a variety of programmes were initiated in the Fourth (1969–74) and Fifth (1974–79) Five Year Plans (FYPs). Some of these were: Small Farmers Development Agency and Marginal Farmers and Agricultural Labourers Agency (SFDA and MFALA), the Command Area Development Programme, the Drought Prone Area Programme, the Desert Development Programme, the Tribal Development Agency Projects and in 1978–79 the Integrated Rural Development Programme (IRDP) (Sudan 1985) that paved the way for the formation of the District Rural Development Agency (DRDA). Pertinently, the DO was made the Chairman of the DRDA and made responsible for the implementation of IRDP and other programmes that accrued.

The tribal sub-plan strategy initiated under the Fifth FYP, identified blocks with concentration of indigenous people for undertaking specific interventions aimed at their socio-economic development. In most states the DO was intimately involved with planning, supervision, and implementation of schemes under the programmes (Singh 1985). The role of the state with respect to social welfare activities expanded steadily from the late 1960s and early 1970s (Rao 1981). The emphasis on development of the weaker sections, especially the scheduled castes and scheduled tribes, through an institutional approach, for instance by the setting up of District Harijan Welfare Committees, and a development orientation marked another significant change in the perspective and role of district administration (Purushottam 1996). It turned the DO into an agent of social change by calling upon him/her to play a much more proactive role than ever before.

If the 1970s witnessed the further addition of development programmes, especially in the area of poverty alleviation and rural development, to the list of DO's duties the late 1980s and early 1990s saw a new mode of development intervention—projects. Two factors may be deemed responsible for this new twist in the nature of the DO's work: first, a conscious effort on the part of the government to introduce management by objectives; and, second, a significant rise in the number of externally aided projects— at the district level. The former resulted in the adoption of the Mission approach to tackling long languishing problems such as illiteracy and unavailability of drinking water resulting in the creation of five special 'Missions'. The latter in the form of increased funding of projects by multilateral and bilateral institutions such as the World Bank, the Department of Foreign and International

Development (DFID), UK, and several organizations of the United Nations system, hastened 'projectization.' In this regard, the DFID funded District Primary Education Programme in six states, the World Bank funded the irrigation and health projects in four states, and the German GTZ funded projects in drinking water and health projects in five states, are cases in point. For implementation of these and similar projects on the ground, international agencies usually insisted upon enlisting the leadership of the DO.

By the 1980s, however, criticism of the DO-based system of district administration resurfaced. With the expansion of the developmental agenda of the government, some observers like Sadasivan (1985: 738) felt that the 'district administration as it now exists is an outworn system, incompatible with modernity and unfit for democratic society.' Other scholars like Mishra (1998) apprehended that the consolidation of democracy and democratic institutions had resulted in the domination of district administration by politicians: 'By the time the country was in its second decade of independence, the Collector had almost ceased to function on the lines of his British predecessor. He had been exposed to interference from higher authorities particularly at the instance of politicians'.[4] According to some commentators, the short and uncertain tenure of DOs in many states, in the last quarter of the 20th century was the most glaring indicator of this interference. This not only created administrative uncertainty and it affected not just the DO's morale but also his/her ability to deliver (Eames and Saran 1989; Mishra 1998; Potter 1986).

Another instance of weakening of the DO's position was seen reflected in the 'generalist versus specialist' controversy, the DO being often cited as a leading example of the generalist administrator (Mukhopadhyay 1983). This conflict was often noted in the DO's relationship with the police, especially because it began to be informed by political considerations. In the words of one comment-ator though the relations between the DO and the SP has always been a sensitive issue, 'After Independence, the police has resented its subordinate role vis-à-vis the District Magistrate in managing the law and order affairs. The political bosses are also inclined to accord independent status to the police officers' (Acharya 1996: 92).

In a study conducted in the late 1980s Eames and Saran found that in the post-Independence period, the perception of the DO being 'overburdened, relatively powerless and inadequately compensated' (1989: 197) existed even among the DOs. We hear iterated the familiar lament from the 1960s: 'On the whole, there has been an increase in his re-sponsibilities, if not his authority' (Singh 1994: 171). While Mishra goes so far as to say that the 'authority of the DO has steadily been eroded and his position in the district as No. 1 is no longer unquestioned' (Mishra 1998: 60).

How valid are these criticisms? How accurate the charges? In the above section we have seen that after Independence not only was the DO called upon to shoulder new responsibilities, his/her existing responsibilities also underwent significant changes within the new matrix of democracy and self-government. There were changes in the nature of the DO's regulatory functions, a diminution of the judicial responsibilities, a significant elaboration of the developmental functions, and an accretion of duties in the area of social change. Indeed, the burgeoning of the DO's duties was a sign of his enduring centrality to the administrative system, and the undeniable political attempts to interfere with the workings of the office an added indication of its importance. It may also be noted that, except for the reduction in judicial responsibilities as mandated under the Constitution, in law there was no dilution of either the DO's authority or his/her jurisdiction.

The most recent and significant changes in the Indian state may be traced to the late 1980s and the early 1990s; these may be grouped together in four categories; first, decentralization through not only the 73rd and 74th Amendments to the Constitution but also through the growth of non-state actors such as non-governmental organizations (NGOs) and grass roots organizations (GROs); second, economic reforms initiated in 1990 that unleashed the forces of privatization such as marketization, contractualization, and public-private partnerships; third, administration aimed at improving the efficiency of government systems; and, fourth, new forces for accountability such as judicial activism, the right to information, and the media. Additionally, incremental growth but increased impetus in the last two decades of the 20th century in the legislation for social change and correction in areas like women's issues, rights of the child, and welfare of the disabled has informed most of these changes. These processes have effected an internal restructuring of the state, amplified its responsibilities, altered the way it discharges its duties, and modified relations between the state and citizens.

Although these developments have generated debate and discussion at the national and state levels, the impact on the administrative machinery at the district level has received no more than passing attention. Yet it is at the district and sub-district levels that the effects of these changes are, if not obvious, most desired. Both, what the state does and how it does it have changed, and are changing. Further, new expectations have been engendered regarding both the form and substance of state action.

At the district level, the role and responsibilities of the DO, often seen as the principal agent of change, are also being transformed. On the one hand, new regulatory frameworks call for stronger rowing while on the other, forces of decentralization and privatization call for more steering and less rowing. DOs must not only adapt to the changing environment of administration but also adopt new methods and practices to effectively perform their new role. In the following chapters we shall explore the impact of public sector reforms at the district level on the duties and activities of the DO and what they mean for the future role of this key functionary.

Notes

1. 'Perhaps no other institution in India is as much shrouded in the mystery and magic epithets as the Collector. He has been variously described as "Annadata," "Maa-Bap," "representative and agent of government," "general manager of all Governement activities," "eyes and ears (and sometimes arms) of government," "the kingpin of administration," "the captain, sometime non-playing, of the team," "the man on the spot," "the area specialist," "the supreme head of

the district administration," and more recently in more benevolent terms, like "friend, philosopher and guide," "the main-spring of development," and "the director of the Rath of Lord Jagannath (the Rath of Panchayati Raj)"' (Dubashi 1965: 614).

2. Various committees and commissions have held up the primacy of the D.O. For details please see: Report of the Royal Commission Upon Decentralization in India, vol. I (1909), para 539; Memorandum Submitted by the Government of the United Provinces to the Indian Statutory Commission, vol. IX, HMSO, London (1930), p. 47; and Indian Statutory Commission, vol. I, HMSO, London (1930), p. 291.

3. 'Why is my district death-rate low
   Said Binks of Hezabad,
   'Wells, drains and sewage outfalls are
   My own peculiar fad.'
   (Woodruff 1954: 96)

4. It is not clear, whether for even a moment the critic questions the desirability of the DO's functioning 'on the lines of his British predecessor' in free India!

Public Sector Reforms: Impact at the District Level

IT IS true that the waves of New Public Management and Reinventing Government did not directly lash the shores of the public sector in India; yet elements of both have found their way to the subcontinent. Spurred on by a severe balance-of-payments crisis and nudged along by the structural adjustment stipulations of the International Monetary Fund (IMF), the wide-ranging economic reforms initiated in the early 1990s hastened public sector reforms in India (Ariff and Iyer 1995; Saxena 2003). Market liberalization and privatization were only two forces, and manifestations of reforms (Ahluwalia 1998). These processes of change have contributed to an internal restructuring of the state, amplified its responsibilities, altered the way it discharges its duties, and modified the relations between state and citizens.

The trend towards decentralization, which had been gathering force in the previous three decades, resulted in 1993 in the 73rd and 74th Amendments to the Constitution that mandated the creation of a three-tier structure of local self government—Panchayat Raj Institutions (PRIs) in the rural areas and municipal bodies in urban areas. Decentralization was accompanied by increasing citizens' participation. Paucity of resources, administrative reforms, pressure of multilateral institutions, judicial activism and advances in information technology also emphasized efficiency and accountability in the public services. In the changing context the district officer (DO) must not only adapt to the changing environment of administration but also adopt new methods and practices to effectively perform his/her new role.

The objective of this chapter is to examine and analyse the impact and the implications of public sector reforms at the district level.

Public Sector Reforms at the District Level

The impact of four main types of reforms may be discerned at the district level. Decentralization and participation are evident not only in PRIs, but also in the involvement of non-governmental organizations (NGOs) in service delivery; creation of government-operated NGOs (GONGOs) at the district and sub-district levels to promote functional and financial autonomy; and, in the promotion by the state of new grass root bodies such as Joint Forest Management (JFM) committees. The impact of market forces may be seen in the trend towards privatization, notably in outsourcing of services; contractualization of not only services but also of personnel engaged in government agencies; introduction of user fees for hitherto free services such as medical facilities; public-private partnerships in the social sector; and regulation of existing, unacknowledged, or newly developed markets. Administrative reforms have also led to greater use of information technology in service delivery; new personnel policies; and simplification of procedures. The concern for accountability of the district administrative machinery has been addressed by increased transparency—especially after the passage of the Right to Information Act 2005; the explosion of media coverage, both print and electronic, of district level governance activities; and the role of civil society organizations (CSOs), National and State Commissions and the judiciary.

Decentralization

Faith in decentralization is founded on the belief that decentralized decision making will make for greater efficiency in the utilization of resources (Chatterji and Ghosh 2003). The avowed aims of decentralization are to '(a) ensure effective governance and equitable political representation through the institution of federalism; and (b) to promote economic growth and social justice' (Tremblay 2001: 216). In India, Article 40 in the Directive Principles of State Policy in Part IV of the Constitution of India, laid the foundations of decentralization[1] (http://panchayat.nic.in). In the wake of the Balwant Rai Mehta Committee recommendations, Panchayat Raj was first initiated in Rajasthan in 1959 followed by the passage of legislation for its establishment by most other states. However, by the early 1970s political tensions, financial dependence on the state government, extended period of suspension and administrative indifference[2] had dissipated PRIs in most states. Sharma (1985) notes that Panchayat Raj before the 73rd Amendment passed through three phases: the phase of ascendancy (1959–64), the phase of stagnation (1965–69), and the phase of decline (1969 onwards). However, beginning in the late 1970s, the political leadership in the four states of Gujarat, Maharashtra, Karnataka and West Bengal paid special attention to the establishment of PRIs; elections were held regularly for all three tiers, efforts were made to decentralize functions, and attempts made to provide them with resources and administrative machinery to carry out their mandate.

The need for viable and responsive PRIs again gathered steam in the country in the mid-1980s, and in 1993 by the 73rd Amendment to the Constitution the creation of the three-tier PRIs in states across the country[3] became mandatory. Conferment of constitutional status on PRIs under Article 243 of Part IX of the Constitution, not only made it binding upon all states to promulgate their own new acts as per the provisions of the 73rd Constitutional Amendment Act, it also created a uniform structure for PRIs. As Mathur (1998) observes, the 73rd Amendment turned PRIs from largely developmental bodies in the pre-1993 years into constitutionally mandated local self-government institutions. The 74th Constitution Amendment Act also passed in 1993, was similarly aimed at conferring constitutional status upon urban local bodies, and ensuring their stability, feasibility and uniformity across the country. Both these Acts provided for greater devolution of functions and the authority of taxation; assured financial support based on recommendations of State Finance Commissions; reservation of seats for Scheduled Castes (SCs), Scheduled Tribes (STs) and women; and compulsory periodic elections for the local bodies.

The impact of the 73rd and 74th Amendments on the existing structure of district administration was foreseen by Dave (1965: 377) who recognized the potential for the introduction 'of diversity in district administration in contrast to the basic continuity and uniformity which has existed over almost a century.' There is little doubt that the establishment of PRIs has led to a fundamental restructuring of the system of governance in India; and the office of the DO is at the centre of both the process of restructuring as well of the restructured system.

The challenge before the state is to reconcile the role and interests of the state government with that of the local self-government bodies. Different approaches to balancing the two sets of interests may be seen in different states. In some states like Karnataka and Maharashtra, the office of the DO has been distanced from that of the PRIs. In other states like West Bengal, a largely successful attempt has been made to utilize the many strengths of the DO's office by appointing him/her as the executive officer of the district panchayat. It is notable that even in those states that have not associated the DO with the PRIs, the state government continues to count upon him/her for overall guidance, supervision, coordination and conflict resolution in the area of development administration.

With great prescience V.T. Krishnamachari had observed, 'The collector's role has changed but not diminished for he now has the function of guiding democratic bodies. Often he has to carry conviction with members of democratic institutions' (Pai 1962: 488). Whether directly involved or distantly associated, the role of the DO in relation to PRIs is an important one that requires a new orientation and new skills.

Decentralization was accompanied by increasing citizens' participation. Apart from PRIs, participation by other non-state entities in the process of governance escalated in the 1990s. In this respect, the second important development in the area of decentralization in India has been the ascendance of NGOs. In India, the term NGO includes a bewildering variety of organizations (Sen 1998) such as community based organizations (CBOs); non-party political groups; welfare, philanthropic, relief and development organizations; GONGOs; and, caste, regional and religious groups. With the tentative engagement in the first two decades of the post-Independence era, involvement of NGOs in development has steadily grown and has been perceived a part of the national planning process since the First Five Year Plan (FYP).

From the beginning, the state has provided space and resources to NGOs, especially in the social sector.[4] As early as 1956, the Central Social Welfare Board (CSWB) started a grants-in-aid programme to encourage social welfare activities among the non-governmental sectors (Kudva 2005). Although outlays were made for NGO-based service delivery in the earlier FYPs, from the Seventh FYP onwards, NGOs were allocated funds to plan their own schemes—on the basis of the needs felt by the people[5] (Roy 1987; Sen 1998). The state in India continues to be the main provider of services, but more and more NGOs are getting involved in service delivery—especially in areas where the state apparatus is either absent or not performing (Clayton, Oakly and Taylor 2000).

A large number of NGOs are also committed to advocacy and research. The Peoples' Union of Civil Liberties (PUCL) and Centre for Science and Environment (CSE) are two such NGOs active in the areas of advocacy for human rights and environmental sustainability, respectively. Apart from seeking policy modification at the central and state government levels these NGOs also exert pressure upon district level government organizations for the effective implementation of developmental programmes— through public interest litigation.

A third category of organizations that have also developed and consolidated their positions in the last three decades may be termed grass root organizations (GROs). They may be distinguished from NGOs in that they do not serve merely as intermediaries for service delivery, advocacy or research. Rather they are organized bodies of direct recipients of certain entitlements for which they engage with and pressure the state. Further, as Mendiratta and Smith (2001: 3) add, they are 'generally membership-based, are struggle-oriented and have few or no paid staff.' These may be single issue GROs such as Pensioners Associations or organizations concentrating upon a cluster of related issues such as Senior Citizens Associations (Nayar 2003) or Slum-dwellers Association. As D'Cruz and Satterthwaite (2006) show some of these associations have formed into federations with membership exceeding two million.

Joint Forest Management Committees (JFMCs) or Forest Protection Committees (FPCs) are also GROs but with a difference; they have been organized largely through government initiative. JFM guidelines were first issued by the central government in June 1990. By 2003, 25 states had passed resolutions for the establishment of the JFM and its institutional framework (Das 2003). The experience in West Bengal and Jharkhand shows that being created through government initiative does not dilute their ability, like other GROs, to either partner with or pressure government agencies; they are also effective in mobilizing people (Tiwary 2003). In several districts in West Bengal, FPCs have been given the responsibility for executing schemes under the National Food for Work Programme and the Rashtriya Sama Vikas Yojana in villages within the forest or on the peripheries.

The role played by grass roots NGOs/CBOs in garnering local support for government programmes is also growing and may determine its success or failure. The Swachchha Grama Yojana is a PRI-based rural sanitation programme in Karnataka; it is an initiative to involve people not only in developing private sanitation infrastructure, but to address basic issues in public health such as diarrhea and dysentery through the process. In the first year of the second phase of the programme, Rs 59 lakh were collected from 59 villages (*The Hindu* 2005). Another example is the establishment of Community Information Centres in Assam, through the joint efforts of district administration, the Assam Small Farmers' Agri-Business Consortium (Assam SFAC), and NGOs. It aims to provide information related to agriculture, agri-business and a host of government services to farmers, traders and NGOs at sub-district levels upon the payment of user fees (*Assam Tribune* 2005).

Thus, the central and state governments have been joined in India by PRIs, NGOs and GROs[6] in providing services and undertaking development at the grass roots. For long it has been argued that social welfare services—such as children's homes, day care centres, services for women and for the welfare of SCs and STs—should be transferred to NGOs (Nanavatty 1996). The experience in some states shows that complementarity of NGOs, Panchayats and the state governments in the field of public service provision, has gradually replaced conflict among them (Arya 1999). For the DO these developments imply a change from previous modes of functioning, a change that is also a challenge.

Market Forces—Marketization

In the Indian context, economic liberalization initiated in 1990 translates into deregulation, de-licensing, disinvestment and privatization. In other words, it means the dismantling of the 'license-permit raj' and the withdrawal of the 'subsidy state,' thus replacing a mixed economy by a market friendly one (Chandrasekharan 1997: 124).

Chandrasekharan also points out that two prominent drivers of change in the role of the state at the field level are democratic decentralization and economic reforms.

The changing nature of public administration and its evolving requirements in the transitional societies like India, in the post-cold war period stem from a variety of factors: the impact of liberalization, globalization and privatization on the structures of administration in these countries; the restructuring of public management systems in the context of both emerging markets and the gradual but steady consolidation of institutions of local self government; the shrinking of state resources; the steady escalation in the number of internationally-aided development programs; the growth of the non-governmental sector and its expanding role in delivery of government schemes; and, new areas of public-private partnership. These trends and pressures ensure the emergence in India of novel modes of administration of government programmes and delivery of public services; in turn, these mandate new personnel arrangements, particularly of recruitment and training, that mark a shift from the paradigm of permanent employment in government to models of semi-permanent, temporary and contractual systems of employment for government programmes. Further, these developments are not re-stricted to a particular sector or a specific policy area in an isolated state. They cut across the entire gamut of regu-latory, distributive and redistributive policies that state governments administer around the country.

However at the national level, privatization of state-owned enterprises and withdrawal of the state from the business of business continues, and continues to spark debates. Market forces have also affected government at the district level. It is possible to identify four important forms in which market forces have come into play: outsourcing of services, contractualization, implementation of user fees and public–private partnerships. As we explore the manifestations of these methods and instruments of the Public Sector Reforms (PSR) at the district level, it may be useful to remember that there are areas of overlap and integration among them. We must also recognize that these forces may not make obvious or grand appearances on an imposing scale but are evident even in routine operations of public management.

An instance of privatization due to failure of state to provide a service or good and consequent regulation is electricity generation. The rise in population and the growth of industry and trade have not been matched by a commensurate increase in electricity generation. To meet the rising demand industries, business firms, trade and residential establishments have resorted to ensuring uninterrupted supply of electricity by setting up electricity generation units that run on diesel. In most urban and semi-urban centres, business establishments and many homes depend on these generators. However, generation of electricity over five kilo-volt (kV) requires payment of duty in most states. The collection of electricity duty is the responsibility of the DO; as a result, in recent years registration and levying of electricity duty from all such generators by DOs in states like West Bengal has increased substantially.

Due to the expansion of government and the shrinkage of resources, there has been a conscious attempt by governments at both the centre and in the states to reduce expenditure by outsourcing a variety of services that other government agencies/units earlier provided. A significant area in this regard is the hiring or lease of official vehicles, instead of buying them, by all departments of government at the district level. This is a strategy to not merely reduce capital expenditure but also recurring costs of vehicle maintenance and expenditure on permanent drivers. In many states several other support services such as printing, photocopying and data entry in the district level government offices, including the DO's office, are being outsourced to private service providers based on a publicized bidding process on an annual basis. Upkeep of government premises, catering arrangements in circuit houses, and renting of generators for back-up electricity supply has replaced the do-everything-yourself approach that earlier burdened district administration.

The same trend is visible in the procurement process. In Karnataka, provisions and school uniforms for students residing in the state-run hostels for SC and ST students were earlier supplied by state-run corporations. Now, local governments have been authorized to make local purchases. Similar devolution of authority for procurement from private sources has occurred in government-run social welfare institutions, short-stay homes and even in schools in West Bengal.

Since the 1990s, user charges have also been introduced in various segments of public service provision around the country. Since the mid-1990s in West Bengal, municipal corporations and municipalities have been encouraged to levy water tax—something not considered politically feasible a few years ago (*Financial Express* 2005). Although entry fee was already being charged in many of the larger parks maintained by the Forest department in West Bengal, in 2003, it was introduced for a majority of the parks even in the districts (*The Times of India* 2003). Even in Orissa, perhaps the most vulnerable state in India, although introduction of user fees for veterinary services gave rise to procedural problems, the government modified the procedures instead of withdrawing the fees (*The Statesman* 2005).

The National Population Policy unveiled in 2002 proposed a user fee in the health sector while the new National Health Policy espoused the levying of a user charge in district hospitals (*The Times of India* 2002). Predictably the proposal raised storms, but over the years has been introduced in many states, especially those implementing health sector revival projects funded by multilateral agencies such as the World Bank, the Asian Development bank and the European Commission.

Contractualization in the health sector started in some states in India in the mid-1990s. It was in response to the shortage of doctors attending patients in remote primary health centres, subdivisional and district hospitals— particularly for engagement of specialists in radiology, anesthesia and orthopedics. The World Bank Health Systems project in West Bengal and Punjab also opened the way for contracting out hospital services such as maintenance, cleaning, emergency power supply and security. In Punjab, corporatization of the health sector was attempted by establishing the Punjab Health Corporation. The creation of GONGOs and projectization of programme implementation (such as universalization of primary education) has also resulted in contractual, instead of permanent employment. Although contractualization and outsourcing have been supported by studies conducted internationally and need to be extended (Jalan 2005), its three main limitations must be recognized: to avail of a service for which a fee is charged, those most in need of the service must have the capacity to pay; private agencies and even NGOs are unlikely to step in remote, inaccessible areas that lack infrastructure; and, social structure may not always facilitate contractualization.[7]

The first instances of public private partnership (PPP) can also be found in the health sector. In each of the 16 districts of Arunachal Pradesh, one Primary Health Centre (PHC) has been handed over to an NGO, including Karuna Trust of Karnataka, Voluntary Health Association (VHA), Future Generation and Prayas. These PHCs became operational in January 2006 with funds provided by the state government. A committee chaired by the district medical officer, including Anchal Samity members and NGO representatives was responsible for its implementation (*Hindustan Times* 2006). PPP is also evident in IT projects. In Uttaranchal, under the 'Arohi' project, computerization of rural schools and computer training to teachers to disseminate computer skills, is being provided. This is a PPP scheme in which Microsoft and Intel, two of the largest multinational corporations in the world, are partners.

Administrative Reforms

Several books deal extensively with the history of administrative reforms in India (Arora and Goyal 1996; Maheshwari 2000), therefore this section shall not attempt to go over the ground again. It deals with efforts made since the 1990s to reform public administration in India. It may also be noted that many of the reforms highlighted below were not necessarily based on enunciated policy. However, the aim here is to examine existing processes and their consequences for reform of administration at the district level.

In November 1996, the Government of India (GOI) organized a Conference of Chief Secretaries of States and Union Territories on effective and responsive administration. The Conference of Chief Ministers on responsive administration followed this in May 1997 (Pradhan 2001). An important output of this conference was an action plan focusing on:

(1) Accountable and citizen friendly administration;
(2) Transparency and right to information; and
(3) Improving performance and integrity of the civil services (Sundaram 1997).

In 1997, the Fifth Pay Commission also recommended several strategies for right-sizing government: restricting government focus on the core functions (policy making, monitoring and coordination in critical sectors) and leaving the rest to the private and the NGO sector; organizational re-engineering; work force control through the abolition of vacant posts (350,000); freeze on recruitment; across the board cuts; statutory control on new post creation; voluntary retirement; compulsory retirement; and use of IT in the government (Dey 1997). In the year 2000, the Expenditure Reforms (Geethakrishnan) Commission also highlighted similar concerns.

Responsiveness

Following the Chief Ministers' Conference in 1997, several steps were taken to implement its resolutions. To achieve responsive and citizen-friendly administration, attempts were made to improve the grievance redressal mechanism at all levels, computerized follow-up and designation of nodal officers from departments down to the districts. DOs, as well as other district level officials were directed to visit remote areas to respond to the needs of the poor. The introduction of Citizens' Charters to enhance responsiveness and accountability was another important step that we shall examine in a later section.

Training

Training of civil servants to improve administrative performance, also identified as a thrust area in the 1990s, led to the formulation of the National Training Policy, 1996 (Pradhan 2001).[8] Consequently, the last decade has seen the setting up within states of regional administrative training institutes at district headquarters with the DO usually heading it. During the late 1990s, the concept of Annual Action Plan and Management By Objectives (MBO) was introduced in the central government ministries and state owned enterprises (Pradhan 2001). It has gradually moved attention away from expenditure targets, a pre-occupation with government organizations at all levels, to performance.

Downsizing—Rightsizing

The attempt to downsize government may be traced to the mid-1980s, when the central government banned recruit-ment in some agencies such as the Postal Department. By the end of the 1990s, the ban had been extended to almost all central departments and also to some union territories. Currently, the prohibition on recruitment affects all depart-ments in almost all states. The shortage of about 25 per cent firemen in Andhra Pradesh (*The Economic Times* 2002) and of prison staff in Pune, are two cases in point (*The Economic Times* 2003). In Tamil Nadu, not only have 150,000 posts not been filled, contractual appointments in a variety of departments such as health and education resulted in poor service delivery because contractors employed under or unqualified persons with inadequate experience (*The Hindu* 2005). Thus, freezing recruitment has been a common strategy adopted by both the centre and the states, to reduce the size of government and non-plan expenditure.

Certain states have undertaken downsizing of govern-mental workforce more openly and systematically. In 2002, as part of its economy measures, the Kerala government resolved to undertake an exercise in downsizing. By the end of 2003, the committee formed for the purpose had identified 17,195 positions in various departments as surplus. By a government order dated 19 November 2003, 3510 posts were abolished in the Departments of Land Records and Survey, Health and Family Welfare, Fisheries, Registration, Industry and Commerce, Fisheries and in the Directorate of Medical Education. Of the 17,195 surplus positions identified, 3,570 lying vacant had been abolished earlier (*The Hindu* 2003). This has also been an exercise in rightsizing, for 2,915 personnel were also redeployed to the local self-government bodies, while 1,663 were to soon follow suit (*The Hindu* 2003).

Simplification

To improve efficiency and quality of service, the government has also attempted to simplify procedures and systems. An instance of simplification of procedures is the enactment of the National Highway Authority of India (NHAI) Act of 1998. Prior to this act, the acquisition of land usually took two to three years. This was seen as a major bottleneck for speedy implementation of the Golden Quadrilateral National Highway project of the GOI. The simplified process under the NHAI Act, 1998 allows acquisition of land for the NHAI implemented road infrastructure projects within one year (Haldea and Mohanty 2003).

Decentralization of authority from the state to the district level has also been used as a means for simplifying procedure. This was a distinctive feature of the District government initiative of the state government in Madhya Pradesh in the late 1990s. Other states have been more cautious and taken measures on a case-to-case basis. For instance, to speed up the process of land acquisition in 1995, Government of West Bengal appointed the District Magistrate of Midnapore ex-officio joint secretary to government in the Land and Land Reforms department.

Information and Communication Technology
The movement in the 1980s for computerization, was transformed by the late 1990s into information and communication technology (ICT) initiatives, and in the new millennium rose the cry for e-governance. IT in the public sector, in India, has been increasingly utilized for both internal support processes and for critical procedures that produce goods or services for citizens. These products may be authorized forms, copy of land records or just information (Vayunandan and Matthew 2001). The former is aimed at improving efficiency of the organizational structure and processes, whereas the latter at effectiveness. E-governance, at the cutting edge, revolves around the computerization of treasury, civil supplies, motor vehicles, land records and land registration. These are some of the key areas in which the citizen customer's interface with government service delivery agencies takes place on a routine basis at the district level.

Simplification of procedure has also taken place due to the use of IT. For instance, in Kundagol Taluk of Dharwad district, Enlog Services, a Chennai-based firm, is investing money for the maintenance of rural information kiosks set up under the 'Rural digitalization service' of the 'Bhoomi' project of the Government of Karnataka. For Rs 25, people may now get a copy of their record of rights from these kiosks instead of travelling several times to the block or district headquarters (*Financial Times* 2005).

The Gyandoot project in Dhar district of Madhya Pradesh, was an attempt at providing a wide variety of services and products to people in rural areas through the application of information technology. Although it proved to be a goal more ambitious than could be supported by the local infrastructure—physical as well as human, it is an instance of an alternative approach to service delivery through a public–private partnership on a very small scale: under the leadership of the DO, state and local governments supplied the funding, technical support while private individuals invested, with the help of banks, in information kiosks (Sanjay and Gupta 2003). The Lokvani model for Internet-based public grievance redressal, developed by another DO and his colleagues, has been accepted and popularized by the state government in Uttar Pradesh.

By the turn of the 20th century, video-conferencing facilities had become available in many states. The National Informatics Center (NIC) as the lead agency developed the network, linking the state capitals with the districts. At the time of writing, monitoring meetings of DOs from the state capital had become a regular feature. These meetings are not only monitored by the Chief Minister or the Chief Secretary, but also by the departmental secretaries and during times of election, by the Chief Electoral Officer of the state. Consequently the DO is under much greater scrutiny than ever before.

New Forces of Accountability

According to Samuel Paul, the problem of accountability occurs due to collusion between executive and oversight agencies, 'asymmetry of information,' weakness of civil society, and corruption (Paul 2001: 2). Paul distinguishes between traditional, vertical and horizontal mechanisms of accountability. Traditionally, the DO's accountability has been of the vertical kind. He/she has been accountable to the government—comprising ministers and in particular the Chief Minister, the Revenue or the Land Minister and the Chief Secretary; to his/her immediate superior—be it the Board of Revenue in the Madras Province, the Chief Commissioner in Assam in the 19th century, or the Commissioner in Uttar Pradesh and West Bengal. The DO is also accountable to the Legislature, although only indirectly and to the judiciary very infrequently; in both these instances his/her accountability comes into question only if there has been a severe lapse in duty or the commission of an excess.

Although largely true, that due to the 'colonial heritage as well as the hierarchical society, administrative accountability in India was always internal and upwards, and the civil services' accountability to the public had been very limited' (Saxena 2004: 4) in the closed system of imperial India this was neither surprising nor illogical. However, as may be seen in the following paragraphs, over the years, with the transition to a democratic system, the DO's accountability to a wide variety of actors in both the vertical and horizontal dimensions, has grown.

Right to Information

Before the passage of the Right to Information Act, 2005 (RTI), it was possible for government agencies to hide behind the provisions of the Official Secrets Act of 1923. In United Kingdom, the counterpart Act was amended in 1989 to promote transparency. Between 1997 and 2001, six states passed RTI Acts—Tamil Nadu, Goa, Rajasthan, Karnataka, Maharashtra and Delhi. Although progressive attempts, these Acts suffered from several drawbacks— such as lists of exceptions limiting their efficacy. However, the RTI Act 2005 that came into effect on 12 October 2005 is a vast improvement on the RTI Act of 2001. Not only is it comprehensive in its scope and reach, it also provides for an institutional mechanism from the central government to the sub-district levels for its implementation and penal provisions in case of non compliance by officials (http://persmin.nic.in/RTI/WelcomeRTI.htm).

The implementation of the RTI Act has bestowed a responsibility and an opportunity upon the DO. In many states under the RTI, the DO has been designated the First Appellate Authority and the Additional District Magistrate (ADM) of the district has been empowered as the Public Information Officer. Upon the DO rests the responsibility of ensuring that the other offices in the district follow the law and arrange for provision of information as per rules. The RTI Act provides the DO the opportunity to ensure a cleaner district administration in his/her role as District Vigilance Officer; for, the RTI Act has enabled him/her to enlist the support of individuals and groups fighting corruption. Experience shows that by utilizing the RTI Act 2005, the DO may be able to improve their role as the District Vigilance Officer, and act against fraud perpetrated in implementation of poverty alleviation schemes such as the Employment Guarantee Scheme (EGS) (Gandhi 2005). In this regard, a vital task that the DO must perform is to inform and educate citizen customers abut the provisions of the RTI Act and related procedures.

Citizen's Charters

Citizens' Charters (CC)—based on standards of performance, quality, timeliness and cost of service delivered to the public—are seen as another means to promote transparency. In 1997 the Department of Personnel and Administrative Reforms (DoPAR), GOI initiated a programme aimed at institutionalizing accountability at the department– citizen interface level by introducing CCs in ministries, departments and enterprises. A CC is a statement of the rights/entitlements of the citizen vis-à-vis an agency (Paul 2001: 5). The DoPAR has also urged state governments to introduce CCs. Although an important step, the introduction of CCs has remained confined largely to central government organizations. Further, not only are the CCs non-justiciable, regular assessment of adherence to CCs is not carried out. States like Karnataka and Andhra Pradesh have attempted to introduce CCs at the district level.

Civil Society Organizations

Increasingly, Civil Society Organizations (CSOs) are play-ing the role of a watchdog in monitoring poverty reduction programmes. In this regard, the Citizen's Juries model on the issue of adoption of genetically modified seeds by farmers in Karnataka, or the Jan Sunwai (public hearing) model initiated by the Mazdoor Kisaan Shakti Sangathan (MKSS) in Rajasthan, are steadily gaining ground (Foresti, Lawson and Wilkinson 2002). The government has also stipulated the formation of Bene-ficiary and Monitoring Committees in rural development programmes for supervising and monitoring individual wage employment schemes. Under the DFID (UK Depart-ment for International Development)-funded District Primary Education Programme (DPEP)—undertaken in a few states from 1994 onwards—Mothers' Committees were formed to interact with the primary school teachers and manaagement; in the year 2000 this forum was integrated in the nationally implemented Sarva Siksha Abhiyan for the universalization of primary education.

National and State Commissions

A number of National and State Commissions have been established since the 1990s. Their main tasks are to pro-tect the interests of specific categories among the weaker sections of society, redress grievances of individuals and groups belonging to the concerned class of people, and advise the government on matters pertaining to their wel-fare and development. Some of the prominent National Commissions are: National Human Rights Commission,

National Commission for Minorities, National Commission for Women, National Commission for the Protection of Children and National Commission for Scheduled Castes. Many states have set up counterparts of the National Commissions at the state level, such as the State Human Rights Commission. These Commissions have come to play an active role in monitoring violations of the rights and entitlements of the concerned section of society and inexorably their scrutiny includes the relevant wing of district administration, and often also the DO.

Judicial Activism

A force multiplier for administrative accountability has been the rapid growth in judicial activism. Chatterji (1997: 11) defines judicial activism as the 'assumption of an active role on the part of the Judiciary'. Seen as the stepping in by the judiciary in instances where the executive fails to perform its duties, neglects its responsibilities, or over-reaches its authority or in cases of arbitrariness, for the most part judicial activism has acquired a positive connotation (Bakshi 1997).

Judicial activism is directly linked to public interest litigation. And the foundations of public interest litigation may be said to have been laid in the Supreme Court's decision in S.P. Gupta vs Union of India. The judgment in this case empowered any member of the public with sufficient interest to move the court for 'judicial address for public injury arising from breach of public duty or from violation of some provision of the Constitution or the law and to seek enforcement of such public duty and observance of such constitutional or legal provision' (Bhattacharya 1997: 39). Moreover, any person unable to file a formal petition, may write a letter to the Supreme Court drawing its attention to such breach or neglect of law. To mention two well known instances, in Dr Upendra Baxi vs State of UP and Sheela Barse vs the State of Maharashtra, such letters were accepted as writ petitions by the Supreme Court. For public administration, particularly at the district level, judicial activism has proved to be another mechanism for accountability.

Increasingly, the courts have also sought individual accountability of public servants in laws related to the protection of child labour and over the issue of right to food. In both these areas, the judiciary has, among others, held DOs to be directly responsible for the implementation of specific schemes and projects. Further, on 'an extensive scale, the courts have played a key role in strengthening prison administration and the administration of correctional facilities' (Menon 1997: 27).

Media

In this age of media explosion, the actions of the DO and district administration are daily under review by the press. Not only has the number of local dailies—even in rural towns—multiplied, national and state level newspapers have one or two sheet inserts based on a single district or groups of districts. The tremendous expansion of the electronic media has also resulted in state-based television channels with district level coverage. Thus, there has been a manifold increase in the number of full-time reporters, stringers and correspondents of both newspapers and television channels. Additionally, in many of the larger towns local news channels are operational. Thus, the DO and his/her actions are continuously under the scanner. More and more, it is being recognized that giving information to the press may be more constructive than avoiding it. Also, officers 'feel obliged to meet the queries of the parties of the press as the refusal [to do so] would be interpreted as arrogance and give rise to suspicion' (Krishna 1988: 995).

Not only has the growth of the media enhanced the DO's public accountability, it has concurrently enhanced his/her accountability to the government—administrative superiors—as well as to judicial and quasi-judicial statutory bodies such as the Human Rights Commission and the Scheduled Tribes Commission. Reports of incidents in the morning newspapers may easily invite queries of superiors by midmorning and of the concerned Commission within the next day or two.

The DO may also utilize the press corps to enforce accountability of the vast district and local government machinery: 'Publicity of administrative policies and actions is another informal way of achieving administrative accountability in a democracy' (Mukhopadhyay 1983: 478). Briefing the press through regular press notes about programme details, implementation schedule and other specific information may create not only transparency but also exert pressure on the grass roots-level functionaries to adhere to programmatic guidelines. As Krishna notes, 'A positive role of press in improving public administration is possible if there is greater cooperation between the press and administrators' (1988: 995). Perceived positively the press, if independent and objective, may prove to be a DO's ally in pursuit of effective and transparent governance at the district level.

Information and Communication Technology

The role of ICT in enhancing accountability at the district level also needs to be recognized. In this regard the creation of video-conferencing facilities between the state and district headquarters has been dealt with in the previous section. Furthermore, the Internet is being used more and more for monitoring programmes at the district level. By 2003 it was mandated that DOs submit periodic progress reports of the Pradhan Mantri Grameen Sarak Yojana via the Internet to the Ministry of Rural Development in Delhi. During the General Elections, not only is the compilation of results computerized, their immediate submission over the Internet has also become routine. ICT has enabled DOs also to oversee the sub-district level programme implementation more effectively due to the computerization of Block offices and the, yet incomplete, extension of Internet access. Even the use of cellular phones has connected remote areas still difficult to reach by a land route to the DO and the district headquarters.

Inter-connection Among Reforms

To speak of the reforms as if they marked a linear, independent and holistic trend in one direction, is a trifle misleading. No single type of reform can be said to be either self-contained or exclusive; most have elements of the others embedded in them. Thus, PRIs meant to serve as units of local self-government may, as Singh (2003) contends, have a major role in promoting transparency by holding regular meetings as well as by creating mass awareness about a variety of schemes.

For instance, the Rogi Kalyan Samity initiative in Madhya Pradesh, the first of its kind, was led by a DO and was accepted as a model by the Planning Commission, Government of India and by UNDP. The committee is a registered society comprising district officials, citizens, representatives of the Indian Medical Association, panchayat members and leading donors. It decides issues pertaining to the levy of user fees and the management of hospitals. The revenue generated through the user charges and donations are used to repair buildings, buy equipment and provide free or subsidized services to those living below the poverty line. The system was introduced in over 600 hospitals in the country (*The Economic Times* 2002). Thus, decentralization through the creation of an empowered GONGO has created a responsive mechanism that through a participatory process and by using market mechanisms such as contractual service, outsourcing, and user fees provides greatly improved services to the citizen-client.

There are also instances where judicial oversight, NGO activism and media criticism have joined forces to intensify oversight and enforce accountability in the field. The most notable example has emerged in relation to the Right to Food issue. In 2001, the People's Union of Civil Liberty (PUCL), a highly regarded civil society organization, filed a public interest case in the Supreme Court for extension and effective implementation of the Integrated Child Development Scheme (ICDS) in India. Over the years, other programmes pertaining to food security were added to the original case and elicited a strong response from the highest court in the land. The Supreme Court appointed Commissioners to monitor the implementation of its direction, who visited districts to verify the effectiveness of government efforts. With the expansion of the scope of the Supreme Court's order to a number of states, the Commissioners appointed Advisors in the states and enlisted the efforts of local NGOs in monitoring the programmes. The media also highlighted the work of the Commissioners and the local NGOs sharpening the glare of attention. This combination of factors appears to have been responsible for the engagement of NGOs by the government for monitoring of schemes under the National Employment Guarantee Act of 2005.

Conclusion

To conclude, the impact of the four forces of public sector reforms—decentralization, market forces, administrative reforms and accountability—are manifest at the district level in India. Although to gauge the full effects of the changes they have wrought in public service delivery is not possible at the moment, it is evident from the above analysis that the influence of reforms is increasingly being felt at the point of interface between the government and the citizen. Yet, the impact of the four types of reforms has

not been evenly distributed across the country. Decentralization, through the 73rd and 74rd Amendments, has
had the most widespread influence. Even if the spirit
of the law may take time to catch up with its letter in
the establishment of PRIs, it has brought about constitutionally mandated structural change by creating local
self-government institutions across the country. The role
of market forces in governance at the district level is
growing but varies greatly from state to state and, perhaps, even from district to district. The implementation
of administrative reforms, although constantly on the
agenda of the Indian state, is also uneven. However,
in the amalgamation of downsizing, management by
objectives and market forces such as outsourcing and
contractualization, an overall trend towards economic
efficiency and programme effectiveness may be discerned.
It is undeniable that the RTI Act, 2005 has created the
strongest and uniform basis for public accountability, thus
far denied to citizens.

One common feature of the reforms is their impact on
the role and responsibilities of the DO. As elicited above,
under the influence of the forces of reform, the DO's role
has been changing from primarily that of a regulator to
the principal change agent in the district. As in the case
of the impact of reforms, the alteration in the DO's roles
and responsibilities has not been uniform across the states.
However, as we shall see in the following chapters, it is
clear that the DO will be called upon increasingly to steer
as well as to row.

Notes

1. It envisaged the creation of village level Panchayats, or local self government bodies and directed that the State 'shall take steps to endow them with such powers and authority as may be necessary to enable them to function as units of self-government.'

2. Please see Statement of Objects and Reasons appended to the Constitution (72nd Amendment) Bill, 1991 which was enacted as the Constitution (73rd Amendment) Act, 1992 at http://panchayat. nic.in

3. Except in the States of Nagaland, Meghalaya and Mizoram, the Hill Areas of Manipur and District of Darjeeling in West Bengal.

4. The earliest GONGOs may be traced back to the 1950s, when through government initiative farmer unions were established to interact with the community development projects; later, in the same sequence, came Legal Aid Societies, Bharat Sevak Samaj, Bharat Krishak Samaj and others (Inamdar 1987).

5. In the Seventh Plan, 17 sub-areas in Rural Development (RD) were identified, where local NGOs could undertake responsibilities and Rs 150 crore were earmarked for NGOs (Roy 1987).

6. Elected rural, local self-government institutions at the district, sub-district and village level promoted first in the 1960s and established firmly through the 93rd Amendment to the Constitution of India in 1993.

7. To take up the example Jalan (2005) uses—Sulabh Shauchalayas— in 1994–95, the author tried and failed in setting up similar facilities in rural areas of Bankura. Reason: unfortunately the maintenance of such facilities is taken up only by members of a particular community/caste and the caste does not exist among Bengalis. Most members of this community currently engaged in this work migrated to Bengal from Bihar, UP and Orissa and are concentrated in the urban centres in Bengal.

8. According to the National Training Policy the five concerns that need to be addressed in training are Responsiveness to citizens'

needs and expectations; Commitment to democratic values; Awareness of technological, social and economic developments; Infusion of scientific temper; and, accountability to for efficient and effective performance and service delivery (National Training Policy 2006).

Chapter Five

New Imperatives and Refurbished Responsibilities

IT IS hardly surprisingly that forces of public sector reform are transforming the role of the district officer (DO)—the chief administrator and representative of government in the district. Addressing the National Conference of Collectors in 2005, Dr Manmohan Singh, the Prime Minister of India observed that in light of economic liberalization and despite the growth of the administrative machinery and the PRIs, 'the role of the Collector has only been transformed into a more powerful one of coordinator, facilitator and a person who is responsible for inter-sectoral coordination of various activities....' (Prime Minister's Speech 2005).

In light of the four major drivers of change and reforms in public administration in India, we shall in this chapter, explore their impact at the district level and the changes in the roles and responsibilities of the office of the DO. The traditional functions of the DO such as maintenance of law and order and revenue collection have also grown. However, in this chapter we shall concentrate on functions new or old that have been altered qualitatively. It is noticeable that the office of the DO is charged with playing a central role in regulation and development of the social sector. The DO's regulatory role now also includes new responsibilities for system maintenance and enhanced supervision and monitoring. Yet from regulation and the implementation of development programmes of government the nodal office of the DO is moving towards promoting development through coordination, facilitation and capacity development.

SOCIAL SECTOR: REGULATION AND DEVELOPMENT

The 'social sector' is commonly understood to consist of aspects of the citizen customers' needs, other than economic, that make for their well being in the society. These include education, health, special needs of weaker sections and social justice—many of these were earlier officially grouped under the heading 'General Social Services.' From the very outset of independence, the Directive Principles of the Constitution have prompted the state in India to frame policies and enact laws not only to protect the interests of the weaker sections in the society but also for their socio-economic advancement. The first aspect, protection of their interests, has led to an expansion of the regulatory responsibilities of the state, and the second its development role. Social change has been on the agenda of the Indian state ever since independence. Initially this concern manifested itself in affirmative action programmes for the scheduled castes and scheduled tribes through reservation of seats in the parliament, state legislatures, and in the civil services.

Over the years state action has not only concentrated upon the socio-economic development for these two sections but also expanded to include other groups such as Other Backward Classes, women, children and child labour, primitive tribes and the disabled. Interventions for the welfare and development of these groups have been attempted through passage of laws, the execution of specific programmes and schemes, or both. Among the programmes for the uplift of the weaker sections may be listed as examples, the Integrated Child Development Scheme (ICDS), which began in 1975, Child Labour Schools initiated in 1996, and the National Trust Act for the mentally challenged, implemented 2001 onwards. As we shall see in a later segment of this chapter, in the operationalization of most such interventions, the DO has been assigned a direct role.

The social sector has become all the more important due to the economic reforms beginning in the 1990s. There is a not unfounded fear that liberalization and the expansion of markets is likely to affect the poor and the weak adversely. As Bhattacharya (1997: 255) puts it, 'Markets are not the natural friends of people; they have to be made people friendly through government interventions.' At the cutting edge of administration, it is the DO's responsibility to ensure that government intervention—either regulatory measures or welfare initiatives—safeguard the interests of the poor and the powerless—who form the vast majority of the Indian populace. This requires greater attention to regulate for social justice with simultaneous efforts for the socio-economic uplift of the targeted groups through development programmes.

Regulation   'Maintenance of law and order' remains a central function of the DO and the district administration that he/she heads. Yet, the phrase no longer refers only to the prevention and control of crime and public disturbance or affray; it has come to include a wide variety of social and socio-economic legislation that have considerably expanded the scope of 'the rule of law' and come to focus on what Amartya Sen calls 'human security.' The police continue to be the main law enforcement arm of the government, but to implement new statutes and legislation, other wings have also been added in areas such as labour, child labour, crimes against women, land ceiling, dowry prevention, and social welfare. Maintenance of law and order also no longer remains a reactive affair; it calls for proactive enforcement of laws for socio-economic change whether for land reforms, prevention of child marriage or the rescue of child labour.

The Minimum Wages Act, 1948 was enacted to ensure that labourers received a legally determined minimum wage and were not exploited. As Srivastava (1989) elicits, although its implementation is the responsibility of the labor department in all states, in a few states like Jammu and Kashmir, Uttar Pradesh and Madhya Pradesh, the district administration has been directly engaged in its implementation. In Jammu and Kashmir, the DO has been made specifically responsible for hearing appeal cases.

Yet, in almost all states DOs are in charge of supervision, monitoring and implementation of the provisions of the Act. Among the statutes passed for the protection of the weaker sections, the Minimum Wages Act of 1948, The Dowry (Prevention) Act of 1983, the Child Labour (Prohibition) Act of 1995, and the Manual Scavengers and Construction of Dry Latrines (Prohibition) Act, 1993 may be mentioned.

Development   Development programmes in the social sector for which the DO has direct responsibility are spread over various areas such as education—the National Literacy Mission (NLM), Primary Education Programme and Sarva Siksha Abhiyan; health and nutrition—the Integrated Child Development Project; the Public Distribution System; and rural development schemes—Jawahar Rozgar Yojana, Employment Assurance Scheme and the National Rural Employment Guarantee Act, 2005 assume additional emphasis. Similarly, the DO has been made responsible for implementing Child Labour Schools project initiated in 1996. Education, health and rural development have all seen significant budgetary expansion ranging from 80 per cent to over 100 per cent between 1992 and 1995. The delivery of services under these sectors is the responsibility of the DO (Katoch 1995: 50).

The role played by DOs in leading the NLM campaign, beginning with the Ernakulum district in Kerala, may provide an idea of the innovative and collaborative potential of the DOs office. The campaign mode of programme implementation started with the Total Literacy Campaign in 1989 and continues until this day. Discussing the central role played by the DO in the National Literacy Campaign, Mishra observes 'while the Collector in effect may be the principal mobilizer, organizer, coordinator and supervisor, he/she has to present the impression of being the first among the equals and has to proceed with his task of mobilization of all sections of the society and masses for the campaign with lots of courage and firmness tempered by a sincerity of purpose and a touch of humility' (1993: 114). Even in the health sector, the DO is expected to play a crucial role in planning and implementing health interventions at the district level due to his/her roles as coordinator of other agencies and facilitator of action (Sharma and Tripathi 1989).

Rehabilitation   The DO's central role in acquisition of private land for public purposes, including for setting up privately owned industrial units is well known. However, economic liberalization has both enlarged this role and also modified it in two major ways. The DO's role has been enlarged in those states and districts where land is being acquired for the setting up of industry in the post liberalization phase because of the magnitude of land being acquired. It has also been expanded because it is increasingly stipulated by various important stakeholders that arrangements for adequate rehabilitation should take place that ensures comprehensive settlement of displaced persons.

This concern for rehabilitating land-losers has been driven to a certain extent by conditionalities of multilateral funding agencies such as the World Bank (Jaamdar 1998) and the pressure of civil society groups. As Jaamdar observes, the extent of land acquisition being done and the imperative of rehabilitation may lead to modification in acquisition regulations allowing for greater participation by the private sector and NGOs in the resettlement process. However, he also acknowledges this will call for overall regulation by the state—which in the field, will mean by the DO. As Sinha (1998) emphasizes, in the increasingly participatory and open administrative environment, to effectively implement a rehabilitation project the DO must approach his/her task with sensitivity, vision and a collaboratively developed strategy. This is in keeping with the move from a command to a collaboration and consensus-based model of governance. It calls for the development of skills in negotiation and conflict management.

SYSTEM MAINTENANCE THROUGH REGULATION

The DO's role in system maintenance is not a new one. However, it has undergone a qualitative and a quantitative change. The shift from the imperial regime to steadily deepening and intensifying democratic self-rule was the main reason for qualitative change in the nature and priorities of the state. The increase in the quantum of work flows from the same source. Maintaining and sustaining a democratic system calls for much hard work from many institutions and individuals.

Katoch observes that all levels of administration are affected by two important elements of economic reforms: first, macroeconomic stabilization and fiscal discipline— translating into downsizing of administrative expenditure;

and second, deregulation and de-bureaucratization. However, he notes that 'there is a flip side, reducing the role of
the government in these areas of economic activity, which
is likely to go hand in hand with increasing the role of government in the regulatory sphere and the social sectors'
(1995: 49). Undoubtedly, for a significant proportion of the
population in India—the poor—these are the sectors that
are more important, particularly in the wake of liberalization. Therefore, although the deregulation of some sectors has lightened the regulatory responsibilities of the
DO, it may be ironical that decentralization and economic
liberalization have added several new regulatory functions
to the DO's existing regulatory responsibilities: most of
which are geared toward system maintenance.

Conduct of Elections

Most prominent among these functions is one that is
basic to the functioning of a democracy: the conduct of
elections—a primary responsibility of the DO from the
beginning of independent India. Under election law and
rules pertaining to General Elections and the elections to
the State Legislative Assembly, the DO is designated the
District Election Officer and District Electoral Registration
Officer. He/she bears ultimate responsibility at the operational level for all activities preparatory to election, such
as revision of electoral rolls, as well as for its conduct.
With the passage of time, work related to elections has
expanded considerably, mainly due to three factors. First,
the enhanced intensity of preparatory activities has turned

election work at the ground level into an around the year effort; almost every year either there is a Summary or an Intensive Revision of electoral rolls, apart from the review of basic arrangements. Second, non-synchronous elections held to the Parliament and to State Legislature, have transformed elections from a quinquennial event to a biannual affair. Frequent change of governments and dissolution of the legislative bodies in some states, and even the national level, in the 1990s, also enhanced the frequency of elections; and, third, due to the multiplication of democratic institutions for rural and urban local self-government.

Decentralization and restructuring of the state at the district and sub-district levels by the 73rd and 74th Constitutional Amendments is premised upon mandatory periodic elections to Panchayat bodies and municipalities. At the state level, a State Election Commission has been mandated by the Constitution. In most states, at the district level, this task of system maintenance through the conduct of elections has been entrusted to the DO. As District Panchayat/Municipal Election Officer, the DO is responsible for all activities preparatory to the elections such as revision of electoral rolls and delimitation, and the conduct of elections. Election to PRIs and urban local bodies (ULBs), now mandated by the constitution, are also held after every five years. Due to the linkages, however tenuous, between the three tiers of Panchayats, elections to PRIs in a state are conducted simultaneously; however, in the absence of any such connection among municipal bodies, election to ULBs are usually staggered across the state.

Although theoretically and legally feasible, due to practical considerations, elections to PRIs and to the Parliament, State Legislature or ULBs are seldom held together in a single year. Therefore, combined with the many phased elections to the Parliament and the State Legislature, the above scenario ensures that the vast majority of the DOs in India are required to conduct elections to one level or another every year. Obviously the DO's role as chief election officer of the district has expanded manifold in terms of activity and importance for the smooth working of a multi-level democracy. It may be pertinent to mention here, that in comparison to the augmented workload in most states, there has been negligible strengthening of the district election machinery causing a severe strain on the DO's resources and their diversion from other sectors to election related work.

Data Collection, Management and Analysis

The growing concern in public management with performance and its measurement has resulted in a dramatic escalation in the DO's work related to data collection, management and analysis. The Census Commissioner of India undertakes the Census operation in the first year of each new decade. In the field, however, it is the DO as the District Census Officer who carries out the census with the help of a district-wide team. Effectively, including preparatory and follow-up activities, the Census engages the DO's energies for only three to four years in each decade.

Yet, the number of other kinds of census or census-like surveys that the DO is asked to conduct or supervise has steadily grown. Some of these like the Live-stock Census are carried out by the related departments but under the overall supervision of the DO. Others, such as the Below Poverty Line Survey, the Economic Census, and base-line surveys for special projects and campaigns, such as literacy mission or polio eradication, are not only led by the DO but he/she is required to play a vital role at all the stages—planning, preparation, implementation, reporting and review. The expansion of the data collection function of the state demands new orientation and skills among the field officials, especially the DO. Not only are data-collection and compilation in focus, but there is the further need to analyse and utilize the data collected.

Integrating Information and Communication Technology

The 1990s also ushered in the information technology revolution around the world. Even in the year 2007, the revolution shows no sign of settling down. At the district level, the impact of Information and Communication Technology (ICT) has been felt in all the wings of administration, some of these have been touched upon in the previous chapter.

The National Informatics Centre (NIC) started setting up a branch service facility in the district headquarters all over the country in the late 1980s. From the beginning it was attached to the DO's office. The early 1990s also saw the beginnings of computerization at the district level that took the form mostly of using computers in offices for day-to-day work—mainly word processing. Innovator DOs and other officials, however, also began to exploit the resource to assist in upgrading and automating their systems of internal accounting, improving certain services like arms licensing, motor vehicle licensing and billing, and monitoring of development programmes.

Gradually, under the National Resource Data Management System project of the central government, even the development of Geographical Information System (GIS) was taken up in 1991–92 in some districts on a pilot basis. The programme for Computerization of Land Records was also initiated by the central government in the early 1990s, although some DOs had already taken it up in Karnataka, Madhya Pradesh and West Bengal. Under the project Bhoomi, Karnataka has moved forward, setting up rural kiosks from where citizen consumers may access land records and get a copy after paying a fee of Rs 15.[1] By implementing the Computer aided Administration of Registration Department (CARD), the state government in Andhra Pradesh simplified registration of property and increased its revenues in the bargain. Andhra Pradesh has also drawn up, and is implementing, probably one of the most ambitious plans for ICT application for improvement of service delivery even at the sub-district levels at Mandal Revenue Offices (Kumar 2004). The Lokvani project in Uttar Pradesh is one of the most recent attempts at using ICT for quick redressal of public grievances.

Overall e-governance initiatives in different states have gathered momentum. These have often been fuelled by innovator DOs as in the case of Gyandoot and Lokvani or by enthusiastic state governments as in Karnataka and Andhra Pradesh. They aim to make governance simple, moral, accountable, responsive and transparent (SMART). Yet the fundamental concern remains the redesign of administrative infrastructure in the field, including the re-engineering of processes.

Standard Setting

Outsourcing and introduction of user fee has enormously enlarged the scope of contractual agreements. However, contracting out 'does not automatically produce satisfying results for the public at large. Contracts also need to be administered properly to ensure high accountability and sound performance' (Bhattacharya 1997: 251). Indeed, to ensure a performance regime it is vital that contracts include standards and indicators of performance. Not surprising, therefore, that contractualization has engendered two types of responsibilities that fall upon the DO at the district level. It has promoted results-based management, and a performance regime that requires quantification of results. Hence, whether for data entry after electoral roll revision, photocopying in offices, or cleaning services in hospitals—normally it is the DO's office that is responsible, first, for the development of standards, measures and framing of the terms of contracts and, then, for enforcing them through monitoring and evaluation. Similarly, with

respect to the introduction of user charges, two new functions have emerged. First, the DO often plays a key role in
the determination of the rates of user charges introduced
at the district level, whether for entry into parks or support
services in hospitals. Second, the administration of user
charges often requires the DOs constant support and
supervision.

DEVELOPMENT PROMOTION

Project and Campaign Management

Compared to long-term programmes and schemes that aim
at routine provision of services, projects are short term,
focused and aimed at achieving a few specific objectives.
Born, buried and reborn several times, the Food for Work programme initiated in 1974 continues to be in operation today.
In its newest incarnation, it has acquired statutory force
as the National Employment Guarantee Act, 2005. Perhaps
the oldest project under implementation is the Integrated
Child Development Services (ICDS) Project. Started in
1975, it has steadily spread to almost all districts in India
and has assumed some characteristics of programmes.

Campaigns may be stand alone events, or may be a
component of a project or programme. They entail the
involvement of a large number of persons in a short intervention converging on a few specific goals. Thus the Total
Sanitation Campaign aims at mass mobilization for construction of latrines for every household and ends with the
achievement of the objective and declaration of the village

as a 'Nirmal Gram.[2] On the other hand, the Total Literacy Campaign first sponsored by the National Literacy Mission in 1988, in Ernakulam district of Kerala, has come to be implemented in the project mode. Campaigns are often undertaken by the state to speed up a flaging programme.

The end of the Cold War presaged the stepping up of development aid by international, multi-lateral and bilateral agencies, which paved the way for projects. Consequently the number of projects multiplied in the 1990s. Most of the funds, and therefore the projects, were for social sector interventions such as improving quality of health care and education, provision of drinking water and sanitation facilities, and social welfare—especially for women and children. Almost invariably, the DO serves as the project manager of such district level projects and campaigns like District Primary Education Project (DPEP) and State Health Systems Development Project (SHSDP). Project administration and campaign management require certain distinct skills and competencies. They require the DO to lead, build teams, negotiate and mobilize customers and service providers speedily. People and communication skills come into prominence. A major change has taken place in this respect: whereas, programmes and schemes are normally prepared at the central and state government levels and implemented in the district, projects are increasingly being formulated *and* operationalized in the district by project teams often led by the DO. Therefore, activities such as project preparation, appraisal and evaluation that, in the context of programme implementation, the DO earlier did not undertake are also important competencies he/she must possess to be effective. Trends indicate that more and more programmes are likely to be broken up into a series of projects with the spotlight on goals and outcomes.

Coordination

In view of the plurality of departments at the district level, and the confusion regarding the chain of command commentators have called for strengthening of the DOs coordinating role (Singhvi 1983). The DO uses a variety of formal and informal mechanisms at the district level to coordinate the work of government departments, NGOs, International Public Organizations (IPOs) and private firms. This may take several forms:

(a) The DO may establish Coordinating Committees at the district level based on the type of service delivered such as Rural Development, Health and Family Welfare, Social Welfare, Women and Child and so forth. These committees, comprising NGOs, concerned Government Organizations (GOs), and representatives of PRIs and municipal bodies jointly develop action plans, implement and/or review progress of programmes, and solve interagency problems. Although few, instances of this type of committee may be found in some districts in the field of Rural Development and Health and Family Welfare.

(b) Joint Action Committees are also set up on the basis of programmes and projects. This type of committee may be found in many districts for such fields as the National Programme for the Control of Blindness or Mental Health.

(c) The DO may also set up a system of periodic meetings and reports and returns of progress for interagency coordination.

(d) Finally, the DO often effects coordination by setting up and maintaining databases that could be utilized by GOs and NGOs to improve service delivery. In view of the significance of this function, the DO's role in inter-agency coordination at the district level is discussed in some detail in a following chapter.

Facilitation and Conflict Management

In the new climate of liberalization and rolling back of the inspection and license regime, the DO is called upon to play an increasingly active role as a facilitator. The DO has the jurisdictional reach, administrative authority, social standing, access to diverse resources, and backward and forward network linkages within and outside the district to facilitate collaboration among government, market and the NGO sector.

The thrust on industrialization in a liberalized economy has promoted competition among Indian states for investments. Simplification of procedure for licensing industries has been attempted in many states by creating a single-window or single-point system for the receipt of applications and the issue of clearances. In both, Gujarat and West Bengal, the states that have led in attracting investment in the last few years, a district-level inter-departmental committee under the DO has been established for the purpose (Government of Gujarat 2006). Another new role that the DO has taken up is under the NHAI Act, 1998. In some states like West Bengal, the DO has been appointed the Arbitrator to resolve disputes over compensation received for acquisition of land.

In most GONGOs, at the district level, such as the District Rogi Kalyan Samity or the District Primary Education Committee, the DO has been appointed either as the chairman or the executive vice-chairman. His/her main role in this position is the facilitation of joint action, dispute resolution and inter-agency functioning. For instance, the DO of Rajnandgaon played the acknowledged role of a facilitator by assisting in the organization of poor women quarry workers into self-help microfinance groups. Not only did the women's groups accumulate savings of over Rs 17.5 million between 2001 and 2003, they also won contracts for working in the stone quarries (Kang 2003). In view of the emergence of various non-state actors in service delivery and the controversial nature of their relationship with the state, this issue and the DO's role in facilitating GONGO collaboration at the district level is discussed in some detail in a later chapter.

Capacity Development

In the context of public sector management, capacity development 'is about providing people and institutions with the ability to identify and meet the challenges of development in a sustainable manner' (Morgan and Carlan in Kapoor 1995: 3). Mandating the creation of local government bodies through the Constitution has expanded the human resource development functions of the DO in a majority of the states. Recruitment of personnel for the three tiers of PRI is one such function. This becomes a particularly onerous task since usually the state government issues little more than the basic guidelines and eligibility criteria for the purpose. The details of the recruitment process are usually left to the DO—either directly or under his/her supervision. The same is true for the recruitment of personnel for GONGOs created for the implementation of such programmes as the universalization of elementary education (Sarva Siksha Abhiyan) and the spread of literacy (National Literacy Mission).

Training is a key area of public sector reform emphasizing improvement of delivery of public services. The National Training Policy (NTP) of 1996 elaborated the need for continuous upgradation of skills of civil servants at all levels. As stated in its preamble, 'Sensitivity to emerging political and social concerns, modernity in thinking and reorientation of administrative systems would require specifically focused training programmes to enable their diffusion throughout the administrative structure' (National Training Policy 2006). Decentralization, constant review and simplification of procedures, and use of IT are three significant causes for ongoing training activities at the district level.

The DO is usually in charge of running of the regional administrative training centres that have been established in some states. Further, regular elections to the PRIs is perforce followed by the need for adequate training of the elected representatives of all three levels. In many states the overall responsibility for planning and implementing this huge task has been placed upon the DO's shoulders. For specific projects in which GNGOs, NGOs or GROs may be involved, often the DO needs to arrange orientation and training for their functionaries; as government–NGO collaboration increases so will this activity. This type of training is of critical importance since without it coordination of joint action would not be possible.

Connected to the Right to Information movement, is the growing recognition in the government that one of the services that the government is responsible for providing, is information about the various development programmes and entitlements under them. This has taken the form of district level awareness campaigns regarding a range of issues such as preventive health care, entitlement to essential commodities, voting procedures upon the introduction of electronic voting machines, and consumer literacy. The importance being given to awareness generation may be gauged from the fact that in the Consumer Affairs department, GOI, Rs 107 crore have been allotted for consumer awareness in 2005–06 alone as against Rs 55 crore in the previous FYP period (Singh 2005).

CONCLUSION

As indicated at the beginning of this study, criticism pertaining to either the diminution or the irrelevance of the office of the DO will appear valid if the present officer is compared to the ideal of an all-powerful, all knowing, all-doing, unchanging creature. As the history of the evolution of this office above reveals, such an officer actually never existed. We have seen that when the DO was supposedly 'all powerful,' during the middle and late 19th century, he was not 'all-doing;' now, when he is supposed to be 'all-doing' he is certainly not all-powerful; and, it is doubtful that he was ever 'all-knowing.' While tracing the evolution of the DO we find the office reworking itself continuously in riposte to the continuously changing demands of the ages. That it has been central to district administration is a testimony to the effectiveness of the office over two centuries; yet a principal reason for its effectiveness and unceasing centrality is its ability to adapt to altering circumstances.

From time to time commentators and critics have called for a radical restructuring of the district as taken up in France in 1982 with the creation of elected district councils (Mukhopadhyay 1997; Sadasivan 1985; Singh 1986). Such critics appear to lose sight of three aspects of governance in India. First, they fail to take note of the 73rd and 74th Amendments to the Constitution that have firmly established institutions of local self-government in both rural and urban areas ensuring intervention for socio-economic development at three levels—district, block and village. Second, they appear blind to the federal nature of India and that the central and the state governments have an abiding responsibility in two fields—social development and system maintenance. Third, they tend to ignore the utility of a fundamentally uniform administrative system responding—in normalcy and in crises—both to the demands of the Constitution and the needs of the populace in providing public goods and services.

Today, it may well be said that the office of the DO serves the state, central and local governments. In a differentiated administrative system with multiple actors and manifold programmes, the DO serves as an integrative force for implementing policy at the cutting edge of governance. Pai (1962) identified two additional reasons why the DO holds and is likely to continue to occupy a key position in the chain of authority: first, selection to the post on the basis of merit and experience; and, second, faith of the people and government in him in normal times and especially during times of crisis.

Rai's (1965: 242) observation that despite reforms in the administrative system the DO remains 'the principal executive agent of government, the one man who can get things done, whether it be suppression of the outbreak of disorder or the initiatives of a child welfare movement' remains as valid today as it was four decades ago. Even critics and commentators like Singh acknowledge that despite frequent talk of reducing the authority of the DO, the government finds the DO to be the most reliable and convenient instrument for executing its programmes: 'Government, whenever in difficulty, has looked to the DO for the execution of its programmes' (Singh, 1986, 252). DOs have been called upon to take up leadership of special programmes ranging from small pox eradication in the 1960s, to presiding over colleges and universities disturbed by severe student agitations in the 1970s (Singh 1986), to enforcing laws for protection of women and children in the 1980s and the 1990s, to implementing the National Employment Guarantee Act in 2005.

Thus, in India as long as all three levels of government have a role in public management, the DO is likely to perform the pivotal role in district administration; particularly, if the office continues to adapt and evolve in response to the changing needs of its environment. In the following chapters we shall examine the new role and responsibilities of the DO in leading change at the district level.

Notes

1. Approximately, US 30 cents.
2. Literally, Clean Village. To encourage communities the Central Government awards a development grant to each such village.

Chapter Six

The Archetypal Administrator

UNDOUBTEDLY, THE district officer's (DO) role of the 'mai-baap,'[1] administrator, operating in the wide spaces of a basic legal framework and restricted social responsibility, exercising overarching discretion has changed considerably. The diffuseness of the role stands greatly clarified. Yet when discussing the responsibilities of the DO, or of district administration, it is still common in the literature to describe his/her work in terms of fields of activities. Early commentators (Khera 1960; Pai 1962; Sivaraman1965) identified three main functions of the DO: maintenance of law and order, revenue collection and developmental administration. By the late 1970s and 1980s disaster management, functions related to local government bodies (LGBs)—urban and local, social welfare and a few other activities were being highlighted (Khera 1979); the number has steadily grown. Such an approach may acquaint us with *what* the areas of the DO's activities are but it facilitates neither our understanding of the diversity of the generic functions that he/she performs nor *how* he/she performs them.

As the chief executive of the district administrative machinery, what are DO's fundamental tasks? And in the context of the impact of public sector reforms at the district level, in what way have these functions been modified? This chapter seeks in part to address these questions.

A POSDCORB PERSPECTIVE

The tasks or functions of administration or administrators have been examined and researched by scholars in the discipline of public administration and management since the last quarter of the 19th Century. Depending upon the perspective adopted, these functions and tasks have been identified and categorized in various ways. However, Gulick and Urwick's (1937)[2] enunciation, towards the beginning of the 20th Century, of the tasks of administration in the form of the acronym POSDCORB remains the most comprehensive formulation. It accentuates the essential functional elements of a chief executive's work. It may be eminently applied to DOs to understand the basic tasks performed by them whatever their area of responsibility—whether maintenance of law and order, development or crisis management. Therefore, the aim here is to use POSDCORB as an analytical tool to sift through the many types of functions that DOs perform and examine the impact that public sector reforms have had on them.

POSDCORB

Without going into the details it may be stated that the acronym POSDCORB stands for:

Planning: Setting the broad outline of objectives and methods

Organizing: Establishing a formal structure of authority through which work subdivisions are set up, defined and coordinated to achieve defined objectives

Staffing: Personnel functions, hiring and training

Directing: Decision-making, and giving specific and general orders

Coordination: Inter-relating various parts of work

Reporting: Keeping the ultimate superior and himself/herself informed

Budgeting: Fiscal planning, accounting and control

In the course of this chapter we shall look at each of these functions as performed by DOs and their elements.

Before proceeding further it may be useful to point out certain general characteristics of these functions of administrators encapsulated in POSDCORB. In some form or the other, all administrators in all organizations carry out these functions to varying degrees to achieve their goals. All these functions are carried out by administrators at all levels in any given organization. Whether one is heading the smallest pyramid towards the bottom or one stands at the peak of the organizational mountain, administrators must carry out all these functions.

Further, POSDCORB is not a sequential listing of functions of the administrator. At any given point of time, administrators carry out two or more functions simultaneously. Indeed one function may include elements of other functions for example, planning a revenue collection drive would include organizing the team, which in turn would require staffing. Not only is POSDCORB not a sequential listing of functions, it is also a dynamic process. A function leads to one or more functions, which may further require the taking up of still other tasks. In view of the above, it is important that an administrator, in this instance the DO, not only understands what his/her functions are but should also be able to distinguish when to do what. For optimizing the machinery of government at the district level, this is one of the greatest challenges that an administrator faces.

Planning

The traditional planning process consists of three stages: definition of objectives; identification of the functions and the processes to be taken up for achieving the objectives; and, identification of the methods to be employed. Planning is one of the basic tasks of DOs and their role in planning includes all sectors—regulatory, development and crisis management.

The DO's role in planning stems from his/her other roles: As Head of Office for the Collectorate and its sub-district level offices; after the 74th Amendment to the Constitution, as a Member Secretary of District Planning Committee, except in a few states such as Karnataka; as Executive Officer of the Zilla Parishad in several states; as Chairman or Executive Vice Chairman of various societies and government-operated NGOs (GONGOs) in the health, education and social welfare sectors; as leader of specific campaigns such as Pulse Polio—for the eradication of polio; as District Project Director or Chief Manager of development projects, including externally funded projects.

Various officials support the DO in discharging his/her planning function. In particular, the Planning Section or Cell of the Collectorate, headed by the district planning officer, works under his/her close supervision and guidance to compile data and information from diverse sources. To carry out needs assessment of the district, the DO may analyse datasets and their inter-relationships, and assess resources available—sources of funds and schedule of availability—for the next plan period. In most states, the District Statistics Officer at the district headquarters also assists in this process.

The DO carries forward formulation of the plan by facilitating consultation among stakeholders such as line departments and local self-government bodies in three sub-tasks of planning: agenda setting, identification of goals and their prioritization. These three tasks are also points where politics and administration meet at the field level; the political aspect of these activities should not be under-played. However, it is the DO's responsibility to ensure that the optimum level of objectivity is maintained in agenda setting, the selection of objectives, and the allo-cation of funds among them. He/she is also responsible for setting the planning process in motion by activating the line departments and convening the meetings of various planning fora, including the District Planning Commit-tee (DPC). Given the stress on decentralized planning, he/she also needs to monitor the planning process at all three levels of the PRIs, especially their standing committees, and the preparation of plans at different levels by the line departments.[3] Compilation and collation of plans of LGBs ascending from the villages to the district level and of the line departments leading to the preparation and finalization of the District Plan in the DPC also requires the DO's supervision.

Organizing

Organizing entails:

(a) the establishment of a formal structure of authority based on the principles of hierarchy, span of control, chain of command and unity of command; and,

(b) division of work and its arrangement for coordination according to the nature and variety of work, constraints of time and space and clientele.

Two questions may be asked in this regard: In light of the fact that DOs 'inherit' the organizational structure of district administration, what is the importance of this function to them? As administrators what is their responsibility in organizing?

The above questions would be valid if one were to accept the notion of a fixed, unchanging district administration. Yet, as the previous chapters have demonstrated, the office of the DO and the machinery of district administration has been constantly evolving. In the face of new opportunities and constraints, DOs of each successive generation confront the task of maintaining and nurturing an efficient and effective organization. In this regard, among the

challenges before DOs today are: downsizing and shortage
of professional staff, accompanied by a steady accretion of
functions and responsibilities; and obsolete, but surviving
age-hardened processes together with the slackening of
routine procedures.

Therefore, the DOs need to re-emphasize the formal
structure of authority by reorganizing and regroup-
ing tasks and subordinate units; by reassigning work
among available personnel or assigning new tasks to existing
units; by setting up new work units; and by delegating
authority where required, and reviewing processes and
procedures—especially in the light of utilization of information and communication technology. Multi-tasking,
a now familiar phrase in management, has always been
practiced by DOs and several of their colleagues in
the Collectorate; the need now is to build capacity and
competence to make multi-tasking more effective even at
the lower levels of administration. Outsourcing of functions
on a contractual basis, discussed in an earlier chapter,
is a new way that DOs have adopted in face of resource
constraints—of man-power as well as funds—and for
greater efficiency. This system maintenance function also
includes establishing or re-emphasizing norms of conduct
and interaction and establishing a system of monitoring
and supervision.

Apart from renovating and maintaining the existing
system, the DO is required to set up new organizations
for new programmes, projects or campaigns. These may be
funded by the central government, such as the Sarva Siksha
Abhiyan or Pulse Polio; by the state government, such as

the Employment Guarantee Scheme in Maharashtra and the Lok Jumbish Project in Rajasthan; by external funding agencies (routed through the central and/or state governments), such as the Health System Projects by the World Bank or the District Primary Education Programme by the Department of Foreign and International Development, United Kingdom; or by the local initiative of the DO such as the Gyandoot project in Madhya Pradesh or the SETU project in Maharashtra. New initiatives of these kinds require the DO to either set up organizations, task forces or detailed procedures for implementation, or both. Although the funding source or government, often one and the same, usually frames guidelines for such programmes and projects, these are usually standard instructions that need to be modified, elaborated or reframed in the context of local resources and limitations. Therefore, the DO's task of organizing is not restricted to maintaining the existing administrative machinery; as seen in the previous chapter, both his/her responsibilities of system maintenance and redesign and of configuring new structures and processes are constantly expanding.

Staffing

In today's terminology, staffing translates into human resource development. As Gulick and Urwick (1937) postulated decades ago, it consists of hiring, training, placement, development and maintaining favourable conditions of work. At the same time, as we shall see later in the chapter, the scope of this function has been considerably expanded. Given the DO's large establishment comprising several hundred members[4] spread over the entire district, staffing becomes a vital function for the DO requiring personal attention on a daily basis.

Recruitment

The elaborate, many-tiered district administrative machinery comprises personnel recruited by three authorities: a) by different departments of the state government; b) by the DO; and c) by a district level agency. Group 'A' and Group 'B' officials are recruited by the state government while group 'C' and 'D', ministerial staff, are usually recruited at the district level or within the district. Therefore, the DO recruits personnel in vacancies created periodically, upon government approval, in the Collectorate and subordinate offices to the Group 'C' and 'D' positions. By persuading government to fill up positions he/she strives to fill up vacancies of officers in Groups 'A' and 'B' in different offices under his/her direct charge such as the Collectorate, and the subdivisional or tehsil offices. If he/she is interested in all round development in the district, the DO also attempts to convince Heads of Departments or Directorates to fill gaps in personnel in *other* district level agencies, be it police personnel, veterinary surgeons in the Animal Husbandry Department, Soil Testing Technicians in the Agriculture Department, or Doctors in the Health Department. Further, the range of recruitments made directly or indirectly by the DO has also increased because of the establishment of the PRIs. With the assistance of the District Panchayat Officer, the DO recruits employees to local government bodies like the District, Block and Village Panchayats.

The impact of public sector reforms may be discerned in the expanding volume of the DO's recruitment function as well as upon the way it is done. A major area of supervision for the DO in this regard is ensuring procedural sanctity and transparency in the recruitment process in subordinate offices. To do this he/she must lay down objective policies and set standards that facilitate hiring of persons of appropriate competence. This involves drawing up qualifications, firming up the recruitment procedure, selecting a panel for conducting examinations or interview—even framing question papers where required and ensuring transparency in the entire process of selection. Added to the existing duties of the DO in this respect are recruitment for contractual appointments in LGBs and various externally aided projects. The success of such bodies and projects often depends upon the quality of personnel recruited for running and operationalizing them, respectively. It may be kept in mind that at the local level there usually are a variety of forces at work for influencing the selection of personnel. Only by working out details of the recruitment procedure on the bases of objective principles and by making the process entirely transparent can the DO ensure selection of the best available people. Finally, the DO is also asked to either participate in or provide officers to participate in recruitment by other wings of the state government at the field level, whether it is selection of police personnel or primary school teachers.

Training

As noted in the previous chapter, training is a key activity for the improvement of the delivery of public services.

However, training in government organizations in India is a low priority task. Its importance has been recognized in the National Training Policy of 1996 but is yet to be fully acknowledged at the field level. Traditionally, the Collectorate, and other district level offices, have relied upon on-the-job training of most freshly recruited employees, especially those belonging to Groups 'C' and 'D'. The DO has had a special responsibility for the field training of IAS and State Civil Service (SCS) officers; training for special administrative events such as elections and Census also have a long history. Such events also involve training of personnel from different wings of the state and central governments. Evidently, the DO's training function has increased considerably over the last two decades.

The elaboration of the responsibilities of district administration noted earlier has focused attention upon capacity building of the personnel engaged in service delivery at the cutting edge of administration. Its importance has also increased with the increase in the pace of change. Not only does the DO need to ensure the training of personnel in the traditional activities of administration but also of the personnel of specific and specialized projects, for example, SHSDP and DPEP. A major responsibility of the DO is the training of staff of PRIs and also of the elected representatives of these LGBs. The enormity of the task may be gauged by the fact that in West Bengal alone, Panchayat representatives of all three tiers number to 59,647 (http://kolkata.wb.nic.in/prd/html/panchayat/ panchayts.htm)—almost 90 per cent of whom are provided orientation and subject training at the district level itself under the supervision of the DO; the remaining attend the State Institute of Panchayat and Rural Development (SIPRD). Training and reorientation of staff for upgradation of knowledge and skills based on even a rudimentary training needs analysis (TNA) has become necessary, especially in view of the promotion of information technology in governance. Indeed, a basic shortcoming in computerization of government department has been the lack of adequate training of employees. More and more DOs are taking advantage of the advantage of State training institutions such as the Administrative Training Institute (ATI) and the SIPRD.

The DO's capacity building responsibilities may not be limited to officials alone. With the entry of NGOs in service, provision at the field level collaboration between them and government agencies at the district level has also increased. For implementing a large number of programmes, for example, the National Blindness Control Programme, Total Literacy Campaign and Child Labour School programme, the DO must take steps to augment the capacity of personnel of participating NGOs by organizing orientation and training workshops or camps. Moreover, the DO's capacity-building function at time extends to the larger body of citizens. For this, technological development may be responsible: In recent times, the DOs in their capacity as District Election Officers have undertaken the enormous task of training voters in the use of electronic voting machines prior to the general elections.

Placement

For the DO, an important aspect of organizing in an era of staff shortage is the problem of placing the right man in the right job, keeping in view the demands of the office and of individuals, and the requirements of the citizen customer. In any organization, and especially within organizations with a monopoly over certain types of services, it is natural for people to have vested interests in certain wings; however, it is unnatural to allow such interests to grow. Transfers contribute to ensuring that such interests, and corrupt practices that they stimulate, do not survive for long and do not damage the interests of the citizen-customer.[5] Therefore, the DO needs to transfer personnel at regular intervals on the basis of a principled and transparent policy. These may be desk transfers within the district headquarters or transfers among separate wings under the DO in the Collectorate—for example, Development, Panchayat and Rural Development, Relief, etc—or even among offices across the district.

Staff Development

Capacity building through training is a necessary but insufficient condition for staff development. The DO must make an effort to monitor and review the work of officers and staff so that corrective measures for improvement may be taken. Job rotation through regular transfers also allows employees to acquire new skills and experiences. This also calls for counseling and mentoring of personnel. Effective DOs usually utilize their team of senior officers to undertake these activities. Also, providing opportunities for external training and study contributes to the development of staff by acting as incentive.

Maintaining favourable conditions of work: Finally, the DO who builds effective teams is usually interested in a continuous process of feedback from his/her colleagues. Finding out about how the officers and staff feel about their work conditions is an important part of the DO's work. Based on the feedback, he/she would also be expected to improve the work environment—physically as well as in terms of inter-personal interaction. This may take the form of setting up water coolers for the employees or organizing informal social events such as annual staff picnic, Collectorate sports or interdepartmental football competition. The danger is in looking at these events as medicine given from time to time to boost employee morale. This approach is fated to fail because while medicines and shots may cure some ills they cannot substitute regular nourishment. Therefore, DOs must look to ways for improving the motivation and morale of their colleagues in the organization—from bottom to top—on a regular basis.

Directing

Directing—literally, meaning to give direction or show the way—involves decision making, issuing specific and general orders and instructions, and leading. Essentially, directing consists of taking decisions. Decisions may be 'routine' or 'critical.'

Routine decisions affect the conditions necessary to keep the Collectorate and other wings of district administration running at efficient levels and refer to the resolution of day-to-day problems. The emphasis is on orderly process, on smooth functioning. Routine decisions are 'technical' in the sense that expertise may be required (and usually is in large organizations like the Collectorate) to take care of these functions, indeed, to make them routine. Such decisions do not alter the basic structure of the organization.

Critical decisions are those that affect institutional development of the Collectorate or other parts of district administration. When making such a decision, the DO is actually framing 'policy' in its traditional sense. Since such decisions are closely related to organizational re-definition and reconstruction, the DO, as the institutional leader, may be seen taking critical decisions to translate into reality the goals and designs of new programmes and projects. A few instances to illustrate these types of decisions have been mentioned above in the section on 'Organizing.'

Specific orders are those decisions that relate to a particular person, section or a task of the organization. General orders are those that affect a large number of individuals or sections in an organization. Instructions are directions given for the performance of specific tasks by members of the organization.

In an earlier chapter we have discussed the reliance upon programmed decision making in most sections of the Collectorate, especially in the regulatory wings. Most such decisions, such as issue of arms license, are processed by assistants in the sections, notes are carried up the hierarchy to be approved or rejected by the DO after scrutiny. However, the crucial decisions taken by the DO are non-programmed decisions made in response to non-routine situations, such as the incidence of a riot or an earthquake. No doubt DOs have been taking routine and critical or programmed and non-programmed decisions since the days of Warren Hastings. Yet at this juncture we need to examine two questions: How is decision making by DOs different today from what it was a quarter of a century ago? How have reforms in the public sector affected it? In these respects, three major developments are worthy of note.

First, we have noted earlier that the workload of the DO has not only increased manifold but that it has also become diversified. Whereas, even twenty-five years ago the DO was called upon to take most decisions almost unilaterally with the assistance of his/her small team of officers, the expansion of the regulatory role and the development functions have also brought a variety of actors into the decision making process. The development responsibilities of the DO, whether in rural development, social welfare, industrialization or crisis management, have not only increased the scale of non-programmed decision-making but also necessitated the interplay of many other government and non-government agencies in the implementation of government programmes. Thus, decision-making at the district level, especially—but not only—in the non-regulatory areas, is no longer the closed process that it was a decade or two ago. Consultation may now be deemed a guiding principle for decision-making in district administration. The DO, the principal maker and shaper of decisions, is called upon to engage the stakeholders in a consultation process to build consensus. This is true for schemes as diverse as the National Employment Guarantee Act, the National Trust Act, immunization programmes for children, the rehabilitation of land-losers, and the Community Based Disaster Management Programme. The flip side of the openness in decision-making is the different pressures that DOs sometimes face from various sources in the district and outside it. These may be best dealt with by laying down, and following, clear principles and objective standards, consultation and transparency.

Second, there has been a quantum jump in the availability of information and data for decision-making. The DO has always relied upon both formal and informal sources of information for making decisions. However, three important changes are noticeable: there has been a phenomenal increase in both the amount of information available and their sources; the quantity of hard, quantitative data within reach has grown significantly; and, with the spread of computerization the ability of data analysis has also improved greatly. Thus, today's DO is in a position to make much more informed decisions than his/her predecessor.

Third, with democratization, growing levels of awareness—especially with the passage of the Right to Information Act 2005, DOs are required to be more transparent than ever in their decision-making.

Leadership is perhaps the single most important function performed by the DO. This has been discussed at some length in the subsequent chapter. Leadership can be exercised either by constant affirmation of the ideology of an organization and its reflection in all aspects of its work or by personal example of the leader. The latter often is the most effective way administrators may effectively lead personnel in government organizations. However, dealing with change in district administration requires a more proactive leadership than ever before. The DO's role as a leader and its growing importance is dealt with in some detail later in this chapter.

Coordinating

Coordination consists of inter-relating parts of work in such a way as to achieve a harmony of effort and attainment of the objectives of the organization. In the POSDCORB framework, coordination may be achieved through: allotment of work, allotment of authority, decentralization and by delegation. It can also be achieved by creating a dominant idea in the minds of employees through reinforcing of organizational values and organizational loyalty, which demand leadership skills.

The DO's role as coordinator at the district level has also grown in significance and scope. He/she is widely recognized by the government as the chief coordinator of government programmes in the district. In this regard, the DO's coordination function includes coordination between different departments of the state government at the district level; different departments of the state government and local government bodies; departments of the state government and the central government; the police and judiciary; government functionaries and public representatives; and government functionaries and NGOs.

Some important areas in which the DO plays a prominent coordinating role in most states are: in preparation of district-level plans and schemes/projects; in implementation of schemes of a multi-agency nature at the district level and at subordinate levels; in ensuring that goals of government policies and programmes are understood and owned by all participating agencies, to prevent misunderstanding; and, in effectively supervising and monitoring schemes of a multi-agency nature.

Due to the importance of the topic, the DO's role in inter-agency coordination has been analysed in detail in a later chapter.

Reporting

Reporting refers to a system of communication in the organization that facilitates the flow of information to the decision centre from various parts of the organization and outside it, and the flow of information to all parts of the organization and its environment. It should also ensure that information not only reaches various parts of the organization but is understood by the people. Communication may be formal or informal.

As the 'eyes and ears' of government, it is the DO's responsibility to ensure that feedback regarding the progress of the numerous regulatory and developmental activities at the district and sub-district levels reaches him/her and the state government on a regular basis. This is achieved through a system of reporting whereby reports are received by the DO from the Gram Panchayat, Block/Panchayat Samity and *thana*, and Subdivisional levels. The vast majority of these reports are periodic. However, certain types of reports pertaining to disturbance of law and order or natural and man made disasters may be episodic. The periodicity of other reports may vary according to their nature.

Law and order and natural calamities are two concerns that require immediate intervention. Therefore, the frequency of periodicity of reports in these matters is high. The Situation Report received by the DO from the SP on law and order in the district, for instance, is usually received twice daily—in the morning and in the evening. In flood or cyclone prone areas, the DO may also receive daily reports regarding weather conditions and water levels in the main rivers of the district from the Meteorological Department and the Irrigation and Waterways Department, respectively. Similarly, a summary of the overall law and order situation from the police is received daily and on a weekly or fortnightly basis.

Matters that are of a routine nature are reported less frequently. Reports on matters such as collection of revenue, status of collection of small savings, status of enquiries, disposal of certificate cases, the stock of relief materials and status of cases under the preventive sections of the CRPC are received by the DO from sub-district level offices on a monthly basis. Progress of rural development programmes, panchayat functions, welfare schemes for SCs and STs, projects for women and child welfare like the ICDS, programmes for preventive health care and incidence of diseases also fall under this category. Certain reports such as on the issue of SC, ST and OBC certificates and the expenditure from Central Relief Fund are also received on a quarterly basis. All in all, the Collectorate receives over fifty reports from sub-district level offices each month.

Certain reports have a seasonal character. Thus, in some of the eastern states, during the monsoon, the DO receives reports on the flood situation and the relief operations on a daily or even a twice-daily basis. Similarly, during administrative exercises such as elections or Census operations the frequency of reports increases since monitoring on a daily basis is desirable.

The purpose of all these reports is to enable the DO to monitor the status of various programmes and take corrective or preventive actions as and when necessary. These reports also assist the DO to formulate plans and special interventions. The reports received by the DO are compiled and sent to various departments of the government. Except a few reports on special projects like the Child Labour Rehabilitation Project or the Pradhan Mantri Gram Sadak Yojana that are sent to the central government directly with a copy to the state government, the DO submits his/her report to the concerned department of the state government. Most of these reports are sent on a monthly basis.

Budgeting

Budgeting comprises fiscal planning, accounting, and, fiscal control; it refers here to the DO's financial management function. Fiscal planning is the process of assessing the financial requirements of the organization in keeping with its functional, establishment and capital requirements.

There is a direct linkage, therefore, between the DO's planning function where the items of work, the various functions, processes and methods are identified and delineated, and fiscal planning that is based upon these item-wise details. The preparation of the annual budget of the Collectorate, section-wise, the collation of the budgets of the subdivisional and block offices, and securing governmental assent is an important annual exercise. A major part of the DO's budget consists of non-planned items highlighting the system maintenance function of the office. In several states the DO plays a central role in preparing the budget of the Zilla Parishad, or district panchayat. Financial planning as part of the other planning functions of the DO, particularly preparation of the district plan, involves attention to details and eliciting the cooperation of the many line agencies whose plans need to be included in the exercise. Both the sources of revenue and the items of expenditure must be dealt with meticulously. To be effective, fiscal planning should be a comprehensive task that provides for contingencies that may afflict district administration.

Increase in expenditure on development by government, and to a lesser degree also by external aid agencies, has made a qualitative difference to the DO's role in financial management. One of the hallmarks of effective DOs of today, and the future, is the role they play in securing financial resources for special projects based upon strong project proposals that highlight a special need of a district. Funds for special need-based projects are often available in several Ministries of the central and state governments, such as Rural Development, Social Justice and Empowerment, and Commerce and their wings, as also in external aid agencies such as UNDP and UNICEF. DOs, with initiative, may be able to address special needs of citizen customers in the district—be it a bridge, a culvert, hand pumps, low cost housing, or preventive health care—by obtaining funds available with these agencies for special projects. Financial management of projects has come to be an added responsibility of the DO and one that is likely to expand.

Fiscal accounting is the process of monitoring the inflow of revenue and the expenditure outflows. It includes the day-to-day maintenance of accounts as well as their periodic review to ensure that both, revenue and expenditure meet the targets set during the fiscal planning stage. The DO carries out financial accounting for government expenditure in the district through the district and subdivisional treasuries. This is of special significance because of the change in the nature of the state; prior to independence, the state was concerned more with the generation of revenues than expenditure of funds. After independence, along with revenue generation expenditure of government funds for developmental purposes, in pursuit of the public interest, has become at least as important; it translates into provision of services to the citizen customer. The monthly accounts submitted by the DO to the state government through the treasuries are crucial for state-level financial management. On behalf of the state government, the DO exercises fiscal control over the other departments at the district level by regulating financial outflows through treasuries. The monthly cash analyses at the Collectorate, subdivisional and block levels enables the DO to monitor the financial management in these offices.

CONCLUSION

Even though public administrators and scholars have become disenchanted with the POSDCORB model, its relevance has not changed. Although it may be accused of being 'inward looking' and of promoting compartmentalization of the administrator's work (Jones et al. 2002) the essential principles of POSDCORB are not to be denied. As we have seen above, it is a useful tool to analyse the tasks of the DO, both the elaboration of the functions as well as their nature.

Nevertheless, in the changed and rapidly changing politico-administrative environment, the DO's role cannot remain that of an administrator. Placed at the centre of the field administration, the DO's responsibility is not restricted merely to *manage* change but to act as the principal agent of change in the district. Therefore, it must be recognized that although management and leadership are often used as synonyms they are not. Well-managed organizations are not always high performance organizations; for high performance organizations need to be well managed and ably led (Kotter 1996). The following chapter explores the implications for the DO's leadership role.

Notes

1. Paternalistic.
2. In this section the basic explication of each of the components of POSDCORB is owed to Gulick and Urwick (1937); therefore, they are not referenced individually.
3. This would depend upon the extent to which PRIs have developed in a given state, the devolution of authority, and the development of capacity at the three tiers. The DOs in some states monitor planning-related activities at lower rungs of the Panchayats with the help of the District Panchayat Raj Officer.
4. Without including even the sub-district level offices under the direct supervision of the DO, this number is large. In 2002, the Collectorate in Cooch Behar district, West Bengal, had a staff strength of 416 persons; it may be noted Cooch Behar is one of the smaller districts of the state.
5. A word of caution: transfers are not the sole means of preventing corruption; they should be accompanied by other measures.

Chapter Seven

The Administrator–Leader

'If you don't know where you are going, any road will get you there.'

Lewis Carrol

TO THE observer of the government, it may appear that the matrix of laws and rules within which district administration operates, emphasizes the one best way of doing things and that one best way is usually narrowly defined. However, district officers (DOs) worth their salt recognize that often not only is there no one best way, depending upon the situation, there may be many best ways of doing the same thing. This becomes even more germane in an era of ongoing public sector reforms. The changes sweeping over India discussed in Chapter Four have not come to a stand still. The restructuring of the state and the process of decentralization that the 73rd and 74th Amendments to the Constitution have initiated, will take time to strike deep roots. It will be a while before the course of social justice runs through the remoter, or even nearer villages.

The benefits of marketization will not be available for some time yet to those who do not have purchasing power; and, administrative reforms will continue to take place at a steady pace. And the new forces of accountability are likely to grow stronger with each passing year. Therefore, although trite, it is true that for the DO, the only constant is continuous change.

Administrative systems functioning within a democratic framework, especially in large countries such as India, do not usually undergo revolutionary upheavals and restructuring. Change is often incremental and adoption of innovations, time consuming. Although the DO has always been an administrator, the changes in the environment and context of administration triggered by the independence of India, have gradually changed his/her primary role from the ruler of the district to that of the administrator–leader. In the wake of public sector reforms in India, the expansion of public service programmes, the pace of change and the multiplicity of actors involved in the inclusive process of governance, the DO is not merely the leader of the team of officers at the district level; he/she must lead change. To be able to do so, there is a need for a shift in his/her orientation and approach to district administration.

On the one hand the DO's tasks—the tasks of administration—aim to establish routine and predictability: to ensure the rule of law, deliver public services and respond to crises. On the other hand, he/she is called upon to confront new challenges in this yet new century: manage compounded uncertainty, shoulder multiple responsibilities, deal with an increasing number of partners and face greater accountability. It follows that the requirements of the DO's job underscore the need for balance—in perspective; flexibility—in adapting to new conditions; agility—in adopting new roles; and openness—to people and ideas. Unlike most other officers in field administration, the DO is not just an office—he/she stands for an institution, for government; of no other office do the people have so many expectations because, for long the DO has acted as the representative of the public interest in the field (Chopra 1978). Nevertheless, if institutions do not change in response to the changing environment they ossify.

The 'issue today is not whether organizations will experience change, but how they will manage that change' (Quinn et al. 2003: 302); today this is a crucial question for the office of the DO. Adherence to fixed mind-sets and rigid systems by the office of the DO without regard to citizen clients may often result not only in inefficient service provision to the citizen but also plain ineffectiveness. The change involved not only calls for modifications in the basic processes but also alteration in the attitudes and orientation of the service providers.

To assess the requirements of the new role of the DO—the administrator–leader—we may apply two theoretical constructs that complement each other to the demands of leadership upon the DO: the Four Frames Leadership Model (Bolman and Deal 2003) and the Competing Values Framework (Quinn et al. 2003). The former emphasizes the four main frameworks or windows

through which leaders may perceive their own organization and its environment: structural, human resource,
political and symbolic. The perspective they adopt or
choose determines their approach to the organization, its
purpose, and relationships within it. In the Competing
Values Framework, the authors describe 'the competing
roles managers play in their organization' (Quinn et al.
2003: 15) that determine leadership effectiveness. The
eight managerial leadership roles that they describe are:
Visionary, Producer, Director, Coordinator, Monitor,
Facilitator, Mentor, Innovator, and Culture Manager.
These leadership styles/roles are especially relevant to the
DO's leadership role; effective leadership by the DO often
lies in reframing changing conditions in the district and
shifting to the role appropriate to the demands of the new
situation.

THE CHALLENGE: DYNAMIC LEADERSHIP

If the DO as the administrator–leader in the district milieu
is to succeed, he/she should be able to use all four frames
mentioned above—structural, human resource, political
and symbolic—to comprehend the organization and its
relationship with its environment and to act accordingly.
A multi-frame approach is particularly relevant because
amidst a fast changing society and growing expectations
of district administration in India, much as companies in
the developed world, DOs need to deal with what is called
'adaptive challenges' (Heifetz and Laurie 1997). To do so,

they recommend that the leader needs to 'go to the balcony' to grasp the larger perspective.

'Going to the balcony' from time to time may enable DOs to distance themselves from the humdrum of routine administration or the frenzy of crisis-management and review the course that district administration may be on. Distancing also facilitates multi-frame thinking that may enable the DO to examine afresh each time the demands upon his/her organization—environmental or programmatic—and inculcate a flexibility to reshape it, or a constituent part, to deal with new demands. This becomes particularly relevant in the context of organization, or reorganization, of the Collectorate in light of new programmes and enlarged duties discussed previously in the sections on Organizing and Staffing. It is remarkable that few attempts have been made to reorganize the Collectorate ever since its inception 150–200 years ago. Functions and sections have been, and continue to be, added to it without regard to systemic needs.

The competing values framework (Quinn et al. 2003), in conjunction with the four frames, stresses the multiple roles played by the administrator–leader in response to the demands of the organization and external forces. It indicates that effective leaders do not remain tied to one role but take on new ones as circumstances change. This is particularly relevant to the DO because rarely does a day pass when he/she is not required to take on more than half the roles enumerated, and sometimes all eight roles in one day. Together, the four frames and the competing values models frame the vision of *dynamic leadership*.

ELEMENTS OF ADMINISTRATIVE-LEADERSHIP

Viewed through this lens, in the context of district administration in India, eight key elements for the DO's leadership role stand out: knowledge management, vision, strategic planning, design, team building, monitoring, coordination and facilitation. In view of the ambiguity and controversy about the DO's role in interagency coordination and facilitation of non-state actors respectively, the last two elements—and functions—have been discussed in detail in separate chapters that follow.

KNOWLEDGE MANAGEMENT

In several preceding chapters, we have touched upon the role in district administration of information in an information age. Several commentators have dwelt upon the importance of information management for effective leadership (Kotter 1996; Valsan 2005). Yet its value as a means is often confused for an end in itself. Hence, it is commonplace but inaccurate to say that information is power. Field functionaries inspired by this dictum often zealously preserve reports and statistics until long after they become obsolete, neither benefiting from these treasures themselves nor allowing others to use them. They fail to see that information by itself is not power; but sharing and using information is empowering. However, the DOs are neither meant to serve as store houses of information nor as data banks. Their role is to utilize the knowledge available as a resource for improved performance. Two aspects of information management are particularly relevant for the DO's role as an administrator–leader: provision or dissemination of information as a public good and service; and, management and analysis of data as a tool for monitoring and as an aid for decision making.

The 'information age' refers to the importance of information in societies powered by information technology. The immediate association of the phrase is with the computer monitor and the internet, business process outsourcing and call centres, satellite radio and cellular phones, and similar high technology gadgets of the world of the upper middle classes. Nonetheless, it is logical and apposite, though perhaps unfashionable, to remark at the importance of information or knowledge to the poor and the deprived in both rural and urban areas. The state may have devised elaborate programmes and projects for regulation and development to benefit the weak and the poor, but they are of little avail if target populations are not able to access the services due to ignorance of governing provisions. Whether it is information about their dues from the public distribution centre (for example, amount of grain per month per head or timings of the fair price shops), the immunization dosage for children and pregnant women from health sub-centres, the many services provided at ICDS centres, or the provisions of the newly passed Right to Information Act—unless citizen consumers *know* what their entitlements are they cannot access them, leave alone demand them. Until then theirs' is a paper entitlement.

Publicity departments in states aim to create awareness about programmes and schemes, but that is not enough. Their efforts usually do not include the details regarding what citizen customers are entitled to or how they may take advantage of them. Therefore, it is necessary to view this information as a product and its provision as a service that the state must ensure at the district and sub-district levels; further, not only should information reach the citizen customer it should prompt them to utilize the related service. The state must create demand for its myriad goods and services by ensuring that the weakest sections in society are aware not only about the programmes but also their entitlements under these programmes *and* how to access them. At the field level it is the DO who can lead this process and monitor it.

We have noted several trends regarding the collection of information and the various kinds of surveys that are conducted from time to time. The many sources of information in the field are: the District Gazetteer, Census data, District Statistics cell, monthly and quarterly reports received by the Collectorate, baseline and other surveys noted in the previous chapter, satellite maps, hydrological and geological data and others. To these sources have been added the immense resource of the Internet through which the DOs and their team may access the latest reports, surveys, and other information that may be utilized for planning and project formulation. Studies sponsored by international organizations like the UNDP, for example, State and District Human Development Index, also provide valuable data and insights. If anything, at any given point at the district level there is not a shortage but an excess of data, particularly if it is not being used.[1]

Not only are there these many sources of data available to the DO, the infrastructure for analysing the data have also grown with the rapid spread of information technology. The NIC branch attached to the Collectorate has proven to be a hub and has often been utilized for introducing computers in other wings of the DO's office. Although initially the use of computers was limited to word processing, over the years, even in the remoter districts of the country computers have come to be utilized for data handling and analysis. The extent of utilization usually depends upon the individual DO and other officers in his/her office; nevertheless, some basic degrees of utilization of ICT have come to be commonly accepted. These include a large body of election related work; generation of reports and returns and their online submission over Internet for central government programmes such as the PMGSY; and, preparation of reports and returns for the state government schemes. Although not uniform across the states, ICT is also being used at district and subdivisional headquarters for improving the performance in certain functional areas such as treasury operations, accounting, land related tasks, registration of land, administration of motor vehicles laws and rules. In some states such as Karnataka, Maharashtra, Andhra Pradesh, Himachal Pradesh and West Bengal, computerization of the PRIs has also been undertaken. Attempts at public grievance redressal and of improvement of services for citizen customers through ICT have been noted in Chapter Five.

The combination of data and ICT infrastructure at the district and sub-district levels is a resource that the DO may utilize to strengthen his/her monitoring function. We have noted in the previous chapter that the DO receives over 50 reports from district level and sub-district offices. However, there has been little progress in integrating the reports through a Management Information System (MIS) to harvest their full potential. Although in some states like Andhra Pradesh, attempts are being made to integrate the MIS at the district and even subdivision levels, there are severe problems of coordination between the MIS of different departments (Kumar 2004). However, there is no centralized and integrated Management Information System (MIS) in the DO's office that may facilitate comprehensive monitoring. At present, all reports received by the DO are dealt with in different sections of the Collectorate. Due to computerization, though DOs in most states may have moved away from manual compilation and computation of reports, there is little evidence of integration of the reports.[2] An integrated MIS would facilitate retrieval, cross verification, and multi-level scrutiny of data for monitoring of regulatory and developmental programmes. This would also enable the DO to provide information sought under RTI by citizen customers more easily.

Apart from using the MIS for monitoring and supervision of regulatory and developmental programmes, it would provide invaluable inputs in the DO's decision making and planning functions. The current system of reporting discussed in the previous chapter leads to the stock piling of data at the district and sub-district levels in most districts. However, the emphasis here is upon data collection, compilation and forwarding—to the next level. Not only is this a time consuming process, often the data thus collected is not subjected to even minimum analysis at either the first point of collection or at subsequent levels. Unless the data is analysed, diagnosis of difficulties in implementing a particular programme is not likely to be recognized. For the DO to take corrective and pre-emptive steps, for example, to control a malaria or diarrhoea epidemic, he/she should be able to speedily analyse the periodic reports. Similarly, the targeting of various schemes in the district may be improved if the Census or baseline data is rigorously examined and analysed. Although the Planning Commission of India has carried out a dozen exercises to identify the most backward districts in the country, identification of pockets of poverty at the village level has not been taken up until recently. In 2004 the identification of over 4,000 villages in West Bengal by the Department of Panchayats and Rural Development focused attention upon the poorest areas in the state. In the same year, the Village Vulnerability Index based on Census 2001 data developed in Paschim Medinipur district enabled the DO to locate clusters of poverty alleviation schemes in the poorest villages in the district.

Thus, knowledge is a key input in administration and knowledge management a crucial function of DOs. It enables them to empower citizen customers and alert and energize service providers; monitor the numerous regulatory and developmental activities in the district for corrective measures; and, strengthens their capacity for effective planning and decision making.

Vision

District administration, and especially the Collectorate, in India may best be described in terms of Henri Mintzberg's (1983) model of a machine bureaucracy. Except the strategic apex of the organization, the other four parts—middle line, technostructure, support staff and operating core—are all well elaborated. Formed by rules and bound by rules, these pyramid shaped organizations run on rules. However, because they lack a common vision, they often function blindly like machines. A shared vision is vital for large and small organizations since, as Bennis and Nanus observe 'Management through vision is the creating of focus' (1996: 30); in their study of 90 successful leaders, they found that all of them had an agenda that they successfully conveyed to members of their organization. For most district-level agencies the focus of the organization is diffused; often because of preoccupation with outputs rather than outcomes and sometimes because of an obsession with means rather than even with output.

A well-communicated vision is the internal drive for progress that enables an organization to make continuous improvements (Collins and Porras 1997). The Collectorate and other district and sub-district level offices of government exist to serve specific public interests; however, the public interest is all too often taken for granted and neglected because usually district-level government employees, particularly at the lower levels, are ignorant of or indifferent to the organizational purpose or direction. This contributes to shortsightedness, delayed action and compartmentalization of the Collectorate with sections refusing to share even stationery articles. Therefore, DOs as administrator–leaders must shoulder the responsibility of communicating a common vision throughout the Collectorate and the district administration that reminds all its internal stakeholders of its ideology rooted in the Constitution so that it 'permeates the organization and gives coherence to its diverse activities' (Senge 2000: 206).

Strategic Planning

Articulation of the vision is often the first step in the preparation of a strategic plan for an organization. Most government agencies in India do not have a vision, a mission or a strategic plan; certainly at the district level very few attempts are discernible. The Government of Assam has made an effort in this regard and in each district in the state the office of the DO has adopted a vision statement; however limited in scope, this is a beginning. Vision and mission help catch the employees' attention. As Bennis and Nanus state: 'Leaders are the most results-oriented people in the world, and results get attention' (1996: 28). To focus on the results, the organization must have goals that are specific, challenging and prioritized for integration in individual and sub-unit action plans (Quinn et al. 2003). However, especially in the development and allied sector, most goals of the Collectorate or district administration are either expenditure targets or statement-of-intentions.

The DO must be able to focus the attention of the organization he/she heads upon performance targets that are more than mere numbers and instead highlight outcomes. It is also vital that in identifying the mission and the goals of the organization, the administrator–leader includes members of the organization.

Earlier in the chapter, we have seen that planning is not only one of the key functions of the DO, but that he is engaged in the formulation of a plethora of plans. However, most of these plans, including the district plan, are annual plans that aim at a set of financial and physical targets with little regard to outcomes. Most such plans are driven by the fund support existing under different programmes of the central and state governments. Yet, assuredly, the development—or other—priorities of a district in Chhattisgarh or southern Orissa are unlikely to be the same as that of one in Gujarat or western Uttar Pradesh. It follows that the strategy for addressing them must also be specific and suited to the locale.

Strategic planning for district administration would enable the DO to segregate the different stakeholders of the district administration or the Collectorate, focus upon the priorities of the district, and develop a plan to deal with them with clear goals and performance indicators. A simple stakeholder analysis shows the large number of citizen customers and other stakeholders who have a stake in the various programmes and schemes of district administration (Appendix 5). Similarly, to identify the mission and vision of the office of the DO, an environmental scan would be useful. It would enable the DO to analyse the external and internal factors that affect the performance of the Collectorate. A simple exercise on strategic planning at the district level has been included at the end of this chapter to illustrate the above points.

Design

As Peter Senge observes, the most 'neglected leadership role is the designer of the ship' (1994: 341). Three reasons make design a priority for the DO in the context of district administration in India:

(a) structurally or attitudinally, most government organizations at the district level, especially the Collectorate, have not changed much in well over a century;

(b) the changing environment of field administration demands modifications in designs of administrative systems; and,

(c) unless government organizations at the district and sub-district levels change they will not be able to serve the people effectively.

Available information suggests that although the spotlight of the government has swung towards district administration from time to time, no comprehensive attempt at redesigning district administration has been attempted. The Krishnamachari Report on the Indian and State Civil Services and the Problems of District Administration (1962) was the first effort to engage with the problems of administration at the district level. It was concerned mainly with the vertical elaboration of the district administrative machinery to the block and village levels, the expansion of the state's responsibilities after independence, and the requirements of personnel for discharging the new functions. However, it did not consider the need to review the structure and mechanics of the DO's office at district headquarters. The Study Group on District Administration of the Administrative Reforms Commission (1966) also reviewed the structure and functions of district administration. Although it underlined the centrality of the DO and his/her coordinating role it did not make any major recommendations for redesigning the structures and processes of district administration. The survey undertaken by Dayal et al. (1976) for reorganization of district administration comes nearest to an organized effort by the government in this direction. Not much appears to have come of it.

The most recent attempt to review the role of the DO and district administration was made at the instance of the Prime Minister in 2005. Organized by the Department of Administrative Reforms and Public Grievances, GOI the National Conference of District Collectors (NCDC) was held in New Delhi in May 2005. It was preceded by four Regional Conferences of Collectors where participants deliberated upon: delivery of services in education and health sectors, delivery of services and role of local institutions, modernization of district administration and capacity building, integrated implementation of rural development programmes at the district level, development of infrastructure, urban renewal and habitat issues, natural resource management and environmental concerns, right to information and transparency in government and public private partnership in governance at the district level. Development of policy and legal frameworks for changes at the district level by state governments, capacity building, reengineering of processes outsourcing of services, monitoring, accountability, and need for collaboration with NGOs and the private sector are some of the common themes running through the conclusions participants reached in all eight topics. This indicates that DOs across the country are experiencing the changes brought about by the reform of the public sector and trying to cope with them.

Changes in district level agencies, particularly the Collectorate, have taken place on an ad hoc, incremental basis in knee-jerk reactions to either deal with crises or to handle additional responsibilities. Yet Goold and Campbell (2002, 24) rightly reject the idea that 'organization design will inevitably be an ad hoc process, paying more attention to personalities and power politics than sound principles and logic.' Such an approach cannot make for strong administrative infrastructure for sustainable development. In the Indian scenario, the administrator–leader must be responsible for designing the organization and its policies by being able to see it as a system 'in which parts are not only internally connected but also connected to the external environment, and clarifying how the whole system can work better' (Ray Strata in Senge 2000: 343). Designing the Collectorate or the larger machinery of district administration is not a one-time drill but a continuous process for which the DO as administrator–leader is primarily responsible.

At no other level in the government does an administrator– leader has quite as much liberty or opportunity to design and redesign systems and procedures for improved performance as at the level of the DO. An important reason for this is the new projects, programmes and campaigns that the DOs are asked to implement from time to time in diverse subject areas. Some of the new projects the DO has been asked to implement within the last decade are: Sarva Shiksha Yojana, Pulse Polio, Rashtriya Sama Vikas Yojana, National Employment Guarantee Act and several externally funded projects.

Organizational support is needed to set up many of these programmes; for all of them procedures and processes have also to be laid down. The department or the ministry in which the programme originates usually furnishes the guidelines for forming the implementation structure and procedures. Since details are often not provided in the guidelines, these have to be prepared by the DO and his/her team in the district. Therefore, designing new systems and putting them in place becomes one of the DO's primary responsibilities. This sometimes leads to outstanding innovations, such as the Lakhina experiment in Ahmednagar in 1982–83 for improving service delivery at the Collectorate; however, unless the state government takes steps to institutionalize these changes, such experiments may neither survive the transfer of the DO nor may be replicated in other districts.

Team Building

The change in the perception of organizations from a hierarchy of individuals to an entity comprising interconnected teams (Likert in Bolman and Deal: 2003) may be traced to the growth of the human relations school in the second quarter of the last century. While highlighting participation, consensus and equality in group activities, the human relations model uncovered the significance of values such as commitment, cohesion and morale for organizational efficiency and effectiveness, and emphasized team orientation (Quinn et al. 2003). Over the years not only have organizations come to be seen as a combination of teams, often forging an organizational team is perceived to be the main challenge of leadership. This is particularly true for DOs.

Thus, the DOs' responsibility for building teams is twice that of other administrator–leaders. Not only must they build a performing team within the Collectorate, and its sub-district offices spanning the entire district, they must also develop and lead the team of district-level officials of line departments. Often DOs rely only upon organizational formality to develop teams or they work with a small team of select officials leading to sub-optimal performance by the larger Collectorate organization. With regard to multi-agency programmes, effective DOs have been seen to build strong teams for specific campaigns and projects; in this regard the total literacy campaigns in Ernakulam district in Kerala and Midnapore district in West Bengal in the early 1990s are cases in point. Similar instances may be seen in respect for focused projects in recent years in crises management, rural development, health, education and other sectors in different parts of the country.

Overall, putting together and sustaining teams for routine administration appears to be a great challenge for the DOs, for although all teams are organizations, not all organizations are full-fledged teams. The challenge before most DOs today is to turn their organizations into teams and their teams into organizations. Yet in India, where within government hierarchy persists, forging an organizational team is one of the main challenges of leadership at the district level. The DOs must appreciate the value of the human resource available to them. For although in large organizations hierarchy and formalism are inevitable, arrogance and distrust are not. As Quinn et al state, 'leadership at any level is a social activity as well as a technical one' (2003 261).

Unless administrator–leaders seek to build empowered teams, 'energies of individual members work at cross purposes' (Senge 2000: 234). Senge further indicates that teams signify the alignment of the efforts of individual members that result in 'a resonance or synergy;' and this 'alignment' is based on an understanding of a shared vision, purpose and of each other's requirements. Therefore, among the DO's primary tasks of teambuilding, is the development through consultation of a vision and mission for the Collectorate and for its wide dissemination among team members. A word of caution may be in order at this point. Developing a vision for the organization is not the same as dictating a vision for an organization. All the members of the organization should be allowed to participate in it. Indeed, if wide consultation is ensured by the DO the visioning exercise may itself turn out to be a crucial teambuilding effort in the Collectorate.

To successfully perform the multifarious tasks that comprise the DOs' responsibilities, they must recognize that like other leader-managers, their effectiveness depends upon the effectiveness of their colleagues at all levels in the administrative system (Kotter 1996). Recognition of this fact may not be enough unless the DO also empowers them by appropriate allocation of responsibility and delegation of authority. According to Senge (1994), leaders do this by creating a learning organization—one that fosters learning in the work place. In the same vein while noting that team-building is a key competency of the managerial leader in his facilitator role Quinn et al. (2003) also emphasize the manager-leader's role in developing a productive environment. This is particularly relevant for the DO when dealing with different line departments and other non-state actors such as NGOs and CBOs, where he/she may adopt a change of role to that of a facilitator—an aspect dealt in detail in a subsequent chapter.

Monitoring

As officer-in-charge of the district, monitoring and supervision are traditional functions of the DO that have expanded because of two reasons: first, the changed nature of his/her responsibilities; second, the elaboration of agencies providing public services to sub-district levels; and, third, due to the changes introduced by reforms. Whereas, monitoring of regulatory activities such as law and order, revenue collection and licensing may be done relatively easily on the basis of quantitative performance indicators; measures of progress and performance of development programmes may not always be a matter of simple numbers. Further, in the post-independence period the cutting edge for public service provision has gradually shifted downwards from district headquarters to block or even village levels. Consequently, the monitoring and supervisory functions of the DO have increased vastly. On the one hand, introduction of IT has simplified monitoring and has also created demands for reports, especially since the focus on efficiency and effectiveness of programmess has sharpened. Therefore, as the office responsible for system maintenance, inter-agency coordination, or facilitation and capacity building, the DO is also responsible for monitoring development and progress of interventions. Increasingly, development projects are encouraging social audit, which in turn needs to be monitored and guided by the DO.

Further, DOs are being required to lead teams for monitoring projects. Two instances illustrate the point. The ADB-funded Kerala Sustainable Urban Development Project taken up in 2005, envisages development of the sewage system, drainage canals and road networks. A key element of the project is the collection of a monthly sewerage charge and periodic revision of user fees; this would ensure a subsidy-free service operated and maintained by the revenues generated. To monitor and supervise the project, a steering committee has been set up comprising the District Collector, Mayor, Corporation Secretary, representatives of state departments and non-governmental organizations (NGOs) (The Hindu, 4 March 2005). Similarly, in 2002–03, Akshaya, a project aimed at total computer literacy in the district of Mallapuram was launched in Kerala. Funded by the District Pancahyat to the tune of Rs six million, the DO as the chairman of the District Level Task Force, was responsible for its supervision and monitoring (Akshaya, http://akshaya.net).

Developments in information and communication technology and their extension even to far-flung rural areas have greatly enhanced the DO's span of control. His/her ability to monitor field-level officials has been revolutionized by mobile telephony, internet and video conferencing facilities. Yet, despite these technological improvements, a substitute for touring and site visits as the most effective mode of monitoring and supervision is yet to be found. Improvements in communication have reduced the time taken by DOs on tours, but to effectively accomplish any kind of responsibility—regulatory, developmental or crisis related—it is inevitable for the DO to tour the district. This ensures not only performance but also enables the DO to receive the valuable feedback of the citizen customer.

CONCLUSION

The forces of the public sector reform in India are steadily and inexorably transforming the way public services reach the citizen customer. The emphasis is on decentralized service provision through governmental, PRI and non-state actors at the district and sub-district levels. Market forces and administrative reforms are altering the way district administration functions and driving towards greater efficiency while new forces of accountability, be it the Right to Information Act 2003, judicial activism or the media, by pressuring the state at the field level goad government towards greater effectiveness. In combination, the forces of reform have created a dynamic and demanding environment of district administration.

The challenge before the DO today is dynamic leadership. It requires him/her to not only switch roles as he/she adapts to new situations and responsibilities, but also to adopt an apt perspective. It calls for DOs who are proactive, outcome-oriented, depend on consultation and persuasion than on command, and value relationships and teams. Although the traditional roles and functions for regulatory administration need to be strengthened, the DO is no more primarily an administrator providing leadership in periods of administrative stress or crisis. To lead change to better serve the citizen customer, the DO must function as the 'administrator–leader.' He/she must employ the burgeoning knowledge resources with the use of ICT to empower citizen customers to demand services; take better decisions; and, develop a strategic plan with clear goals for the Collectorate and the district administration. To this, he/she must help forge a vision that may guide his/her teams through a consultative process; to lead change the DO must first lead teams. As administrator–leader, a fundamental function of the DO is in designing and redesigning organizations and processes in response to needs of the citizen customer. The coordination and facilitation functions underscore that the DO's overarching job is to ensure that components of district administration function as one. The two subsequent chapters explore these roles—that are also areas of responsibility—in detail.

Strategic Planning for the District: An Exercise

In the introduction (suitably titled 'Embarkation') of their book *Strategy Safari* Mintzberg, Ahlstrand and Lampel (1998) point out how over time scholars and practitioners of strategic management have chosen to focus on a part of the whole. Consequently, like the *Blind Men of Indostan*, they too have mistaken a part for the whole elephant. The result is the development of at least 10 schools of strategy formation based separately on: Design, Planning, Positioning, Entrepreneurial, Cognitive, Learning, Power, Culture, Environment and Configuration. Since this writer is also from the fabled Indostan, to avoid the pitfalls of any one school, we have attempted to take a holistic view of strategic planning at the district level in India.

This exercise shows how to prepare a simple strategic plan for the office of the DO of a given district. The office of the DO is known as the Collectorate. In the course of this exercise we shall undertake a stakeholder analysis that enables us to explore the mission of the Collectorate in the context of the variety of functions performed by it. Thereafter, we attempt an environmental scan through a short external and internal analysis of its strengths, weaknesses, opportunities and threats. We then suggest a Vision for the office of the DO and identify a few goals and measures of performance.

For the purposes of this exercise, we shall focus on the Collectorate, the principal administrative organization in a district. If we apply Henry Mintzberg's framework (in Bolman and Deal 2003), we find that the DO forms the strategic apex of a huge machine bureaucracy which stretches in several tiers from the district to the sub-district, block and, for certain functions, to the village level. Developed from the perspective of the DO's office, the proposed strategic plan could be for a period of five years.

It is worthwhile to note that currently, neither a vision/mission statement nor a strategic plan is prepared at the state or the district levels in the vast majority of the districts in India; most departments of government at the state and central levels also do not engage in this exercise. Although at the district level DOs implement a wide variety of functions on a day-to-day basis, the aim usually is to achieve certain stated or unstated targets. As the list of departments in Table 1 of Appendix 1

elicits, the DO is directly responsible for a variety
of regulatory, developmental and social welfare programmes. Apart from this, in several states, he/she is
also in charge of implementing numerous rural development schemes as the Executive officer of the Zilla
Parishad, the district level local self-government body,
or otherwise.

Stakeholder Analysis

For government organizations and non-governmental
organizations (NGOs) stakeholder analysis (SA) is
a vital step in the process of mission clarification; it
illuminates who the key stakeholders are and, therefore, what satisfies them (Bryson 1995). In this instance,
since the Collectorate is the centre of district administration, it would be easy to lump all stakeholders
under the term 'citizen'. However, a quick stakeholder
analysis (Table 7.1) reveals the different categories
of stakeholders with distinctive needs and who have
dissimilar expectations from the office of the DO.

Table 7.1 reveals the existence of not only multiple
stakeholder types but their dispersal over the entire
district. The most vulnerable stakeholders—BPL persons, children and women—with the weakest voice are
virtually immobile. Satisfaction of their needs requires
a timely response where they live. To serve them, the
Collectorate needs to be proactive—it must reach out.
The SA also highlights the expectations of entities not
usually considered part of the system such as NGOs,
international organizations and business firms.

TABLE 7.1 Stakeholders of District Administration

Sl. No.	Stakeholder	Served at Location	Service Received	Source of Satisfaction
1.	Below poverty line people	Village; Slums	Employment; Assistance in self-employment; Services	Income; Timely provision of services
2.	Children	Village; Block; Subdivision; District	Variety of services	Timely provision
3.	Women	Village; Block; Subdivision; District	Variety of services	Timely provision
4.	Disabled	Village; Block; Subdivision; District	Variety of services	Timely provision
5.	Complainants	Block; Subdivision; District	Redressal of grievance; Early response	Redressal of grievance; Early response

Note: (A longer table is provided as Appendix 5; it may be noted that both the above and the longer tables are illustrative, not exhaustive.)

Environmental Scan

To identify the mission and vision of the office of the DO, it would be useful to analyse the external and internal factors that affect the performance of the Collectorate by conducting an environmental scan.

External Analysis

The state government depends upon the DO to act as its eyes, ears and limbs. The people of the district have great faith in the office of the DO. As seen earlier, there is a wide variety of stakeholders or customers of the Collectorate. However, these may be recast in four broad categories of customers: local citizens, other agencies of state and central government, NGOs and international organizations (IOs), and entrepreneurs seeking to invest in the district. Government funding for various activities, investment by NGOs, IOs and entrepreneurs are the three main sources of resource. Emerging thrust areas are: employment generation—with emphasis on poverty alleviation, total health and education coverage—with special focus on women and children, and industrialization. Although there is no competition in core areas, there is likely to be pressure for greater accountability due to the passage of the Right to Information (RTI) Act; the rise of advocacy groups; the growing awareness in the citizenry; judicial activism; and competition for industrial investment.

Internal Analysis
The office of the DO is the statutory and traditional nodal point of authority in the district. The DO has the overall responsibility for the coordination of different government agencies. By and large, across the states there is an absence of a shared vision in the Collectorate, and different units are often competing for resources. Lack of punctuality, delay in completion of tasks, low morale, callousness towards needs of citizen customers and lack of integrity and accountability are some of the ailments of the Collectorate. There is a shortage

of staff, and most of the existing staff need training in traditional skills and new skills. It would not be uncommon to discover pride, bordering on arrogance, in being part of the Collectorate among the employees. Many of the sections within the organization either do not have, or are unaware of performance targets.

Mission

The mission of an organization defines its identity and purpose. It serves as a constant reminder of its *raison d'etre* and acts as the touchstone to provide meaning for the actions of the organization, its sub-units and its individual members. Bryson (1995: 75–78) elucidates that clarification of organizational mission may be achieved by answering six questions about the organization. We shall also use these six questions to clarify the mission of the Collectorate. It may be noted that the answers given below are not prescriptive but only suggestive.

Q.1. Who are we?

Ans. We are the nodal government agency responsible for maintaining order and ensuring improvement in the quality of life of the people of the district.

Q.2. In general what are the basic social, economic or political needs we exist to meet?

Ans. A variety of needs—to maintain peace, enforce laws, alleviate poverty, to provide and ensure provision of social welfare services, to facilitate development.

Q.3. What do we do to recognize, anticipate and respond to these needs or problems?

Ans. Utilize existing information, data sources and technology to implement laws and development programmes; proactively seek feedback from our stakeholders to respond to their needs; and, encourage their participation.

Q.4. How should we respond to our key stakeholders?

Ans. Quickly, sensitively, efficiently and comprehensively.

Q.5. What are our philosophy, values and culture?

Ans. We believe in—citizen focus; providing before we are asked; compassion; reaching out; promptness; integrity; efficiency; participation; partnership; and accountability.

Q.6. What makes us distinctive or unique?

Ans. We provide services to those who cannot get them from any other source; we implement laws that cannot be implemented by any other organization.

In view of the above the mission of the Collectorate may be stated as the following:

To administer the law, provide and ensure provision of services, and facilitate development for improving the quality of people's life through an administration that is proactive, transparent, efficient, participatory and responsive to people's needs.

Vision

An organization's vision has an umbilical link with its core ideology which is the source of its internal drive

(Collins and Porras 1997). Any government exists to serve its people. The core ideology of the Collectorate is 'service to people' by responding to their needs, if possible before they are forced to approach the government agency. This is an ideology that often gets lost in the rule-bound, self-motivated, hierarchical maze of government organizations. As leader of his/her organization and of the district administration, it is one of the primary responsibilities of the DO to communicate a common vision throughout the organization that reminds all of this ideology that '...permeates the organization and gives coherence to its diverse activities' (Senge 2000: 206). In view of the jurisdictional vastness and the multi-functional but citizen oriented nature of the responsibilities of the Collectorate, its vision may be stated as:

Peaceful district, prosperous people, healthy children.

Values

As discussed earlier the philosophy that informs this organization is 'service to the people' to realize Mahatma Gandhi's dream to 'wipe every tear from every eye.' To that end the values that anchor the Collectorate are: Integrity, Compassion, Responsiveness, Efficiency, Participation, Equity, Efficiency, Commitment and Accountability.

Goals

Vision and mission help catch the employees' attention. As Bennis and Nanus (1996: 28) state: 'Leaders are the most results oriented people in the world, and results get attention.' To focus on the results the organization must have goals that are specific, challenging and prioritized and should be integrated in individual and sub-unit action plans (Quinn et al. 2003). A few illustrative goals that may be adopted for the Collectorate are:

(1) The most vulnerable rural and urban population groups in the district are identified within one year.
(2) By 2010, there is no shortage of drinking water in any habitation.
(3) By 2010, 100 per cent of the children 5–14 years of age are enrolled in schools.

Performance Measures

Performance measures enable one to assess whether the goals set out for the organization have been met.

(1) Based on the Census data, using latest computer technology, identify and rank in order of priority the most vulnerable villages and urban wards by 31 June 2006.
(2) By 2010, 100 per cent habitations would have one drinking water source per 50 families
(3) All children in the age group 5–14 years are enrolled in school.

Although the above exercise is only an elementary attempt, we find that a strategic planning exercise can enable an administrator–leader to grab attention of his/her people through vision (Bennis and Nanus 1996), reinforce values, resonate the purpose, and set challenging objectives before them; it may help align the entire organization.

Notes

1. It must be pointed out that the quality, especially the reliability, of the data available in the districts is usually uneven.
2. Attempts at creating a paperless office and an integrated MIS have been made in the districts of Sivaganga and Tiruvarur in Tamil Nadu and Kerala, but these are not comprehensive.

Chapter Eight

Coordinator: Multi-agency Operations

THE PROLIFERATION of government agencies and development programmes since independence in 1947 has greatly altered the nature and scope of district administration in India. An important aspect of this transformation is the heightened need for coordinated action by multiple agencies to implement an improbable variety of programmes in the field. As we have seen in an earlier chapter, the district officer's (DO) role as a coordinator of government activity is almost as old as the office itself. Yet the scope of DO's role as coordinator has grown manifold. However, as an issue or an activity, inter-agency coordination at the district level in India has not been studied widely or in detail. The few existing studies restrict themselves to examining coordination among the departments of state government—i.e., interdepartmental coordination—operating at the district level and below. Very few of them are empirical studies, most are speculative; hardly any of these engages with the what, why, who and how of inter-agency coordination.

Indeed, in the present context, inter-departmental co-ordination is a limiting term. It precludes from its ambit, departments of the central government, local government bodies—both rural and urban, international public organizations (IPOs), non-governmental organizations (NGOs), foreign governmental organizations (FGOs), citizens groups and citizens, and the private sector. Increasingly, all these entities have come to play significant roles in the implementation of developmental programmes on the ground. Therefore, the presence of all these 'agencies' needs to be taken into account in any study of inter-agency coordination (IAC) at the district level; for we recognize that district administration does not necessarily act *upon* these other bodies—it increasingly acts *with* them.

In the aforementioned context the objectives of this chapter are:

(i)   to examine the concepts and strategies of inter-organizational coordination in public administration;

(ii) to examine the evolution of the coordinating function of the DO; and,

(iii) to identify the mechanisms and processes for inter-agency coordination at the district level, and to suggest ways of enhancing it.

This chapter comprises two sections. In the first section, we explore the theoretical and conceptual issues of co-ordination and their development in public administration. Also, in the international context, the factors facilitating and hindering inter-organizational coordination are identified and different models of coordination scrutinized.

The second section begins with a review of the evolution of the role of the DO as coordinator of state action. The chapter then investigates the mechanisms of inter-agency coordination, how they function, and the role and responsibilities of the DO in this process. It concludes by analysing the barriers to IAC and with a few suggestions for improving it.

EVOLUTION OF COORDINATION: A SURVEY OF LITERATURE

Coordination: Plain and Simple

Recognized both as the first principle of organization and as a function of the executive/administrator, coordination is widely recognized as a determinant of organizational efficiency and effectiveness. It consists of interrelating parts of work to achieve a harmony of effort and attainment of organizational objectives.

One of the first explications of coordination was made by Luther Gulick in his 'Notes on the Theory of Organization' (in Shafritz and Hyde 1987). Gulick explained that coordination may be achieved principally in two ways: through organization, i.e. through the allotment of work; the allotment of authority; decentralization; and delegation. Other scholars like Simon, Smithberg and Thomson also emphasized the importance of hierarchy, group supervision, planning and goal setting to ensure coordinated action (1961: 434). Mooney, while discussing coordination through sharing of commonly held ideas or doctrine, states, 'Every member of an organization should not only know its doctrine, but he should feel it and absorb it until he lives in its atmosphere and makes it the guide of all his acts' (1953 88). The second way in which coordination may be achieved, is by the creation of a dominant idea in the minds of employees through reinforcement of organizational values and loyalty to the organization.

While building upon the previous work on coordination Mintzberg (1983) identified three fundamental coordinating mechanisms: mutual adjustment, direct supervision and standardization. Mutual adjustment through informal communication is common in very small, simple organizations or for highly complicated tasks. Direct supervision is a predominant form of coordination in complex and hierarchical organizations; it takes the form of division of labour, specialization, decentralization and delegation. And, standardization is defined by Mintzberg as a process of building coordinating mechanisms in the planning stage through standardization of work processes, outputs, and workers' skills. Although Mintzberg was probably thinking of firms involved in the production of goods, the principle of standardization may well be applied to government organizations providing goods and services to citizens based on standard rules and procedures.

Inter-agency or Inter-organizational Coordination: Horizontality

Although the focus of this paper is on inter-agency co-ordination at the district level in India, in this section, we explore the concept of inter-organizational coordination (IOC) as developed in public administration literature. From time to time, IOC has engaged the attention of scholars and practitioners alike in both public administration and public management. It may be noted that we have opted for the term 'inter-organizational coordination' in this section over either inter-departmental coordination (IDC) or inter-agency coordination (IAC) in deference to its prevalence in the literature. Further, different types and areas of IOC such as inter-governmental coordination and IOC in the entirely private, not-for-profit and NGO sectors remain outside the purview of this enquiry. As we shall see, at the level of field administration and in the context of government and governmental activities, the concept of IOC has been transformed over time.

The elaboration of the public sector in the second half of the 20th century led to the creation of a number of agencies. Simultaneously, there grew a concern for coordination among organizations at the cutting edge of public administration, the point where services are delivered. It came to be recognized that public administrators have two types of management responsibilities, institutional and trans-organizational. The former refers to management of and within one organization; the latter refers to management of interdependencies across boundaries of various types of organizations—profit, non-profit and governmental (Wise 1990: 145). As Peters puts it, this interest in the 'horizontality' of government is for 'working across programmes within a single level of government' (1998: 22).

In the United States of America, the most concerted, conscious and consistent attempts at IOC started in 1960s in human services integration. The goal was to create a system that responded to multiple needs of the victims of the most severe social problems (Arganoff 1991). Almost at the same time attempts were being made towards IOC in the spheres of rural development and health services. These developments are not surprising since the social services were a sector in which private investment and expansion was the least feasible. Several Acts, programmes and regulations—often initiated by the federal government—also encouraged the services integration movement. Notable among these are Economic Opportunity Act 1964, Services Integration Targets of Opportunity, 1972 (Department of Health, Education and Welfare) and the Partnership Projects in 1974 (also of the Department of Health, Education and Welfare).

Integration in human services sought to bring about IOC not only between agencies but also in large umbrella agencies providing multiple services through rigid divisions (Vigoda 2002: 16). It is characteristic of this field that human services have always been delivered by multiple providers at the local level, whether by local governmental agencies, non-profit organizations or for profit firms. Due to the multiplicity of actors in the area, the need for a common administrator was seen as a significant administrative issue to effect programme administration coordination (Austin 1982: 17). Due to the nature and range of services in this department service integration was pursued both as a way to provide clients a large number of services from a single point, and also to increase the efficiency of the service, especially in terms of better value for funds available and staff deployed (Milward et al. 1993: 319; Vigoda 2002: 13). In view of the importance of IOC there has been a call for a new paradigm, a form of trans-organizational management that can go beyond the traditional 'single organization authority structure' to develop and operate multi-organizational systems (Arganoff 1991: 541). It is a demand echoed in many areas of public administration.

What then is inter-organizational coordination?

Rossi et al. offer a simple but useful definition of inter-organizational coordination as 'people from two or more agencies working together to improve services to clients' (1982: 9). A more comprehensive definition is provided by Mulford and Rogers (1982: 12) who define inter-organizational coordination, 'as the process whereby two or more organizations create and/or use existing decision rules that have to be established to deal collectively with their shared task environment.' Vicki et al. (1994: 172) characterize IOC as 'a pursuit of coherence, consistency, and comprehensiveness and of harmonious or compatible outcomes.'

These definitions indicate that IOC comprises agreed-upon, joint or coordinated action by two or more agencies to achieve a common or shared objective. However, IOC may also be brought about by the coordination of two organizations by a third party through voluntary agreement among them (Chaturvedi 1988: 53).

Most writers on coordination have chosen to clarify and emphasize the distinction between cooperation and coordination. One of the most comprehensive comparisons between cooperation and coordination is presented in a tabular form by Mulford and Rogers (1982: 13) as follows:

TABLE 8.1 A Comparison of Cooperation and Coordination Processes

Criteria	Cooperation	Coordination
1. Rules and formality	No formal rules	Formal rules
2. Goals and activities emphasized	Individual organization's goals and activities	Joint goals and activities
3. Implications for vertical and horizontal linkages	None, only domain agreements	Vertical or horizontal linkages can be affected
4. Personal resources involvement	Relatively few— lower-ranking members	More resources involved—higher- ranking members
5. Threat to autonomy	Little threat	More threat to autonomy

Based on the above, it is possible to state that cooperation is often founded on informal personal relationships between individuals at various levels in different organizations; it is by nature temporary; and due to its informality, bypasses issues of accountability. However, due to its formality and more demanding nature—in terms of joint commitment of resources and efforts towards a shared goal—IOC is also a more permanent and value creating function.

Several benefits, some obvious others less so, of inter-agency coordination have been highlighted in the literature. Some of these are: improved staff effectiveness—due to pooling of skills, knowledge, equipment and facilities; reduced fragmentation of services—due to provision of multiple services to individual clients; greater efficiency—due to better use of resources and time by both agencies and clients; and improved public image of agencies (Milward et al. 1993; Rossi et al. 1982; Vigoda 2002: 13).

Collaboration: The More the Merrier

It is possible to trace the transformation of IOC into collaboration in the 1990s. The distinction between the two is not always clear because the two terms are often used interchangeably. For instance, Gray (1985: 912) defines collaboration as:

(i)   the pooling of apprehensions and/or tangible resources, for example, Information, money, labour, etc.,
(ii) by two or more stakeholders,
(iii) to solve a set of problems which neither can solve individually, within inter-organizational domain.

Similarly, according to Vicki et al. (1994: 174) 'Collaboration is a process of interaction in which two or more parties intensify mutual interests and freely agree to work together towards a common goal.'

The main difference, however, lies in the greater inclusiveness of collaboration—the involvement of not just organizations, but also individuals or groups of individuals in joint action to achieve a shared goal. Collaboration entails not merely responsiveness to citizens' needs but also their active involvement in government programmes

(Vigoda 2002: 529). This is not only a shift from the Total Quality Management model which projects citizens as customers but proposes a three-cornered model of joint action among government agencies, citizens and other social players such as media, private sector, NGOs and academia. The advocates of privatization see collaboration and particularly partnership, as the means of reducing governmental involvement, increasing public ownership governance and increased efficiency of public service.

By and large, the process of collaboration is seen as having three phases: the problem setting phase—is an exercise in both, the identification of other stakeholders and the joint definition of the problem. This stage also exposes the organization to the interdependence among them. In the second phase—direction setting—the various entities share and develop their common objectives or common solution of the problem. Structuring—the third phase—is the development of routine processes among the stakeholders through appropriate regulations (Gray 1985: 915–16). It can be argued reasonably accurately that IOC also passes through the same three phases. However, in comparison to IOC, the presence of the citizen/client in the process makes collaboration a more intense, demanding and elaborate process.

Another distinction may be found in the diversity of goals pursued through collaboration. Three levels of goals may be discerned in a collaboration: one, the meta-goals, which are the stated aims of the collaborative effort; two, the goals that each organization aims to achieve along with the stated goals; and three, the hidden objectives of each party (Huxham and Vangen 1996: 8). Multiple actors negotiate for a multiplicity of goals; hence, often there is difficulty and delay in the formulation of joint goals.

Although we are conscious of the crucial differences in IOC and collaboration, due to the numerous characteristics that they share, for the purposes of this exploration, we shall treat the two terms as interchangeable.

Three Models for Inter-organizational Coordination

Making a distinction between managed and unmanaged coordination, Mulford and Rogers (1982: 19) discuss three models of coordination strategies: mutual adjustment strategies, alliance strategies and corporate strategies. An analysis of the three strategies suggests that they may be ranged on a spectrum with mutual adjustment strategies occupying one end and corporate strategies the other, while alliance strategies occupy the middle ground. As Mintzberg (1983) also notes, mutual adjustment strategies focus on the agency or its clients; are managed by professionals; and, action is mostly taken on the basis more of norms than the few rules that bind the organization with a minimum commitment of resource. Power is decentralized and agency goals are the main objective of joint action.

Alliance strategies focus on both, the agency and the inter-agency system and are managed by professionals and administrators through negotiated rules with a medium level of resource committed. Decision-making may or may not be centralized and decisions have to be ratified.

Alliance strategies aim at both agency and inter-agency or collective goals.

On the other end of the spectrum, corporate coordination strategies are highly formal, run by administrators centrally, on the basis of regulations. The focus is on the inter-agency system with high-resource commitment and the aim is achievement of collective goals.

Facilitators of IOC and Collaboration

The essential methods for achieving IOC are not very different than that used for achieving coordination in an organization. The difference lies in the ways of negotiating goals, decision-making systems and boundaries of the organizations involved. Several factors have been found to facilitate IOC.

Two basic ingredients of inter-organizational coordination or collaboration, as emphasized by human services managers, are leadership and interpersonal relations (Jennings and Krane 1994: 347). Unlike cooperation, that is an informal compact between individuals, IOC is a formal arrangement for joint action among two or more organizations. Leadership and interpersonal relations between the key representatives of the different organizations play a critical role in the processes of goal setting and direction setting. They lead to rational planning—another factor that facilitates IOC by creating a framework of guidelines for action (Vicki et al. 1994: 174). Other significant elements identified as conducive to IOC are: co-location of services; combining part of the staff structure; common rules and procedures; common points of access for records and reports (Austin 1982: 18–19); not surprisingly, these factors recall the earlier models of coordination—organization and standardization. The clarity, workability and durability of commonly agreed upon goals also depend upon the negotiation process.

The importance of standardization in coordination is highlighted by Halpert (1982: 62), 'Organizations with highly standardized procedures are better able and prepared for a concerted joint endeavour than organizations with a low degree of standardized procedures.' Standardization facilitates routinization of transactions, supervision and accountability, and is enhanced by a high level of professionalism in an organization.

Effective communication between organizations at every stage of the IOC process becomes vital for its success. Access to core information, or information necessary for inter-agency coordination, and its timely communication is a determinant of levels of coordination and, therefore, of efficiency and effectiveness. This is more so in emergency situations like a disaster (Comfort et al. 2004: 311–12).

Barriers to Inter-organizational Coordination

Factors inhibiting coordination abound; the list is long and in it one may often find the very factors identified as facilitators of inter-organizational coordination!

Among the technical barriers to coordination are programme regulations, specialization, training, state and federal laws, and regulation and technical requirements such as audit. Organizational barriers arise from the differing goals, processes and structures of the organizations as well as due to absence of clear definitions and identifiable starting points, and the lack of positive benefit-cost ratios (Comfort et al. 2004: 311–12; Jennings and Krane 1994: 342). Organizational structure, elaboration of rules and professionalism may all, separately or together, make communication difficult leading to failure of coordination between organizations.

Perhaps a key barrier to IOC is the perception that there is no interdependence between organizations that necessitates coordination of their actions (Arganoff 1991: 541); such a perception in any one of the organizations would ensure that the IOC process is frustrated before it is initiated. It is worth noting that the issue of IOC among two or more organizations could not be mooted if there was no interdependence at some level or in some aspect or another.

Perceptual barriers to IOC are often rooted in the history of relations between organizations; a common issue is fear of loss of prestige due to coordination with an organization with a poor service record. Memories of past interaction may create a perception of the other organization as a threat and attempts at turf protection may defeat IOC (Halpert 1982: 62–66; Jennings and Krane 1994: 342). These kinds of factors, also classified as political factors, may be a product of the internal politics of an organization or its external political linkages. Both may translate into the failure of leadership which, once again, may be either political or bureaucratic. As Ledwith observes (1999: 245–46), 'Even though at the agency planning and staff levels conditions may be conducive, lack of support of superior levels of government or policy change may also prove to be a barrier to collaboration.'

Networks

A discussion on IOC and collaboration would be incomplete without at least touching upon the phenomenon of Networks. They are best described by Considine and Lewis: 'This new ideal of network governance is thus a form of organization in which clients, suppliers and producers are linked together as co-producers' (2003: 252). Networks are seen to work on the basis of a new rationality, a new found organizational culture—in place of rules and plans—are aimed at greater flexibility and treating citizens as 'clients.'

It may be said that networks belong to the lineage of collaboration, IOC and coordination. However, while retaining some key features of their precursors, networks mark a crucial departure in several respects. First, they are based not in or on organizations or groups but chiefly on individuals in organizations and groups. For instance Sarason and Lorentz (1998) favour informal coordination, 'having no explicit powers' and on the creation of networks of individuals across organizations. Second, as indicated, they are based on informality—in all transactions, decision making, communication and action. Third, as a consequence of the aforementioned two features networks appear to be unaccountable to any rule or law except the members therein. Fourth, they are projected not as a new form of joint action but as a new form of governance.

Few empirical studies of network effectiveness are available. Provan and Milward (2001: 421) have attempted one of the few available but are tentative about the results. They find that evaluating effectiveness of networks to be extremely difficult but both find it reasonable and desirable.

INTER-AGENCY COORDINATION AT THE DISTRICT LEVEL

The District Officer as Coordinator: A Review

The central role played by the DO in inter-agency coordination at the district level has come about due to several reasons: partly due to the traditional role of the office of the District Magistrate, partly due to the multiplication of government agencies—and absence of a formal binding/inter-relating cord—giving rise to the need for a coordinating entity; partly due to statutory responsibility; and, partly due to the expectations of the government and the people.

The establishment of the role of the DO as the integrator/coordinator of state activities in the district has a historical and functional rationale dating back to 1786. In that year, following the Mughal tradition of area administrators, the Court of Directors of the East India Company decided not only to retain the collector as 'the permanent feature of local administration but also combined in him the offices of Revenue Administrator, Civil Judge and Magistrate' (Rai 1965: 238). By 1859 the office of the district magistrate and collector was established not only in Bombay, Madras and the north-western provinces but was further consolidated in Bengal. In his office was unified the judicial, magisterial, revenue and police functions of the imperial regime. However in 1861, the transfer of governance of the Indian Empire from the East India Company to the direct control of the crown brought about slow but significant changes in the functioning of the administrative system in the field.

As we have noted in Chapter Three, the second half of the 19th century saw the emergence of two seemingly opposite trends: progressive functional differentiation of state activities on one hand and their coordination and control through the office of the DO on the other. The thrust for specialization resulted in the creation of the office of the superintendent of police, the public works department and health departments. Yet the collector's office as the general controlling officer was strengthened by Sir George Campbell, Lieutenant-Governor of Bengal. While the direct, executive administration of these separate departments was withdrawn from the collector, he continued to be responsible for general control and supervision. Campbell was quite clear that as the head of the district, the collector 'was to control the local departments not as the drudges of so many departments and master of none, but as the general controlling authority over all departments in each district' (Mishra 1970: 495). The sentiment was iterated by the Famine Commission of 1880 (Mishra 1970: 497) and the Royal Commission Upon Decentralization in India in 1909 (Rai 1965: 20).

Although the Morley-Minto Reforms of 1909 and the Monatagu-Chelmsford Reforms of 1919 aimed at the creation of legislatures in the centre and the states, they left an impact on district administration also. Creation of legislatures and provincial autonomy, however watered down, gave impetus to the elaboration of specialized state functions and to relatively independent ministerial control in transferred departments such as education, agriculture, industries and cooperative credit. The Act of 1935 added rural upliftment, cooperative banks and village Panchayats to the list. Although, these developments were seen by many as contraction of the authority of the DO, it led to the enhancement of his duties for he continued to be responsible for general supervision, control and co-ordination. The introduction, along with diarchy of the new agenda of the government 'led gradually to the DO becoming increasingly the coordinating rather than the unifying agency for the different departmentalized and other components of district administration' (Khera 1964: 249).

Administration in post-independence India has experienced wide-ranging changes in both its environment and its context; gradually, it has been transformed from a closed, colonial system to an open, democratic framework. Independence in 1947 witnessed an upsurge in the concern for development, particularly rural and agricultural development, and social welfare. The plethora of development programmes introduced mostly by the central government also created certain changes in the structure of administration. The first of these was the Community Development Programme initiated in 1952 that saw the

establishment of community development blocks. The
Balwant Rai Mehta Committee, the architect of the initiative was of the firm opinion that:

> At the district level, the collector or the deputy commis-
> sioner should be the captain of the team of officers of
> all development departments and should be made fully
> responsible for securing the necessary coordination
> and cooperation in the preparation and execution of
> the district plans for community development. (Dave
> 1965: 377)

The following decade saw the establishment of Panchayat
bodies as institutions of local self-government in the rural
areas.

In 1955, the District Planning Office was created (Dayal
et al. 1976: 14). With the national emphasis on a planned
economy, it was designed to be a mechanism to aid the
DO to coordinate the planning process at the field level.
The DO was called upon to 'inspire and coordinate development, a function which rarely formed part of his
principal concerns' (Mishra 1986: 350). Initially it included
the departments of Panchayat Raj, minor irrigation,
animal husbandry, cooperatives, harijan and social welfare, and agriculture.

Meanwhile, many new and old departments launched a
variety of development programmes and projects through
newly created or extended offices in the districts. The setting up of these departments also saw the development
of line control—or control of these departments in the

district directly from state directorates or secretariats; the DO was not involved with most of these programmes. However, implementation of these programmes faltered. The Prime Minister of India lamented the state of affairs in his address to the Indian Institute of Public Administration on 23 October 1964 (Prime Minister's Speech 1964). He recognized that divorcing the DO from his role as coordinator of the new programmes had been a mistake. A few days later, while addressing the National Development Council on 27 October 1964, he urged the Chief Ministers to restore 'the status of coordinator of all government activities in the district' to the DO (Dave 1965: 39).

After the First FYP, several state governments issued clear orders giving the DO the central position in district administration and making him responsible for co-ordination of the functions of all district-level departments engaged in development. The 'redefinition' circular issued by the Chief Secretary, Bihar in September 1955 (Dayal 1988: 183–84) is a case in point.

In the almost six decades of independence, the functions undertaken by government and the agencies created to perform those functions have multiplied. A variety of departments have come into existence to implement programmes in the areas of rural development, social and infrastructure sectors. In the last decade, there has also been a remarkable increase in externally aided projects, especially in the social sector, that usually require multi-agency cooperation. Simultaneously, committees, councils and other bodies have been formed to perform supervisory and coordinating functions for given programmes schemes. The Working Group on District Planning chaired by Dr Hanumantha Rao recommended in 1984, that in the district planning bodies, the DO should not only play the role of the 'Chief Coordinator' but that he should accordingly be endowed with adequate 'status, powers and responsibilities' (Planning Commission 1984). The establishment of Panchayat Raj institutions, initiated in the 1960s and given a constitutional mandate in 1993, is another significant development that added administrative tiers at the district and sub-district levels. However, instead of reducing the centrality of the DO's position in most states, they have enhanced it.

From a simple, relatively closed administrative machine that focused overwhelmingly on regulatory administration during the colonial era, district administration in the 21st century India has turned into an open and complex administrative system that requires considerable effort and administrative skill to ensure effective performance. However, the DO continues to play the role of coordinator of government functions in the district. The extent of his involvement in IOC may vary from state to state but not its importance. As Sadasivan observes, 'It is the pivotal locale of the collector in the district administration that projects him as the principal coordinator and enables him to perform the task of coordination' (1988: 14).

INTER-AGENCY COORDINATION: A GROWING NEED

From the perspective of public administration, inter-agency coordination at the district level may be defined as coordination among a number of actors, official and non-official, to achieve the objectives of state policy and the public interest.

As we have seen, the number and types of actors involved vary depending on the programme and the objectives to be achieved. The actors may be departments of the central and state governments, local government institutions, international public organizations, non-governmental organizations, citizens, citizens groups, political parties and private firms that have an interest in a public programme at the district level. In short, virtually all active stakeholders are potential parties in the joint action. The categories of programmes also vary based on the various activities of the government.

Over the last century, inter-agency coordination has become progressively necessary because of five emerging trends in public administration and its one constant requirement. These trends that gathered brisk momentum in post-independence India are: the elaboration of government functions and structures; growth of non-governmental actors; increasing complexity of tasks; specialization of departments; and, mounting interdependence among the various actors. The constant requirement of public administration is the need for more efficient and effective programme implementation with limited resources.

Elaboration of Government Functions and Structures

In the earlier sections, we have indicated how independence in 1947 spurred government to take up a variety of functions in its new role as builder of a welfare state. Development was the defining word and basic orientation of most new and of many of the older departments. The process of elaboration of functions and structures was based upon differentiation of the existing functions and identification of new needs. To illustrate the former, the single Public Works Department (PWD) branched into several divisions such as PWD Roads, PWD National Highways, PWD Construction Board, PWD Electrical and PWD Bridges; depending upon the size of the district, all or most of these divisions maintain offices in each district and some have superior regional offices also. Newly identified needs gave rise to new functions and departments such as Refugee Relief and Rehabilitation (in the states bordering Pakistan and Bangladesh), Public Health Engineering and Horticulture.

Specialization of Government Agencies

A number of forces have given rise to specialized organizations. Development in technology has led to differentiation of functions resulting in specialization. To return to the PWD example, the construction of a public building may entail three different wings of the PWD—PWD Design Division located in regional centres and state headquarters, PWD Civil and PWD Electrical Divisions. Specialization may also be driven by field of operation; therefore, both PWD Construction Board and PWD Bridges may be manned by civil engineers but the former constructs buildings while the latter builds bridges.

Complexity of Tasks

The chief reasons for the growing complexity of tasks are nature of programme/scheme objectives, specialization and multiple sources of funding. Just one of the self-employment schemes implemented by the Backward Classes Welfare Department entails a large number of processes: scheme development, beneficiary selection, his/her training, financing and hand-holding during the initial period of the scheme and evaluation; it also necessitates the coordination of a variety of actors, official and unofficial. Although multiple actors are involved in a relatively simple task, such as the excavation of a water-harvesting tank under the Food for Work Programme, the need for coordination in the former scheme is of a higher order because of the greater complexity of the task due to the nature of the objective—the development of an entrepreneur.

Specialization may also contribute to the intricacy of a task because it may increase the number of actors involved in a scheme; an example is the construction of a district hospital under an internationally-aided programme. Multiple sources of funding of a programme—from a combination of central, state, IPO, FGO, and NGO sources—can result in making the financial aspect of a task a complicated process requiring coordination.

Complexity has also been caused by the duplication and overlap of activities, personnel and programmes. Dayal et al. found that agricultural credit in the district of their study was being administered by three agencies: the Cooperatives, Agriculture and the Revenue departments. Only the Agriculture and the Revenue departments were involved with the distribution of credit while all three were engaged in its recovery.

Growth of Non-governmental Actors

As noted in earlier sections, independence transformed the system of public administration in India from a closed system to an open one. If the thrust by the government on development resulted in a burgeoning of government departments, the development of democracy resulted in the rise of numerous non-governmental actors. The development of the Panchayat Raj bodies has been already noted. The development of public consciousness resulted in the growth of citizens groups and NGOs. The growth of the UN has found the presence of IPOs in state headquarters. In the post-cold war period the expansion of development assistance programmes of various OCED countries has found them making a way down to even the district headquarters.

Increasing Interdependence Among the Various Actors

The differentiation of governmental functions may have created many government and non-government agencies but it also created the need for coordination between them due to their interdependence. Chaturvedi's study of inter-departmental coordination among four departments in four districts revealed that the agency perception of interdependence varied from department to department and changed 'across the disaster and the non-disaster prone districts' (Chaturvedi 1988: 281).

Often interdependence has been recognized and encoded in statute, as in maintenance of law and order, or in executive instructions, regulations and government guidelines as in instances in development administration. In recognition that government programmes are meant not for government but for the people, formal space has been created and reserved for public representatives and citizens in bodies charged with planning or implementation of government programmes.

Thus, we find that the above trends in public administration along with its constant requirement—the need for more efficient and effective programme implementation with limited resources—create the need for coordination of the plethora of programmes and projects planned and/or implemented at the district level.

OBJECTIVES OF INTER-AGENCY COORDINATION

The government has one basic objective—ensuring the welfare of the people. Although different departments alone may produce different outputs, they are all meant to contribute to the one outcome, and they are to pursue it in concert with a variety of other actors. Therefore, the chief objectives of inter-agency coordination at the district level may be identified as:

- System maintenance because the maintenance of rule of law at times of disturbances—political, social or any other—is contingent upon the smooth joint action of a number of law enforcement wings such as the magistracy, police, armed forces, and other enforcement agencies.
- Effective planning for development because district is a basic unit for planning, and without local input from official and non-official sources, a district-level plan is unlikely to be optimal in terms of either coverage or workability.
- Effective implementation of development programmes that benefit the people either individually or as a group.
- Facilitation of development by non-state actors such as private firms and NGOs in the industrial and the social sectors, respectively.
- Provision of prompt relief in times of crisis.

MECHANISMS OF INTER-AGENCY COORDINATION AT THE DISTRICT LEVEL

Due to his/her central position in the district, one of the principal tasks of the DO is inter-agency coordination. For this purpose he/she uses a variety of mechanisms which recall the methods and models of coordination discussed in the earlier sections on coordination and IOC, whether it is a combination of organization and standardization, mutual adjustment or direct supervision. We also find reflections of the three models of IOC presented by Mulford and Rogers (1982) in the structures and processes of inter-agency coordination in the district. Perhaps the weakest and least used mode of IOC is coordination though the dominance of an idea. It would appear that in government organizations inspiring coordination on the basis of ideas or a vision is more difficult than in the public and NGO sectors. It may be kept in mind that to coordinate actions of district-level agencies, the DO sometimes needs to take up the issue with the state-level functionaries of concerned agencies; this often happens with centralized line departments.

Office of the District Officer

The office of the district magistrate and collector or the DO serves as a coordinating mechanism; he/she is invested both by law and tradition to carry out the role. In this role as chief government representative of government in the district, he/she uses direct supervision, standardization and mutual adjustment to coordinate the activities of different kinds of agencies.

Regulatory issue In maintenance of law and order, all three modes of coordination may come into play. For instance, if a riot between two communities occurs, the DO would be expected to coordinate the actions of the police and paramilitary forces through direct supervision on the site on the basis of laws or rules. However, the process of coordination on the ground may call for mutual adjustment based on informal communication and the existing inter-personal relationship of the actors. The role of these non-formal factors would increase if he or she, along with the superintendent of police, were to initiate a return of peace in a given area with the help of a peace committee. The peace committee, convened as and when required, is a body consisting of prominent citizens belonging to the warring communities and representatives of political parties whose help may be enlisted to restore peace and order. If the riot cannot be brought under control by the local police and paramilitary forces, empowered by law, the district officer may call in the military to quell the rioters; thus, resorting to an increased use of standardization. This instance illustrates the complex nature of the DO's task of inter-agency coordination; in such dynamic situations, not only does one find no single mode of coordination to be adequate, but also that there is no substitute for leadership and interpersonal relationships in inter-agency coordination.

Ad hoc issues   Agencies, government or otherwise, often approach the DO to resolve a conflict with other agencies and to coordinate the agreement. Thus, the PWD Roads department may seek the DO's intervention if the construction of a particular road, funded by the district development fund, has been held up due to certain grievances of the local people with the tacit support of the Gram Panchayat leaders. After meeting the parties separately, the DO could convene a meeting of the parties concerned to resolve the issue and draw up an agreed upon plan of action that all the actors would be expected to follow. Mutual adjustment would be the coordination model followed in this instance. Such coordination mechanisms are usually ad hoc, loosely structured, semi-formal and temporary. The minutes of the meeting or the resolutions recorded form the basis of joint action and reference. Such coordinating devices may be used often in a variety of cases but are short-lived as the issue that prompted their creation.

Field Visits

The most direct manifestation of direct supervision as a means of coordination, field visits are relied upon extensively by the DO for the coordination of programmes—especially those that are being carried out by multiple agencies. Field visits may be undertaken in connection with a regulatory issue, such as the conduct of a raid against evaders of minor mineral royalty by personnel of the land department and the police; the disbursement of pension to old people (under a Social Welfare department scheme) through the Panchayat Samity; the excavation of a flood embankment by the irrigation department through a private agency and in consultation with the beneficiary committee; or the implementation of flood relief measures by the staff of the Relief department, the Panchayat, the local NGO, and citizens groups.

In the implementation stage of regulatory or developmental work direct supervision in the field is the most effective form of coordination. However, field visits also require close familiarity with programme details and procedures. DOs often find it effective to make joint visits with the functionaries of concerned agencies so that decisions may be taken up on the spot. Field visits also entail personal monitoring and follow up by the DO of corrective or supplementary action.

Standardization of Procedures

Not all regulatory issues are as fluid as the law and order situation referred to above. Indeed, regulatory administration comprises mostly routine activities that are standardized on the basis of clear rules in great detail, such as the issue of permits and licenses. Thus, the issuing of an arms license, that involves verification of the antecedents of the application by the police—sometimes by two of its wings—is coordinated by the use of standardized procedures and practices by the office of the district magistrate with a minimum of direct supervision. The most telling example of coordination through standardization of procedures is the process of elections to the Parliament or to the State Legislature. Each and every step of the process is spelt out and the room for discretion is virtually non-existent. Census operations also fall in the same category. Yet it must be noted that however clear the rules and procedures, leadership is required to ensure that the procedures are followed. Further, to ensure that all participants in the process understand their roles, other coordinating mechanisms such as meetings and field visits become necessary.

Committees, Councils

A large number of Committees, Councils and Boards facilitate IAC at the district level. Almost all of them have the DO either as the presiding or the executive head or both. Almost all these committees are set up either under statute or by government orders that usually lay down the functions, structure, periodicity of meetings and responsibilities of the committee. The last two decades have witnessed the trends in many states to appoint a minister of the district or the head of the District Panchayat Parishad as the chairperson of various district level committees. However, it inexorably falls upon the DO as the executive of this committee to actually carry out IAC (Basu 1990: 51). In this section we shall briefly look at some of the key committees and how they operate.

District Planning Committee   Established under statute in 1994 and based on the constitutional provision, each district has a District Planning Committee (DPC) which is responsible for the preparation of the annual district plan. It consists of peoples' representatives—Members of Parliament (MPs), a selection of Members of the State Legislative Assembly (MLAs), members of the district level LGB, a selection of members of the Zilla Parishad (ZP) and the chairpersons of municipalities—and the DO, the only government official in the DPC. In West Bengal, the head of the ZP is the Chairperson of the DPC, although in other states a state minister from the district usually presides. The DO functions as the Member-Secretary of the DPC with the assistance of the District Planning Office (DPO) that is a part of his office. The DO's responsibility is three-fold. First, he/she facilitates the emergence of the priorities of developmental district through discussion in the DPC. Second, he/she ensures that the district-level heads of departments and the three-tier Panchayat and municipal bodies prepare and submit plans for their departments timely to the DPO which compiles and collates them before presenting them to the DPC for its approval. Third, he/she presents the progress of the previous year's plan to the committee for discussion and review. It is a vital and difficult coordinating role because of the number of actors involved and because expenditure on several items of development cannot be incurred without approval of the DPC. Further, in this task the DO coordinates not only among different actors but also between two significant sets of actors in the district—people's representatives and government functionaries.

District Disaster Management Committee   The District Disaster Management Committee (DDMC) has been mandated by a government order in most states. The DO is the chairperson of the DDMC, which includes the heads of a large number of departments—police, irrigation and waterways, health, animal husbandry, and others—sub-divisional magistrates, heads of Panchayat bodies and NGOs active in the area of disaster relief. The disaster management micro-plan, prepared in advance by each department from its viewpoint, and collated by the District Relief Officer of the DO's office, is discussed in detail and roles and responsibilities clarified and allocated. In areas affected by annual crises such as floods, cyclones and thunderstorms, the meeting is held ahead of the likely period of disturbance, for example, for flood-affected areas, the committee meets in April or May, well ahead of the monsoons. The committee serves several functions: it clarifies roles and distributes responsibilities of the actors in relation to each other; it establishes a standardized system of response to a crisis; and, it signals that the different agencies must ready themselves for the imminent crisis.

The DDMC may not meet immediately after a disaster has struck; at that point coordination is done by the DO by direct supervision and/or through a small task force set up for the purpose. In a crisis, recognition of the DO's role is unhesitant. Whether flood or drought, earthquake or mud slide—all departments of government look to him/ her for direction and leadership. In such crises, he/she is also empowered to requisition such local resources as he/ she deems necessary to combat the problem (Chaturvedi 1976: 182).

District Coordination Committee   In a few states like Karnataka and Uttar Pradesh, a District Coordination Committee has been set up by statute. Chaired by the DO, it includes the heads of the departments of all government agencies in the district. It is supposed to meet once a month and all issues pending before two or more departments, problems and conflicts, are brought up and steps are taken to resolve them. In Orissa, the District Development Committee set up by government with heads of the development departments in the district as its members, plays this role in the area of development (Padhi 1990: 85).

Task Force

Task forces are often set up by the DO to deal with non-routine problems that involve two or more agencies. These may be: the apprehension or occurrence of a disaster; the apprehension of disturbance of law and order by a category of people, for example, a political party or a social group; the outbreak of a disease; the need to collect data; the dissemination of a body of information; and so on. Task forces last only as long as the problem exists and are characterized by mutual adjustment and standardization of response.

The composition of a task force is determined by the task it is meant to address. For instance, a task force to tackle a likely breach of peace by a group of people on the India-Bangladesh border is likely to be composed of law enforcement and paramilitary agencies of the central and state government. A task force to combat an outbreak of malaria is likely to be more broad-based—including health personnel, LGB representatives, IPOs and NGOs.

Review Meetings

Periodic review meetings are a very important instrument of IAC (Sadasivan 1988). Usually meetings lack the sanction of statute or government order; often, they are initiated by the DO and sometimes are discontinued by his successor. However in most districts, several review meetings are regularly held for: rural development; industrial development; health and family welfare; civil supplies; and social welfare. These meetings are fora for ventilating and sorting out inter-organizational problems and resolving disputes on an ongoing basis. Resolutions and minutes of the meetings serve as record for reference and guidance. Decisions taken in these meetings are binding.

Reports and Returns

An unobtrusive means of IAC coordination is through the institutionalization of reports and returns, particularly in the case of developmental programmes. At the planning stage itself, a commonly agreed upon schedule of reporting progress or problems ensures that vital information is collected without convening meetings. The collection of reports must be followed by their collation—if from multiple sources—analysis and follow-up action. Reports and returns become most effective when they are combined with field visits.

BARRIERS TO INTER-AGENCY COORDINATION IN THE DISTRICT

The main hindrances to IAC at the district level spring from perceptions and attitudes. As we have seen, the DO is designated the pivot of administration at the district level by statute, government direction, tradition and popular expectation. Yet he/she normally faces a variety of barriers in his coordination tasks. Often he/she faces challenge to his/her role from specialized agencies such as police and the technical departments. The technical departments perceive him/her as a generalist bereft of the specialized technical knowledge needed in their domain; while the police perceive the DO as a rival for administrative eminence and social prestige. The fact that DOs normally are much younger than the heads of the district level technical agencies—who have put in many more years in government service than the DO—also affects the attitudes of the former (Seth 1999). Matters are usually made worse if the DO's behaviour betrays arrogance and/or insensitivity to the position and age of other officials and non-officials. The perception of an organization as a habitually poor performer may also come in the way of IAC. Such barriers to IAC may be described as social-psychological factors.

The pyramidal structure of government machinery shapes the hierarchical orientation of government personnel—an orientation supported by the hierarchical structure of Indian society in general. Officers often tend to view each other not in terms of their respective roles in achieving a common purpose and the public interest, but in terms of junior or senior, more or less powerful, holding larger or smaller jurisdictions, or more and less important in relation to each other in the government structure. They tend to slot themselves and others in the overall or immediate hierarchy on the basis of the type of service, type of agency, designation, rank, and so forth. Needless to say, that such perception militates against mutual adjustment and/or consensus building.

Poor communication also debilitates coordination in several ways. Negative perceptions may be strengthened and attitudes hardened if communication between the actors decreases, especially between the DO and the others.

Regular and unambiguous consultation can change perceptions and help towards building a common goal that unites the efforts of different government departments. Although there is an elaborate system of reporting in every department, these reports are rarely analysed at the district level; thus, they also cannot be utilized for pur poses of coordination and supervision. It has also been found that there is no coordinated system of reporting that may lead to better coordination; often the reports are made only to create records (Dayal et al. 1976). Furthermore, often decisions taken in the IAC mechanisms discussed above are not always communicated down the line in the concerned agencies; this not only fails in creating a common goal in the respective organizations, but also leads to misunderstandings between functionaries at the cutting edge.

In the district, there are several political barriers to IAC. Internal politics of an organization may be the cause of its reticence or inability to collaborate; these usually take the form of denial of inter-dependence. Problems of coordination may emerge between two government departments in a district due to the nature of relationship between the ministers in charge of the departments: political rivalry, poor interpersonal relationship, and—in case of a coalition government—affiliation to different political parties at the secretariat level, may all foil attempts at IAC in the field. Poor relations between the administrative heads of departments may also have the same effect. Hence, the DO needs to interact with heads of departments often to convince them of the need to collaborate at the district level. That, however, may only resolve part of the problem unless joint decisions are communicated down the line to the staff of the concerned departments by the heads.

Among the technical barriers to IAC, the most important are financial rigidities. The inability at the district level to make alterations or adjustments in resource allocations (Basu 1990); regulations pertaining to the drawal and disbursement of funds; and, accounting rules are some of the factors in this regard. Similarly, disparity in procedures relating to operationalization of schemes, involvement of the beneficiaries, and evaluation may also pose problems for joint action by a number of agencies.

IMPROVING IAC AT THE DISTRICT LEVEL

The history of district administration in India reflects the changing nature of the state. From the feudal days of the Mughals to the Raj days of first the Company and then the Crown to the light of independent India, administration at the district level has changed in orientation, form and process: from regulation to development, from unity to differentiation and from control to collaboration. Although changes may have taken place in role of the DO, its centrality to the extensive administrative machinery in the district remains. The DO's role as the principal coordinator has been acknowledged time and again in statute and executive orders; despite apprehensions to the contrary, in most states, the establishment of Panchayat Raj institutions has reaffirmed this role. One of the main reasons for the growth of the DO's role as coordinator is that he/she is uniquely positioned to coordinate the actions of inter-governmental and local programmes. Therefore, it is in the fitness of things to examine ways and means of ensuring that the DO is able to perform his/her responsibilities as a coordinator in the most effective manner.

Leadership is the cornerstone of the DO's role as a coordinator. This the DO must acknowledge before he/she expects other functionaries to recognize him/her as the co-ordinator. From the DO's point of view, leadership is not merely leading through taking initiative, marshalling of available resources, knowledge of rules and expression of authority. It also lies in valuing relationships, and in utiliz-ing the appropriate mechanism of inter-agency coordin-ation in the myriad functions that he/she performs.

In many areas of regulatory administration, standardized processes facilitate the task of coordination. In recurring administrative events such as elections and census and in routine administrative tasks such as issuing of licenses, and collection of taxes and duties, the elaborate standardization of rules clearly demarcate the rules and responsibilities of the agencies involved. This approximates the Corporate Strategy model of Mulford and Rogers discussed in an earlier section. However, even in this model, the role of interpersonal relations and communication cannot be underestimated.

Increasingly however, in development administration, the model that produces best results is the Alliance Strategy. This strategy calls for a collaborative approach to programme implementation. In India, there is more and more recognition of the need for participation of the stakeholders themselves, including non-state actors such as NGOs, citizens groups and the beneficiaries of government programmes. This is reflected sharply at the policy level; the guidelines of different government programmes mandate the involvement not only of PRIs but also of the beneficiaries. In the social sector, there is a growing tendency to pass on the responsibilities of the delivery of certain types of services to NGOs or even to private firms. These developments call for coordination of the different agencies involved so that successful collaboration is possible. The mechanisms suited for this purpose are committees, task forces and review meetings. However, these mechanisms are unlikely to prove useful if the following elements are missing in the process they follow: inclusiveness; genuine respect of views of all participants; a consensus building approach; appropriate frequency of meeting; and clear communication of decisions taken.

Field visits are a traditional means of IAC that appear to be underutilized due to the technological advances in communication. However, although video conferences may replace meetings, there is no substitute for a field visit and it is unlikely that there ever will be. Field visits enable the DO to directly supervise and monitor the implementation of programmes and to take corrective steps. Joint field visits, including functionaries of other agencies, can be very useful because immediate decisions may jointly be taken to prevent delay.

Finally, the importance of communication in any kind of coordination mechanism bears repetition. The DO must make full use of formal and informal channels of communication available at the district level to keep in touch with other district-level functionaries. Sharing information and ideas about new programmes can only help him/her develop common purpose and consensus among partners in development. As noted earlier, information is empowering only if one shares it.

CONCLUSION

In the course of this chapter, we have seen that in the United States over the last century, the concept of coordination has evolved in tandem with the evolution of public administration. Thus, the spotlight moved from coordination within organizations in the first few decades of the 20th century to IAC from the 1950s to the early 1980s to collaboration and collaborative management in the late 1980s and into the new century. The development of networks, a turn of the century phenomenon, is in the same sequence but still too amorphous to be deemed part of public administration in the absence of a unifying constant, structure and continuity.

Interestingly, the evolution of the task of coordination at the district level in India has also traversed the same path although not at the same pace. We have found that the DO's role as chief coordinator of state activity at the district level has also evolved and utilized a variety of mechanisms of IAC. Yet, the efficacy of any model of IAC used would depend upon the DO's leadership and the value he/she places on relationships.

Although beyond the scope of this book, it is tempting to compare the nature of coordination in the Indian and the American systems of public administration. Across India, the DO provides an integrating constant at the cutting edge of administration; on the other hand, the absence of a uniform administrative structure and a variable leadership precludes the possibility of any single office effecting IAC in the United States at the field level. This becomes highlighted in times of crises such as the failure of relief agencies to meet the requirements of the victims of the hurricane Katrina in New Orleans in September 2005, primarily due to the failure of intergovernmental coordination at the local level. The emphasis in the United States is on collaborative management because state action is limited and resources of the other entities considerable. In India, the emphasis is on IAC because the state has most resources and state action is pervasive.

Chapter Nine

Facilitator: Collaboration at the Cutting Edge

THE ONGOING transition towards inclusive governance has brought a variety of operatives in the area of service delivery at the grassroot level. Although some new entrants are related to government many are not. The growth of these 'non-governmental organizations' (NGOs) and the rapid expansion of their activities at the ground level draws attention to the need for facilitating their operations.

The principal questions that this chapter seeks to answer are: Is collaboration among government organizations (GOs) and NGOs necessary for effective service delivery in India at the district level? If so, how may it be achieved and what role if any, may the district officer (DO) play towards this end? Since this long debated topic is known to raise both eyebrows and hackles, we hasten to demarcate the boundaries of our enquiry by making three qualifications. First, although the chapter briefly appraises the discord over this issue, in the global context it concentrates on the NGOs in India. Second, among the bewildering organizations that fall within the category of NGOs in India, we focus sharply on those engaged in service delivery in the development field. Third, this chapter seeks to examine the GO–NGO relationship at the cutting edge of development.

To answer these questions, we begin by briefly examining various perspectives on the state–NGO relationship. In the next section, the spotlight is on the nature of the relationship in India *at different levels—central, state and the districts.* We then explore the desirability of GO–NGO collaboration by scrutinizing the assumptions in the Indian context. What are the consequences of isolation for both GOs and NGOs and what benefits can collaboration bring to the service delivery is the question addressed next. Based on the discussion, the chapter proposes a typology of collaborative relationships among GOs and NGOs that may facilitate an appreciation of the range of options for collaboration. Finally, it indicates how different types of collaboration may be achieved through the office of the DO.

State–NGO Relationships: Perspectives

Economic theory has long argued that 'the inherent failures or limitations of both the market and government in providing public goods' is the primary reason for the existence and growth of NGOs (Gidron et al. 1992: 7). No doubt there is truth in this explanation; yet increasingly we find that growth of both state and markets has promoted and not contained NGO activities (Fernando and Heston 1997). Although voluntary public and charitable organizations have existed since the middle of the 19th century in the West, the term 'NGO' was introduced by the UN in 1949 (Fernando and Heston 1997). Not only are they the least understood segment of today's society, 'this set of institutions takes quite different forms in different national settings, reflecting differences in culture, traditions, legal structures and political histories' (Gidron et al. 1992: 3).

Without digressing into the rich history of NGOs globally, we must acknowledge the extraordinary range of organizations that may potentially fall under the heading of 'NGO.' Therefore, in the interests of clarity, and this chapter, we accept the following defining characteristics of NGOs—on which there is considerable agreement: they are formal, voluntary, non-governmental, not-for-profit, and legal entities functioning within legal frameworks (Fernando and Heston 1997; Hulme and Edwards 1997; Martens 2002; Streeten 1997) in pursuit of the public interest and public good.

Three types of NGOs may be discerned: first, those that serve as intermediaries between donors and beneficiaries in development; second, those that focus on empowerment through networking such as energy, gender and environment; and third, those that undertake both types of activities (Sen 1998). A UNDESA study in 2005, found that almost all the NGOs surveyed—77 from 44 countries—were engaged in more than one type of the nine identified activities. However, service delivery through partnerships, and capacity building/training are two areas that engage a majority of the NGOs in the developing and least developed countries (23 of 25) as well as in the developed (OECD) countries (13 out of 23) (Karaboni 2005).

The tension in relationships between the state and NGOs is based on several factors: First, on the purported conflict between them due to the perception of a competitive relationship between government and NGOs characterized by a zero sum game (Gidron et al. 1992).

Second, NGOs receiving funds from government are seen as part of a principal–agent relationship (Hulme and Edwards 1997) that compromises their mission by reshaping their agenda, engenders corruption and reduces their independence (Clark 1995).

Third, it is perceived that the influence of neo-liberal economics in a globalizing age has turned NGOs into 'contractors,' bidding for contract-based service provision, especially in Africa and Latin America; although contracting by NNGOs is more the norm in Africa, the Latin American governments are also contracting out services to NGOs (Robinson 1992). However, NGOs have collaborated with the state in service delivery in the social sector—health, education, welfare—in Africa also; yet the state tends to restrict direct service delivery preferring that NGOs provide services through the government machinery (Oyugi 2004).

Fourth, further afield under the authoritarian regimes, as in the case of the Arab world, the growth of NGOs has been limited, even in service delivery, and their relationship with the state is either precariously tenuous or so strong as to co-opt them, transforming NGOs into parastatal organizations (Marzouk 1996).

Fifth, in the context of the countries of the South, the greatest danger of the NGO engagement with the GOs is seen as the legitimation of the system, the status quo (Kothari 1987).

However, since the 1990s, around the world more and more NGOs are choosing to collaborate closely with governments in the interests of participatory development— both, by contributing to informed policy-making and to its implementation (Clark 1995). While discussing the expanding engagement between NGOs and government, Alsop (1998) discusses three types of relationships: consultative, contractual and collegiate. In the first, views of NGOs are heard but not necessarily acted upon; the second is a formal relationship based on receipt of remuneration by NGOs for performing specified tasks; and the third is based on equality.

Yet in the context of NGOs engaged in public service delivery in India, how valid are these perceptions?

Foremost, the view that GOs and NGOs are competing with each other in the field of public service delivery presupposes the existence of a sufficiently large body of NGOs capable enough not only to deliver services effectively but also to deliver them to populations spread over large areas. Comprehensive data regarding the total number of NGOs engaged in different fields in India is scarce (Mohanty and Singh 2001); yet in terms of the vast area and population, NGOs are comparatively few. For instance, the state of West Bengal with a population of 80 million has the largest number of NGOs receiving government funds in the area of rural development in any state: they number 804. In the same state, in the health and family welfare sector, only

107 NGOs receive funds from the Government of India (Planning Commission of India at http://164.100.97.14/ngo/ conference/stdy_voluntary.pdf). Thus, in West Bengal, in the rural development and in the health and family welfare sectors the number of NGOs working for each million of the population stands at eight and one, respectively. Without going into the question of their capacity, even if there were to be a dramatic expansion in the number of NGOs in the two fields, it would be difficult for them to cover the population of the state in the foreseeable future. Therefore in India, competition between the government and NGOs appears to be an improbable contention.

The perception of a principal-agent relationship between the NGOs and the GOs, the second cause of tension, is also the principal criticism against close collaboration between the government and NGOs. Indeed, if the NGOs act solely on the basis of government funds, are bound by the latter's regulations, and if such funding causes them to lose sight of their mission—then such criticism is unexceptionable. No doubt in India, a majority of the NGOs receives funds from government; three of the five large Indian NGOs studied by Uvin et al. (2000) received more than 50 per cent of their funds from state governments while the other two received a smaller share of government funds. Sooryamurthy's (2002) study of 371 NGOs in Kerala also shows that more than 50 per cent were dependent upon government funds and almost 75 per cent were engaged in service delivery. Further, it is entirely credible that curtailment of NGO autonomy due to financial dependence on government is inevitable (Inamdar 1987) and that donor pressure or influence often re-shapes NGO activity (Hulme and Edwards 1996: 20). Chowdhury (1987) notes that the grant-in-aid programme of the Government of India in the social welfare sector during the 1950s and 1960s created such a principal-agent relationship between the GOs and the NGOs.

However, in the Indian context, three trends affecting the GO–NGO relationship need to be noted. First, the constraints upon NGO autonomy started changing in the Seventh FYP under which, autonomy was given to NGOs to decide the nature and the details of their activities in broad fields of work (Roy 1987; Sen 1998); the trend has continued. Second, studies by Uvin et al. (2000) and Sooryamoorthy (2002) also indicate that NGOs are also increasingly utilizing other sources of funding to implement schemes in the area of service delivery indicating diversification of funding source (Kudva, 2005; Ministry of Home, http://www.fcraforngos.org/intro.htm). Third, although there are legal requirements common to all NGOs—pertaining to registration, audit and external funding—which NGO spokespersons would also like to see abolished (Mohanty and Singh 2001), there is no evidence to suggest that the GO funds are tied to stipulations directing changes in the internal management or overall operational framework of NGOs receiving funds. Therefore, as long as NGOs remain dependent solely upon government funds, the possibility of a principal-agent arrangement and the attendant distortions in GO–NGO relationships cannot be denied. However, the existing policy framework does not mandate it. To the contrary, as we shall see in the next section, at the central and state government levels, attempts to encourage genuine partnership between the GOs and NGOs have escalated over the years.

The third charge based on the perception of GO–NGO relationship as an exchange model, with the latter performing a job for the payment of a certain amount based on a competitive bid, is even more severe. As Robinson (1996) shows, this kind of practice has followed the rapid increase in the numbers of NGOs in the wake of increased aid-based development in Latin America. In a situation where bidding over contracts for services becomes a matter of course, it is difficult to distinguish between the non-profit and the for-profit sector; this well may indicate the privatization of public service provision and the transformation of the NGOs into private firms or 'contractors.' Such a GO–NGO relationship based on market principles falls outside the perimeter of our enquiry.

Marzouk's (1996) analysis of NGOs working under authoritarian regimes of the Middle-east, and heavily dependent for their resources upon the state, focuses upon consequent limitations of such entities to function with any degree of autonomy. The description of such NGOs as parastatal organizations may be appropriate. However, discussion of such NGOs and their comparison with others must occur within the context of the authoritarian state, and not in the matrix of democratic regimes—as in the case of India.

Finally, as Kothari (1987) warns, close relationships between the government and NGOs may lead to the legitimization of the former. This is a serious charge and may well be valid, especially if the legitimacy of the government in question is in doubt. However, there is little evidence to suggest that effective service provision to the weakest segments in society has had a direct effect upon either the survival of an authoritarian or an illegitimate regime. Perhaps, the criticism may be more valid if applied to NGOs engaged in activism or advocacy, where aligning with the state in any way may result in, or may be seen as, co-optation and compromise. As noted at the very beginning, this chapter focuses upon NGOs engaged primarily in service delivery.

Since the 1990s, around the world, more and more NGOs are choosing to collaborate closely with governments in the interests of participatory development—both, by contributing to informed policy making and to its implementation (Clark 1995). While discussing the expanding engagement between the NGOs and the government, Alsop (1998) discusses three types of relationships: consultative, contractual and collegiate.[1] Gidron et al. (1992) propose an interesting typology of government–NGO relations in the area of service delivery on bases of two fundamental activities that comprise service provision: financing and authorizing of services, and actual delivery. Based on the share of or dominance over the two activities by government or the third sector, they construct a spectrum of models ranging from the Government Dominant to Dual, Collaborative to Third Sector Dominant model. In the Government Dominant model—typified by the welfare state—government agencies both, finance and provide services relegating the third sector to the margins.

In the Dual model, government and NGOs are involved in both, financing and provision of services with the latter either supplementing or complementing the former's efforts. In the Collaborative model, financing is principally the government's responsibility while NGOs are responsible for service delivery. Gidron et al. (1992) distinguish between the collaborative-vendor and the collaborative-partnership models. Finally, in the third sector, dominant model financing and service delivery are both dominated by non-profits.

Several other scholars such as Clark (1995), Streeten (1997) and Sanyal (1991) have also suggested models and bases for GO–NGO relationships and collaboration. However, before examining the desirability of collaboration let us examine the situation in India.

NGO–STATE RELATIONS IN INDIA

In India, the term NGO includes a bewildering variety of organizations (Anheimer and Salamon 1998; Sen 1998) such as, community-based organizations (CBOs); non-party political groups; welfare, philanthropic, relief and development organizations; government-operated NGOs (GONGOs); and caste, region-based and religious groups. However, for the purposes of this paper, the term NGO refers to an organization with the characteristics noted in the above section.

It may not be an exaggeration to claim that in post-Independence India the state has encouraged the growth of NGOs. In post-Independence India, a large number of Gandhian organizations initiated work in the field of community regeneration and social work. Involvement of the NGOs in development has been a part of the national planning process since the First Five Year Plan (FYP). The earliest GONGOs may be traced back to the 1950s when, through government initiative, farmer unions were established to interact with the community development projects; later, in the same sequence, came Legal Aid Societies, Bharat Sevak Samaj, Bharat Krishak Samaj and others (Inamdar 1987).

As early as 1956, the Central Social Welfare Board (CSWB) started a grants-in-aid programme to encourage social welfare activities among the non-governmental sector (Kudva 2005). The Third FYP reiterated the importance of Gandhian organizations in development. In 1977, financial incentives to donate to NGOs working in the field of rural development was provided for the first time to the corporate sector, which was, however, withdrawn after a few years due to its abuse by some business houses. In the early 1980s, consultative committees on voluntary organizations were set up in several states at the initiative of the Prime Minister. Yet only from the Seventh Plan onwards have they been given the liberty to plan their own schemes—that is on the basis of the felt need of the people in their operational locales. In the Seventh Plan, 17 items under Rural Development were identified where local NGOs could undertake responsibilities and Rs 150 crore earmarked for spending through NGOs on anti-poverty programmes (Roy 1987).

From mid-1980s, the involvement of the NGOs at the national and state levels was consciously promoted by the GOI. In 1986, the Council for Advancement of People's Action and Rural Technology (CAPART) was created under the Ministry of Rural Development as a nodal agency 'for catalysing and coordinating the emerging partnership between voluntary organizations and the government for sustainable development of rural areas' (http://capart.nic.in/). Its importance as a funding agency may be gauged by the fact that in 2002–03, CAPART distributed over three billion rupees to more than 10,000 NGOs (Kudva 2005).

The Eighth FYP also invited greater participation of NGOs in service delivery in the social sector and in expanding participatory micro-planning. The rural development, social sector, social welfare and housing policies of the 1990s also envisaged a greater role for NGOs in these areas (Sen 1998). This is evident in a number of efforts made by the state. By the mid-1990s, not only had many of the Ministries—such as Rural Development, Social Justice and Empowerment, Social Welfare, and Health and Family Welfare—set up NGO coordination cells, NGO involvement had also been built into more than 200 centrally-sponsored programmes (Kudva 2005). Apart from involving NGOs in planning and implementation of projects, their training and capacity building is also taken up, for example, National Institute of Social Defence (http://ncdap.nisd.gov.in/charter.php).

The flow of funds from agencies of GOI to NGOs attests to the growing collaboration between them. According to the NGO Database of the Planning Commission of India (http://164.100.97.14/ngo/default.asp accessed on 22 March 2006), as per June 2005 figures, 16,430 NGOs were receiving assistance from 17 agencies of the GOI. Of these 6,541 or 39.5 per cent received funds from the Ministry of Rural Development, 2,074 (12.6 per cent) from the Ministry of Human Resource Development, 2,944 (17.9 per cent) from the Ministry of Social Justice and Empowerment and 1,343 (8.2 per cent) from the Ministry of Health and Family Welfare. Thus, more than 88 per cent of the total NGOs assisted financially by the Government of India are funded through these ministries. It is noteworthy that all three ministries fund NGOs to implement developmental activities and provide services at the field or district level.

Data from the Home Ministry, GOI attests to the growth in the numbers of NGOs and the scale of their funding over the years. Some 22,924 NGOs were registered to receive foreign funds in 2000–01 under the Foreign Contribution (Regulation) Act, 1976. In terms of aid, the largest amount was received for rural development (Rs 547.74 crore) followed by health care and family Welfare (Rs 432.98 crore), and relief for natural calamities (Rs 339.77 crore) (http://www.fcraforngos.org/intro.htm accessed on 22 March 2006).

State governments have also openly adopted a collaborative approach towards NGOs in service delivery, especially in rural development and the social sector, for example, the Bhagidari (literally 'partnership') programme of the Delhi government for setting up of a Juvenile Justice Home in partnership with CRY and SAMARTH, and for running institutions for the mentally retarded—their education, vocational training and rehabilitation is a case in point (http://socialwelfare.delhigovt.nic.in/bhagidari. htm accessed on 15 February 2006).

The central and state governments in India have been joined by Panchayat Raj Institutions (PRIs) and local self-government institutions, in providing services and undertaking development at the grassroots. It is noteworthy that the Balvantray Mehta Committee (1957), the Committee on Rural–Urban Relationship (1966), and the Ashok Mehta Committee (1978) all foresaw an increasing role of NGOs in assisting the government generally and PRIs specifically in the task of rural development. Providing technical support to PRIs was seen as a vital responsibility of the NGOs (Bhattacharya 1987). Traditionally, PRIs and NGOs have viewed each other as competitors of NGOs; often they may also approach each other as adversaries. However, as the experience in some states shows, complementarity of NGOs, Panchayats and the state governments has gradually replaced conflict among them (Arya 1999).

The pattern of the state–NGO relationship in India indicates the development of interdependence marked by brief periods of unstable relationships during the emergency and the early 1980s. 1990 onwards, the GOI has steadily sought to involve NGOs in more and more of its programmes aimed at service delivery in development and social sectors. Not only has the Indian state continuously increased outlays to NGOs for service delivery in several sectors, the trend of foreign aid is in a similar direction (Kudva 2005). At the state level also there is some evidence of greater collaboration between the NGOs and the governments, particularly in urban areas. The logical extension of this trend is enhanced collaboration between government agencies and NGOs at the district level for more efficient and effective implementation of programmes.

The policy instruments that affect GO–NGO relations are: good governance policies; regulation and fiscal legislation; opportunities for operational collaboration; policy debate and formulation; fostering sensitive coordination and training; and, government funding (Clark 1995). All these policy instruments may be found in India in a wide var-iety of sectors. However, it is noticeable that these policy instruments relate to GO–NGO relationship at the national or state levels—not at the district level.

NGOS AT THE DISTRICT LEVEL

For the federal and the state governments in India, the district is the cutting edge of administration. It is the unit of planning, implementation and evaluation of a var-iety of federal and state programmes in regulatory and developmental administration. A combination of state government, local self-government and central government machineries working together with a variety of non-government organizations at the district and sub-district levels in totality comprise administration at the district level. All these government organizations implement state and central government programmes through their different functionaries; NGOs engage and interact with the work of these government bodies in matters of governance or with implementation of development programmes.

It is true that the relationship between government organizations at the central and the state levels has received considerable attention (Clark 1995; Muttalib 1987; Mencher 1999; Roy 1987). NGO coordination organizations like Association of Voluntary Associations for Rural Development (AVARD) and Coordination Council of Voluntary Association (CCVA) have also developed at national and regional levels. However, the relationship between government agencies and NGOs at the field level, at the point of project implementation, has received little more than a cursory glance and coordination or collaboration at the grassroots is minimal. Yet it is at the district and sub-district levels that developmental programmes and services are delivered.

Whether located at the district headquarters or in a remote village, all NGOs implementing projects or providing services within a district may be designated as 'local NGOs.' Several streams of funding of local NGOs may be noted:

(a) Direct funding by International bilateral and multi-lateral organizations and transnational NGOs;
(b) direct funding by national NGOs or foundations;
(c) direct funding by central or state government agencies;
(d) direct funding by a district level agency or Panchayat body; and

(e) indirect funding by bilateral, multilateral or inter-
     national organizations through the central or state
     governments.

In the first three types of funding arrangements NGOs
are relatively independent and may work in isolation;
however, in the remaining three there are varying degrees
of interdependence.

Local NGOs are small in size, operate in a small area,
usually have one main area of operation (Lawani 1999),
and are most often engaged in service delivery as opposed
to advocacy or institution building. As Gidron et al. (1992:
11) note '... advocacy is more likely to be promoted at the
national level and service provision in the locality'; however, there may be notable exceptions to this norm. Most
NGOs in a district are also likely to be local and depend
largely on government funding. A study of 140 voluntary
organizations/NGOs in Solapur district, Lawani (1999)
found that 50 per cent of them were dependent almost
entirely on government funding, 58 per cent were local,
22 per cent were regional and 20 per cent were branches
of national and international NGOs.

THE WAGES OF ISOLATION

From the discussion thus far it is evident that the GOI
policy framework not only envisages but also actively
promotes collaboration between the government and
the NGOs in development. However, the scenario at the

field level does not quite live up to expectations. The relationship between GOs and NGOs at the district and sub-district levels is marked by mutual suspicion and distrust (Muttalib 1987; Roy 1987), both ploughing their separate furrows. Nevertheless, both GOs and NGOs suffer from a variety of limitations in implementing several development programmes independent of each other.

Even in India where the administrative machinery is large, in difficult terrains—forests, mountains, riverine belts and deserts—there are gaps in government machinery for service provision in areas such as education, health and allied sectors. Even where infrastructure in terms of buildings have been put up and personnel sanctioned the deployment of staff is usually not adequate; either staff are not posted or if they are posted they may not join, and even if they join they are often not to be found at their posts. An easily proven thumb rule is: the closer the service facilities, such as health centres and schools, are to urban areas the greater the number of employees deployed. It is hardly surprising then that often facilities located in towns are overstaffed. Similarly, it is difficult to retain professionally qualified employees for specialized services in remote areas. Usually, government employees are also perceived as poorly motivated, a consequence attributable to poor training, low morale due to unsatisfactory working conditions or to an eroded system of accountability.

Deployment of permanent government employees in places where their services may be utilized only on a part-time basis also makes service provision by government very expensive. Multitasking is not common in GOs.

Therefore, within the matrix of inflexible rules and job design, the implementation of a programme usually entails the deployment of a full complement of personnel instead of a team customized as per requirements of the situation. Further, schedules of work of government agencies, such as the Public Works Department, are by nature conservative, rigid and difficult to modify; they are also more expensive.

Responsibilities of GOs in India have consistently grown. However, the hardened organizational structures in government are oftentimes unsuitable for the performance of certain types of services. Advocacy for entitlements and awareness generation functions are not necessarily best delivered through GOs; they are not always outfitted for it—by orientation, training or equipment, for example, advocacy regarding food entitlement under the Public Distribution System and rural development programmes. Similarly, there are a variety of training and capacity building functions that GOs perform which they are also not equipped to take up optimally, for example, training of PRI functionaries after each election.

By keeping NGOs at arms length, district level agencies are also unable to take advantage of the innovations that they may have developed or the feedback that they may provide.

On the other hand, NGOs keep their distance not only from GOs but also from other NGOs. It has been noted that NGOs, often seen as models of cooperation, are usually unable to cooperate with each other (Clark 1995; Sanyal 1991). Community development, their common objective, does not often enable them to rise above competition for scarce donor funds (Lawani 1999; Sanyal 1991) and achieve inter-NGO coordination because 'their energy is decentralized and small scale' (Streeten 1997: 198). Not cooperating with either NGOs or government severely circumscribes their impact. As Sanyal notes, 'At best their efforts created small, isolated projects that lacked the institutional support necessary for large scale replication' (1991: 30).

The strength of NGOs is often their small size, flexibility and location on the peripheries (Farrington 1997; Sanyal 1991). However, due to their preference for splendid isolation, NGOs often do not reach the poor and seldom the poorest who are marginalized, dispersed and difficult to reach (Edwards and Hulme 1996; Streeten 1997). Often due to the nature of their project and the need for demonstrable achievement of targets, as in micro-finance, NGOs usually focus on groups 'above the lowest income decile' (Sanyal 1991: 30).

Isolation also leads to difficulties in organizational development. Lawani's (1999) study shows that 74 per cent of the organizations surveyed in Solapur faced problems in accessing government grants of which 15 per cent had no inkling about the procedures followed. Inadequately trained personnel are one of the chief problems faced by NGOs. By working independently at the district level, NGOs have encountered administrative corruption to be a severe hindrance to their work leading even to the collapse of a project (Joseph 1997). Also, prominent among problems faced by NGOs are absence of funds, inadequately trained personnel and lack of coordination/cooperation among NGOs. The last often leads to overlapping and duplication (Lawani 1999). Further, it has been noted that NGOs often face problems with local power groups and vested interests who collude with departmental functionaries to hinder developmental programmes (Dasgupta 1997).

Thus, for GOs not collaborating with the NGOs often results in: vulnerable populations not being provided services; duplication of development investment in some areas; inability to provide or meager provision of certain types of services; expensive and inefficient service delivery; and wastage of scarce resources. On the other hand, by not collaborating with GOs, NGOs may not be able to access a variety of resources—financial, managerial and technical. They may also be unable to utilize the authority of the state to combat vested interests. Upscaling and mainstreaming innovations would also be limited without the active collaboration of GOs (Wils 1996). Therefore, by not collaborating, both GOs and NGOs fail to effectively deliver vital and basic services to the people for whom they are supposed to be working—the poor and the unheard.

To Collaborate or Not to Collaborate?

In light of the above discussion we are faced with the question: do GOs and NGOs need to collaborate at the district level? According to one view, 'There is no overriding imperative for NGOs to develop working links with GOs or vice versa' (Farrington 1991). Independence of NGOs ensures their purity of purpose and action; collaboration with GOs—therefore, interdependence—is polluting and may well be the kiss of death.

This extreme view is based on the following set of assumptions:

(a) The state is essentially interested in the status quo while NGOs are the true agents of change. The state not only constantly needs to be reformed but unable to do so itself, it needs NGOs to help reform it.

(b) NGOs are above the law and beyond regulation. Therefore, attempts by developing countries to regulate NGOs are seen as influencing them with 'sticks (closure, deregistration, investigation and coordination) and carrots (tax exempt status, access to policy makers and public funding)' (Edwards and Hulme 1996: 3).

(c) NGOs are the true champions of the poorest of the poor while the state is designed to ignore them.

(d) NGOs have a participatory, bottom-up approach to development while the state has a top-down approach.

(e) Finally, all NGOs are simultaneously engaged in service provision, institutional development and advocacy. Sometimes this assumption carries with it a normative baggage—that not only is this so, it *should* be thus.

The assumptions appear to be founded on the 'New Policy Agenda' (NPA) on development policy and aid transfers from the north to the south. Inspired by neo-liberal economics and liberal democratic theory, NPA espouses market principles and democratization (Moore 1993). As Hulme and Edwards (1996: 6) note in the context of development NGOs, according to NPA, that they are: (a) the 'preferred channel for service provision in deliberate substitution for the state' and (b) 'a vehicle of democratization'. The NPA approach itself seems to be premised upon channeling development assistance to developing countries with weak, democratic or authoritarian regimes dependent for development on aid transfers from the north.

In the case of India, these assumptions do not ring true.

The strength of the Indian democracy, developed over less than six decades of independence, is an oft quoted example that needs no additional attestation. The establishment of PRIs has resulted in an internal restructuring that strengthens democracy at all levels, especially at the grassroots. The Indian Constitution has been a source of stability as well as change. The Directive Principles of State Policy (Part IV of the Constitution) have guided a variety of reforms (http://lawmin.nic.in/ncrwc/finalreport/v1ch3.htm) of the state and society, which goes beyond the scope of this chapter. Indeed, it is to implement many of these reforms that the GOI has sought to work with the third sector.

There is no reason to suppose that the NGOs are or should be above the law. In the north, NGOs utilizing public funds are subject to the law of the land as well as oversight of their activities by other NGOs. Any organization in the public arena using either public or private funds to address public requirements needs to be accountable to the public.

Scholars have noted that NGOs often do not reach the poor and seldom the poorest who are marginalized, dispersed and difficult to reach (Edwards and Hulme 1996; Streeten 1997). Often due to the nature of their projects and the need for demonstrable achievement of targets, as in micro-finance, NGOs usually focus on groups 'above the lowest income decile' (Sanyal 1991: 30).

Experience shows that the record of NGOs in participatory approaches is not as sound as assumed. For instance, GOI and state governments have, even if cautiously, sought the involvement of NGOs in JFM and a number of NGOs have responded. However, the NGOs addressing basic needs have normally been more effective than those engaged in 'generating' people's participation in programmes such as JFM (Tiwary 2003).

Neither is it true that all NGOs are simultaneously into the business of advocacy and policy initiation or change. Indeed, as Karaborni's (1995) study shows, although NGOs may be engaged in more than one activity, most of them in the countries of the south are involved in service delivery and capacity building. Arya (1999) has indicated that it is only the experienced, stable and mature NGOs that are in a position to provide policy inputs. Further, as the experience of Myrada and Urmul suggests, a combination of advocacy and collaboration is possible, especially in non-sensitive social sector (Uvin et al. 2000); this may especially be possible because in India, NGOs may often be engaged in pursuing not so much policy reform as the implementation of existing but partially implemented or unimplemented law/programme. The assumption that NGOs pursue multiple objectives appears to be neither an accurate description of fact nor a justifiable moral prerequisite for the functioning of NGOs.

Lawani's (1999) study of 140 NGOs elicits that almost all NGOs identify and work in one main field; in Solapur district, he found that more than two-thirds of the NGOs were engaged in service delivery. As noted earlier this chapter focuses upon the relationship between GOs and NGOs engaged in service delivery at the district level.

Finally, the development process in India is far from being dependent on aid transfers from the north. Comprehensive studies in this regard are hard to come by. However, an examination of the inflow of foreign funds to NGOs working in rural development, the sector receiving the largest amount of foreign funds, clarifies the point. In the year 2000–01, NGOs in the Rural Development sector received Rs 5.47 billion (Ministry of Home http://www. fcraforngos.org/intro.htm) whereas, the budget of the Ministry of Rural Development for 2002–03 (for which figures are available at http://rural.nic.in/Budgetframe. htm) exceeded Rs 182 billion; that is, the total inflow of foreign aid for rural development through the NGOs is less than 3 per cent of the budget outlay of the Ministry of Rural Development. Tandon (In Kudva 2005) estimates the total inflow of government funds to NGOs in all sectors to be Rs 40 billion in 1999–2000, less than 4 per cent of the Central Plan Outlay of the Union budget of Rs 1,052 billion for the year.

278   Public Sector Reforms in India

Thus, it would appear that in the case of India, the assumptions on which barriers to collaboration between GOs and NGOs are proposed do not hold good.

As noted in an earlier section, since the 1990s, globally there has been a growing trend of collaboration between state and NGOs in the delivery of services (Alsop 1998; Clark 1995; Streeten 1997). In the context of developing countries, Sanyal (1991: 31) appeals to NGOs to forsake their 'autonomy fetish' thus underlining the need for government-collaboration: 'just as development does not trickle down from the top, pushed by the state alone, it cannot effervesce from the bottom, initiated by NGOs alone. The state and NGOs must work together and include market institutions in their joint effort to alleviate poverty.' The reasons for collaboration between GOs and NGOs in service delivery have also been widely debated. From the churning have emerged a not uncontested set of reasons for partnership between the state and the Third sector. Viewed through the framework developed by Gidron et al. (1992), the relationship is seen as essentially collaborative with the state and the NGOs supplementing and complementing each other.

The strength of governments flow from their authority, command over resources, elaborate machinery and reach. The state brings many positive elements to the partnership with NGOs. First, only the state can provide a constructive policy framework in which effective partnerships between GOs and NGOs may be formed (Streeten 1997; Sanyal 1997). Second, whether directly or indirectly, the government is the main source of NGO resources—financial or technical—either directly or through bi-lateral and multi-lateral aid (Arya 1999; Streeten 1997). Third, replication, scaling up and mainstreaming of NGO innovations and activities can be made possible only through collaboration with the state (Arya 1999; Farrington 1991; Streeten 1997; Uvin et al. 2000). Fourth, the state can play a critical role in developing capacity of local NGOs, especially regarding procedure and methods for getting government grants (Lawani 1999: 245). Fifth, collaborating with government can also help NGOs acquire legitimacy (Arya 1999).

Among the identified strengths of local NGOs are: thorough knowledge of the area and environment, community development experience and experimentation with new forms of service provision. NGOs have greater operational flexibility regarding minimum qualifying standards of personnel, remuneration packages and procedural leeway regarding recruitment.

First, NGOs can assist GOs in improving delivery of services either by complementing government's role in remote areas, substituting it or by bringing specialized technical skills to the partnership (Arya 1999; Lawani 1999). Second, they may facilitate replication of innovations and alternative approaches to development (Arya 1999; Farrington 1991). Third, NGOs collaborating with GOs may induce institutional reforms—transparency, bottom-up planning and accountability. Fourth, NGOs can contribute grassroots knowledge to policy debates (Streeten 1997).

Fifth, NGOs with an extensive local presence can serve 'as brokers or catalysts, linking families and communities with the institutions of the wider society' (Streeten 1997: 198). Sixth, NGOs can play an important role in training and capacity building programmes. Seventh, advocacy related to issues of social change—legislated upon but unfulfilled—can be best undertaken by NGOs, for example, PDS, health, women's and children's welfare. At times it may be possible to combine service delivery and social advocacy within the governmental policy framework. A case in point, is the provision of low-cost sanitation and promoting scavengers' rehabilitation in Tamil Nadu (Centre for Rural Technology 1997).

DANGER OF CO-OPTATION?

The question whether GOs and NGOs are too close for comfort, arises if there is a conflict of interest based on either ideology, methodology or objectives. There is little evidence to suggest that NGOs occupied in service provision to deserving and needy populations and GOs engaged in the identical or similar tasks are ideologically distinct. Regarding methods and approaches, not only are GOs and NGOs not expected to follow identical processes, NGOs are encouraged and expected to innovate and disseminate innovations. From the policy perspective also, GOs and NGOs in the area of service delivery are not competing with each other for resources; indeed, they are working to achieve common objectives.

Is it desirable for NGOs and GOs to work independently if it results in neglect of deserving target groups, duplication of effort, wastage of scarce resources, stifling of initiative and innovation, inefficiency and ineffectiveness? In the Indian context the answer can only be a firm 'No'. For we find that collaboration between NGOs and GOs at the cutting edge may help them to transcend their constraints, employ each other's strengths to negate weaknesses and serve to strengthen society. Working together would not only help GOs and NGOs to employ each other's strengths, to negate their weaknesses, but also strengthen society. Therefore, the above analysis indicates that strong reasons exist for collaboration between GOs and NGOs at the district level.

COLLABORATIVE RELATIONSHIPS: A TYPOLOGY

By acknowledging the need and desirability of GO–NGO collaboration, this paper does not for a moment prescribe either interference in the NGOs' activities by GOs or the co-optation of the former by the latter. Collaboration between GOs and NGOs need not translate into a marriage of the organizations. The objective of GO–NGO collaboration is to nullify each other's limitations in the interest of improved delivery of services. The extent of collaboration would depend upon the need for collaboration (Farrington 1991); and the need for collaboration may vary from time to time.

Indeed, based on this principle it is possible to propose a range of collaboration types between NGOs and GOs.

(1) *Primary* A primary collaborative relationship between GOs and NGOs is ad hoc, based on the needs of the project, and lasts for the duration of the project or crisis. They are dependent not so much on policy, guidelines or joint resolutions but upon the nature of the problem, personality of the principal actors and urgency of the situation. At present, most collaborative relations at the district level belong to this category. A ready example is collaboration between district administration and NGOs in the event of a natural disaster. The collaboration is characterized by sporadic interaction over the short term, with minimal commitment of resources, and based on the need to solve a problem or a crisis.

(2) *Secondary* In secondary collaboration, the main aim is a basic stability in interaction to preclude duplication of development investment in the same geographic or technological area. For instance, NGOs involved with micro-finance may not require much assistance from GOs; however, by indicating their area of operation they can help the DO to redirect micro-finance initiatives and schemes by public sector banks and District Rural Development Agency (DRDA) in other villages or blocks of the district. Similarly, information about progress of the micro-finance schemes can also help the DO not only to monitor the scheme comprehensively but also to

plan for potential investments in the coming years. Periodic interaction, minimal commitment of funds, and strengthening of organizational capacities for better planning and implementation of service delivery characterize this type of collaboration.

(3) *Supplementary* In this type of collaboration, NGOs provide assistance in delivery of a service or good that a GO may be unable to provide comprehensively or vice versa. The setting up of counselling centres ('Santwana') for women in distress in Karnataka is one such example (Economic Survey of Karnataka 2002–03). The collaboration is characterized by regular interaction over a short period, small commitment of resources and one party, usually the NGO, provides an additional service in a programme.

(4) *Complementary* Collaboration takes place when NGOs provide a service in an area not serviced by the GO; NGOs provide one segment of a programme; or, GO helps to replicate an innovation or initiative developed by an NGO. A case in point is the establishment of child labour rehabilitation schools through close collaboration with NGOs (Child Labour in India). The collaboration is characterized by regular interaction over a long period, large commitment of resources, with one party providing a key missing service in a programme.

(5) *Partnership* In a partnership, a GO and NGO join forces to design and provide a new service. An example is the setting up of a mobile medical service in remote forest areas of Paschim Medinipur

District in West Bengal in 2004. The collaboration
is characterized by regular interaction over a long
period, large commitment of resources, with both
parties jointly providing either a new service or an
old service in an improved way.

The essential features of the typology may thus be sum-
marized in tabular form:

TABLE 9.1 A Typology: Collaboration between GOs and NGOs

Type of Collaboration	Frequency of Interaction	Commitment of Resources	Period	Need
Primary	Periodic	Nil	Long term	Share information to plan and assess
Secondary capacity	Irregular	Minimal	Project Period	Share information and skills to improve
Supple-mentary	Regular	Some	Short term	One side adds to existing service
Comple-mentary	Regular	Large	Long term	One side provides missing service
Partnership	Regular	Large	Long term	Jointly provide a service

This typology does not envisage water-tight compart-
ments; there may be overlapping areas and one NGO
may simultaneously be engaged in more than one type of

collaborative arrangement with more than one GO, and vice versa. It is noteworthy that the typology is based not on possible collaborative relationships but existing ones. Categorization facilitates an appreciation of the range of options available for GOs and NGOs and underlines that commonality of objectives demand collaboration but not necessarily always on the same terms. A common element of all five types is that they are based on joint decisions.

In this regard, as noted by Brinkerhoff (1999), formal instruments such as agreements and charters are necessary to facilitate both partnership and joint-project implementation and lead to more sustainable relationships between the state and NGOs rather than ad hoc arrangements. Such mechanisms are vital for both stability and sustainability of GO–NGO collaboration; by demarcating parameters of the relationships, they can also prevent state interference and co-optation of NGOs. Further, instruments such as agreements and charters clarify mutual expectations of GOs and NGOs.

Brinkerhoff (1999) states that all partnerships and collaboration-based project implementation require coordination and coordinating hubs. This begs the question: who or which office can serve as the facilitator and coordinator of GO–NGO collaboration at the district level?

ROLE OF THE DISTRICT OFFICER

By statute and by government notification the DO in India, as discussed at considerable length in earlier chapters, is the representative of the governor in the district. As the 'officer in-charge of the district', he/she is also responsible for coordinating the task of the numerous agencies at the district level (Chaturvedi 1987). In most states, he/she is responsible for effective implementation of development programmes and for supervising most of the concerned departments, including those that disburse majority of government aid to NGOs such as Rural Development, Social Welfare and Empowerment, and Health and Family Welfare. As Member Secretary of the District Planning Committee, the DO is intimately involved with the formulation of the district plan that covers all sectors.

The DO is also the only district level functionary with administrative reach down to the village level on the one hand, and to the heads of directorates, departmental secretaries and even the chief secretary of the state on the other. He/she is also either the chairperson or the executive vice-chairperson of a number of multi-agency committees and task forces. Consequently, the DO is often called upon to resolve inter-agency conflict and to coordinate multi-agency programmes from both within the district and from the state head quarters. By tradition, the DO is usually also at the helm of several district level GONGOs, nonprofit organizations, associations or charitable bodies such as the District Red Cross, governing bodies of educational institutions and sports associations; this enables him/her to activate a network, if required, outside the government.

The role of the DO as the chief coordinator and facilitator at the district level, especially in developmental administration, has been emphasized by a variety of committees and personages (Dave 1965; Planning Commission 1984). While addressing the National Conference of Collectors in 2005 the Prime Minister of India observed that despite the growth of the administrative machinery and the PRIs, '... the role of the Collector has only been transformed into a more powerful one of coordinator, facilitator and a person who is responsible for inter-sectoral coordination of various activities....' (Prime Minister's Speech 2005).

Through an analysis of 13 cases from Asia and Africa, Brown and Ashman (1996) illustrate that whether programmes are GO-initiated and NGO-supported or vice versa. Success and sustainability of programmes depends upon ensuring participation of the target population. PRIs, especially Gram Panchayats—the lowest tier—can facilitate participation. The Rural Sanitation project in Midnapore district, initiated in early 1990s, is an instance of collaboration between district administration, NGO (the Ramkrishna Lok Shiksha Parishad) and PRIs that has led to acceptance of sanitation facilities as integral part of a rural house in the district. The DO's role as coordinator and provider of funds, the NGOs role in providing technical inputs and education, and the role of PRIs in mobilizing local support have made the programme a model (UNICEF http://www.unicef.org/india/wes1433.htm).

The above noted features of the office of the DO make him/her the logical choice to serve as the facilitator and coordinator of GO–NGO relationships in a district. The DO has the jurisdictional reach, administrative authority, social standing, access to diverse resources and backward and forward network linkages to facilitate the collaboration between GOs and NGOs for effective service delivery.

At this juncture we are faced with the question: how would the DO facilitate the collaboration of the five types of collaboration between GOs and NGOs? It must be pointed out that the DO is already involved in coordination of GO–NGO activities. During calamity relief operations he/she coordinates Primary collaborative relationships among GOs, NGOs and PRIs within the legal framework; however, he/she may also be called upon to facilitate GO–NGO action by resolving conflicts by dint of personal initiative, leadership and official position. For instance, LEAD, an NGO in Trichi district found strength and support from the collector in liberating and organizing bonded labor in stone quarries (Dasgupta 1997).

Yet as noted by Brinkerhoff (1999), it is formal mechanisms such as agreements and charters that facilitate both partnership and joint-project implementation and lead to more sustainable relationships between the state and NGOs rather than ad hoc arrangements. Such formal mechanisms are necessary to ensure stability and sustainability of the GO–NGO collaboration; by demarcating parameters of the relationships they can also prevent state interference and co-optation of NGOs. Further, instruments such as agreements and charters clarify expectations of both GOs and NGOs.

However, only a few programme guidelines issued by the central or the state governments—as in case of watershed management programmes, micro-finance and family welfare—create fora for interaction and bases for collaboration between GOs, NGOs, PRIs and other organizations. By and large there is a paucity of formal mechanisms that could institutionalize collaboration and render it a sustainable process.

The DO is authorized to develop formal mechanisms at the district level to facilitate collaboration among NGOs and GOs. This may take several forms: (a) The DO may establish Coordination Committees at the district level based on the type of service delivered such as RD, H and FW, SW, W & C and so forth. These committees, comprising NGOs, GOs concerned, and representatives of PRIs and municipal bodies could jointly develop action plans, implement and/or review progress of programmes, and solve inter-agency problems. Although, few instances of this type of committee may be found in some districts in the field of Rural Development and Health and Family Welfare. (b) Joint Action Committees may also be set up on the basis of programmes and projects. This type of committee may be found in many districts for such fields as the National Programme for the Control of Blindness or Mental Health. (c) The DO may in consultation with NGOs and GOs develop standardized formats for agreements on the basis of which the two parties may enter into collaboration. (d) The DO may also set up a system of periodic meetings for facilitating GO–NGO collaboration. Finally, (e) the DO may facilitate collaboration by setting up and maintaining databases that could be utilized by GOs and NGOs to improve service delivery.

However, even though the DO is authorized to develop formal mechanisms in a district, lack of state-wide policy intervention would lead to much experimentation with form and little lasting substance. The instruments developed by one DO may not last beyond his/her tenure in the district. To ensure institutionalization of the DO's role in facilitating sustainable GO–NGO collaboration it is necessary, therefore, that the state government issue policy guidelines for the establishment of formal mechanisms.

At present, only a few programme guidelines issued by the central or the state governments—as in case of watershed management programmes, micro-finance and family welfare—create fora for interaction and bases for collaboration between GOs, NGOs, PRIs and other organizations. By and large at the point of programme implementation, there is a paucity of formal mechanisms that could institutionalize collaboration and render it a sustainable process. Therefore, to facilitate GO–NGO collaboration at the district level, a policy framework needs to be developed by the state or the central governments.

CONCLUSION

In fine we confront the initial questions: Is collaboration among GOs and NGOs at the district level in India necessary and desirable for effective service delivery? If so, how may it be achieved?

The above analysis indicates that GO–NGO collaboration may acquire the character of a principal-agent relationship;

however, liberalization of NGO funding by GOs, lack of restrictive stipulations and escalating diversification of NGO funding sources detract from the danger. For both GOs and NGOs, the wages of working in isolation are sub-optimal service provision and wastage of resources.

Therefore to answer our initial questions, we may conclude that in the Indian context GO–NGO collaboration for public service delivery at the district level is both necessary and desirable for maximum coverage of the population and optimum resource use. Collaboration can result in mutual reinforcement, heightened programme/ project effectiveness, and improved and sustainable service delivery. However, there is no one best way of GO–NGO collaboration.

Based on existing practices, the chapter presents a typology of collaborative relationships as options of bases for GOs and NGOs to join forces upon. The typology emphasizes that under conditions of resource constraint, common objectives and widespread need demand GO–NGO collaboration at the cutting edge; yet collaboration may not always be on the same terms. In all five types of collaborative relationships envisaged, the DO may play a key role as a facilitator due to his/her central role and mandate. However, while opening up the possibilities of GO–NGO collaboration facilitated by the DO it is also vital that the state or central governments develop a policy framework that promotes and helps institutionalize stable collaborative relationships at the district level for effective delivery of public services.

Note

1. In the first, views of NGOs are heard but not necessarily acted upon;
   the second is a formal relationship based on receipt of remuneration
   by NGOs for performing specified tasks; and the third is based on
   equality.

Chapter Ten

Looking Ahead ...

THE OPENING years of the much-celebrated new millennium have witnessed the effect of reform initiatives undertaken in India at the beginning of the previous decade. Their impact on the economy has received widespread attention and led to much self-gratulation within the country and even a little clapping of hands outside. True, the loosening of the license-permit regime and the unshackling of the market have unleashed energies of the private sector with far-reaching impact upon the production and provision of goods and services. A wide variety of services and goods, ranging from telecommunications to cement—erstwhile solely provided or regulated by the state—have become easily available in the market.

Yet, despite the hoopla of an information technology-led booming economy and the hyperbole surrounding India's almost-achieved status as an economic 'superpower,' the benefits of the new prosperity, enjoyed primarily by the urban middle class and the rural elite, are slow in trickling down to those most in need—the poor, particularly in rural areas. According to NSS data, at the turn of the century, the per capita daily expenditure of over 87 per cent of the rural population was Rs 30 or below (Sagar 2006). While applauding the expansion of the private sector, it is necessary to remember that only those with money are welcome in the market. The fundamental services that contribute to quality of life often cannot be accessed by those without purchasing power. Therefore, it is the responsibility of the state to provide such public goods and services.[1] Although not a novel inference, this is true and central to our purposes here.

The undeniable responsibility of the state in providing public goods and services to the vast majority of the population in India draws attention to the wide-ranging reforms of the public sector and demands an assessment of their impact upon the service delivery machinery at the cutting edge. The impact of the four broad forces of reform on the manner in which the state provides these services at the district level has been discussed at length in Chapter four. While the thrust upon decentralization has not merely restructured the service delivery system and brought in several quasi-state and non-state actors, forces of marketization have introduced new modes of transacting the business of government such as outsourcing, user fees, contractualization, and public-private partnerships. Further, administrative reforms have emphasized right-sizing, process simplification and introduction of ICT for speedier service delivery; while a host of new external mechanisms for accountability constantly goad the system towards more responsible action. The focal point of this combination of reforms is on improved service delivery to the citizen customer.

The first requirement, however, is to redefine the work of grassroots level government agencies. It is common in government to speak of state activities in terms of implementation of programmes and schemes, of working for the uplift of society, of meeting plan and budgetary targets, of performance expenditure. Such ambiguous functional labels seldom clarify what state action means to those at the receiving end of government programmes. It matters little whether we look at: a child attending, or not attending, a primary school; a pregnant woman receiving, or not receiving, an immunization shot at a health sub-centre; or, a victim of theft lodging, or not being able to lodge, a First Information Report in a police station. These instances beg two simple questions: what did each receive, or not receive? At what cost?

The obfuscation of the end product of state action is further enhanced by appeals to vacuous idealism. Thus, civil servants for long have been exhorted to sympathize with the people they are meant to serve, especially the poor. Let there be no doubt that citizen customers prefer speedy service to sympathy; idealism, after all, is best expressed in action not words. Therefore, a fundamental need is to recast state action in terms of products and services and its 'beneficiaries' as citizen customers, and to reorient individuals in the government machinery to perceive themselves as professional service providers. This recognition would help re-orient the role of the government in service delivery, to focus upon not merely processes but also on their immediate output and final outcome and to measure performance.

The forces of reform also highlight the need to re-engineer processes and institutions for service delivery at the district level. The re-engineering of processes attempted thus far has in most instances been piecemeal and driven by individual rather than systemic initiative. Following the recognition of the products and services offered by the state to its citizen customer, a wide-ranging review of processes and procedures at the district level and below needs to be undertaken as a matter of policy. This requires clarity of objectives, appropriateness of process selection, and a consistent commitment to standardization at each stage.

The institution central to the state service delivery mechanism in the district is the office of the district officer (DO). The evolution of this office over the ages has been discussed at length in Chapter Three. Not only has the office of the DO adapted itself to the new challenges posed before it and the added responsibilities, it has emerged as the one integrative office that serves the central, state and local governments during times of both normalcy and crises. Social sector regulation and development, system maintenance through regulation and development promotion are three areas of responsibilities of the DO that require him/her to take on the role of the administrator—leader. DOs across the country have been reinventing themselves to take on their new role which require them to manage knowledge, create a vision, plan strategically, design and redesign new and old systems, build teams, coordinate, facilitate and monitor performance of service delivery in the district. Their roles as coordinators and facilitators are of particular significance due to three reasons: their mounting responsibilities; the increasingly consensual nature of decision making; multi-agency activities; and the expanded role of non-state actors in service provision at the grassroots.

However, the state needs to acknowledge and act to recast the new role of the DO as the administrator–leader. If the claim of the citizen customers on basic public services is to be met, if their entitlements are to be honoured, if the service delivery is to be effective and efficient, if an acceptable degree of uniformity of public satisfaction is to be ensured, the state must take steps towards institutionalizing the new role of the DO and bringing about the changes discussed above in district level service delivery system. This would require policy modification and statutory initiative that enables stable, systemic changes. Both the central government and the state governments have a crucial role to play, the former as the prime mover and the latter as the principal actor. Without doubt, the final call on improving service delivery to citizens at the cutting edge is that of the state.

Note

1. In an earlier chapter we have seen the wide variety of public goods and services provided by government either directly or indirectly at different levels within a district.

Acronyms

ADM	Additional District Magistrate
ARC	Administrative Reforms Commission
DA	District Administration
DFID	Department of Foreign and International Development (UK)
DO	District Officer
DPEP	District Primary Education Programme
FGO	Foreign Government Organization
GO	Government Organization
GOI	Government of India
GONGO	Government-operated Non-governmental Organization
H&FW	Health and Family Welfare
I&CT	Information and Communication Technology
IPO	International Public Organization
LGB	Local Government Body
NGO	Non-government Organization
NNGO	Northern Non-governmental Organization
NPA	National Policy Agenda

PPP	Public Private Partnership
PRI	Panchayat Raj Institutions
PWD	Public Works Department
RD	Rural Development
SCS	State Civil Service
SC&ST	Scheduled Castes and Scheduled Tribes
SHSDP	State Health Systems Development Project
SIDA	Swiss International Development Agency
SJE	Social Justice and Empowerment
SNGO	Southern Non-governmental Organization
SW	Social Welfare
W&CC	Women and Child Care

Appendices

APPENDIX 1

Sections of the Office of the Collector and District Magistrate, Paschim Medinipur, W. Bengal (2005)

1. Establishment
2. General
3. Nezarath
4. Pool Vehicles
5. Election
6. Excise
7. Motor Vehicles
8. National Child Labour Project
9. Sarva Siksha Abhiyan
10. Land Acquisition
11. Revenue Munshikhana
12. Refugee Relief
13. Judicial Munshikhana
14. Normal Relief
15. Cinema Licence
16. Census
17. Jails and Probation
18. Forms and Stationery

19. Treasury
20. Compensation
21. Refugee Relief and Rehabilitation
22. District Record Room
23. Tank Improvement
24. Certificate
25. Freedom Fighter Cell
26. Library
27. Citizenship Registration and Passport
28. Panchayat and Rural Development
29. Health and Family Welfare
30. Development and Planning
31. Social Welfare
32. Integrated Child Development Scheme
33. Literacy and Immunization Mission
34. Minority Affairs
35. Public Grievance Cell
36. Arms Licenses and Explosives
37. Municipal Affairs including DUDA
38. Vigilance
39. Office of District Registrar
40. BCW (including SC/ST Development and Finance Corporation)
41. Food and Supplies

Appendix 2

Other State Government Offices at the District Headquarters, Paschim Medinipur, W. Bengal (2005)

1. Additional Registrar, Cooperative Societies
2. Animal Resources Development (including Veterinary)
3. Agricultural-Mechanical
4. Agricultural Income Tax
5. Agricultural Marketing

6. Agri-Irrigation
    (i) Agri-Irrigation, Midhapore Division
    (ii) Agri-Irrigation, DPAP
7. Agriculture
8. Commercial Taxes
9. District Industries Centre
10. Education
    (i) District Inspector of Schools (SE)
    (ii) District Inspector of Schools (Pry)
    (iii) Primary School Council
    (iv) District Mass Education Extension
    (v) District Physical Education Office
    (vi) Regional office of Board of Secondary Education
    (vii) Regional office of H.S. Council
    (viii) District Social Education Office
11. West Bengal State Electricity Board
    (i) Superintending Engineer
    (ii) Zonal Manager
12. Employment Exchange
13. Forest
14. Fire Station
15. Fisheries (Including Fish Farmers Development Agency)
16. Food and Supply
    (i) District Controller Food and Supplies
    (ii) Essential Commodities Supply Corporation
    (iii) Weights and Measures
17. Consumer Forum
    (i) Consumer Affairs
    (ii) Assistant Controller, Metrology
18. Health
19. Handloom Development
20. Horticulture
21. Industries
22. Information and Culture
23. Irrigation and Waterways

24. Khadi and Village Industries
25. Municipality
26. National Cadet Corps
27. Public Health Engineering
   (i)   Civil
   (ii) Mechanical
28. Public Works Department
   (i)   a) PWD, SE, South-Western Circle Midnapore Division I, Mid
         b) PWD, Midnapore Division II, KGP
   (ii) PWD (Roads), Midnapore Division I
   (iii) PWD (Electricals), Midnapore Division
   (iv) PWD, State Highway Division
29. Police headquarters
30. Soil Conservation
31. Sericulture
32. Small Savings
33. W.B. Seed Corporation
34. Youth Office
35. Zilla Sainik Board

APPENDIX 3

Central Government Offices

1. Food Corporation of India
2. National Highway Authority of India
3. National Informatics Centre
4. Station Manager, SE Railways, Midnapore
5. National Sample Survey Organization
6. Income Tax
7. Post and Telecom
   (i) Sr Superintendent, Post Offices
   (ii) SDO, Telecom
8. Air Force Base, Kalaikunda
9. Divisional Railway Manager

APPENDIX 4

Chart 1: Organogram: Collectorate, Paschim Medinipur, West Bengal

Organogram: Collectorate,
Paschim Medinipur, West Bengal

Appendix 4
Chart 1

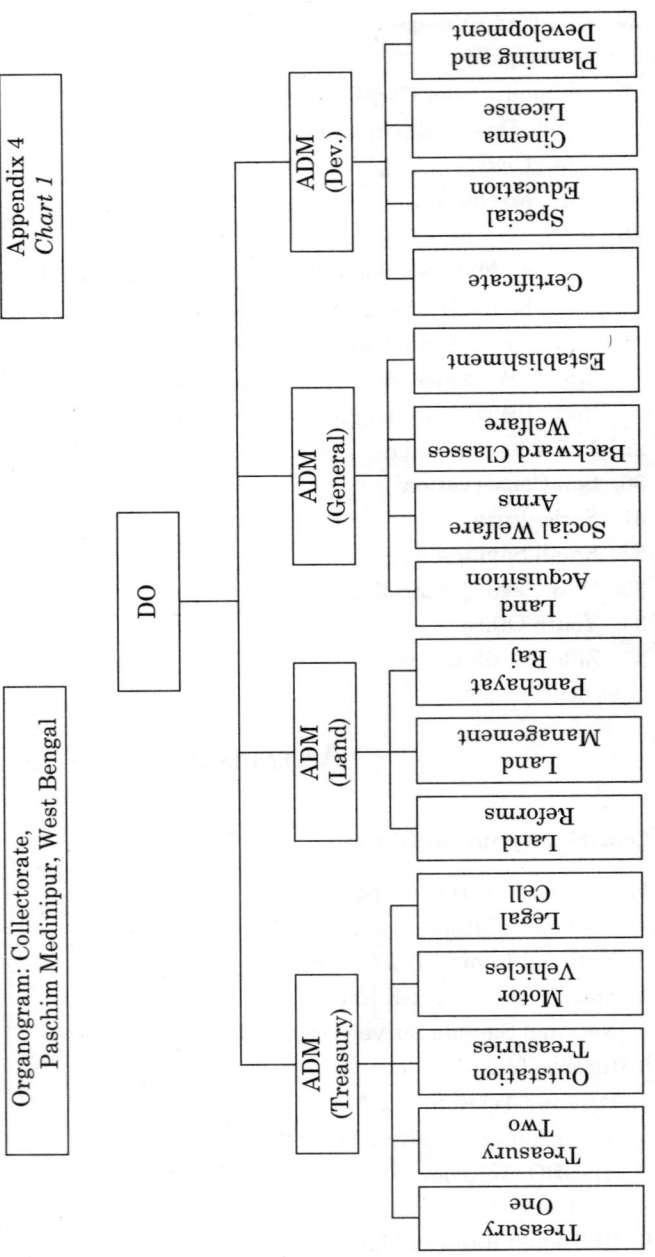

APPENDIX 5

Stakeholder Analysis* for the Collectorate of Paschim Medinipur District

Table A

Sl. No.	Stakeholder	Served at Location	Service Received	Source of Satisfaction
1.	Below poverty line people	Village; Slums	Employment; Assistance in Self-employment; Services	Income; Timely provision of services
2.	Children	Village; Block; Subdivision; District	Variety of services	Timely provision
3.	Women	Village; Block; Subdivision; District	Variety of services	Timely provision
4.	Disabled	Village; Block; Subdivision; District	Variety of services	Timely provision
5.	Complainants	Block; Subdivision; District	Redressal of grievance; Early response	Redressal of grievance; Early response
6.	Scheduled Tribe persons	Village; Block; Subdivision	Certificate; Employment; Scholarships; Other Schemes	Receiving the benefit within a short period
7.	Scheduled Caste persons	Village; Block; Subdivision	Certificate; Employment; Scholarships; Other Schemes	Receiving the benefit within a short period

No.	Stakeholder	Level	Expectations	Response
8.	License/Permit applicants—Individuals	Block; Subdivision; District	License/Permit	Receipt of License/Permit within a short period
9.	License/Permit applicants—Firms	District	License/Permit	Receipt of License/Permit within a short period
10.	Other departments—Local	Block; Subdivision; District	Cooperation; Conflict resolution; Resources	Cooperation; Resolution; Receipt of funds
11.	Other departments—External	District	Verification of personnel; Miscellaneous	Quick verification
12.	NGOs/International Organizations	Village; Block; Subdivision; District	Cooperation; Collaboration; Funds; Respect	Cooperation; Collaboration; Sanction of funds; Respect
11.	Entrepreneurs/Firms	District	Land; Facilitation; Coordination	An early response; Facilitation; Coordination
13.	Employees	Block; Subdivision; District	Financial dues; Respect; Development opportunities	Timely receipt
14.	Suppliers	District	Payment	Timely payment
15.	Government	Across the District	Implementation of law and policy; Periodic performance reports; Feedback	Effective implementation; Timely reporting

Note: * The above list is illustrative not exhaustive.

Bibliography

Acharya, M.K. 1996. 'Changing Role of the District Collector', in D. Sundar Ram (ed.), *Dynamics of District Administration: A New Perspective*. New Delhi: Kanishka Publishers.

Administrative Reforms Commission (ARC). 1966. *Study Team on District Administration*. Delhi: Government of India.

Ahluwalia, M.S. 1998. 'India's Economic Reforms: An Appraisal'. Available at http://planningcommission.nic.in/aboutus/speech/ spemsa/msa018.doc. Accessed on 12 March 2006.

Alsop, Ruth. 1998. *Coalitions and the Organization of Multiple Stakeholder Action: A Case Study of Agricultural Research and Extension in Rajasthan, India*. EPTD Discussion Paper No. 34. Washington, DC: Environment and Produuction Technical Division, International Food Policy Research Institute.

Anheimer, Helmut K. and Lester M. Salamon (eds). 1998. *The Nonprofit Sector in the Developing World: A Comparative Analysis*. Manchester: Manchester University Press.

Arganoff, Robert. 1991. 'Human Services Integration: Past and Present Challenges', *Public Administration Review*, 51 (6): 533–42.

Ariff, M. and T.K.K. Iyer. 1995. 'Privatization, Public Sector Reforms and Development Strategies of Developing Countries', *Asian Journal of Public Administration*, 17 (2): 322–44.

Arora, Ramesh K. and Rajani Goyal. 1996. *Indian Public Administration*, 2nd edition. New Delhi: Vishwa Prakashan.

Arya, Ved. 1999. *Toward a Relationship of Significance: Lessons from a Decade of Collaboration between Government and NGOs in Rajasthan, India.* Network Paper No. 97, London: Agricultural Research and Extension Network, DFID.

Assam Tribune. 2005. 'Farmers Urged to Utilize New Agriculture Web Portal', *Assam Tribune* (Guwahati), 6 July. Retrieved 18 April 2006 from Lexis-Nexis Data.

Austin, David M. 1982. 'Administrative Issues in Improving the Provision of Human Services', in Harold Orlans (ed.), *Human Services Coordination.* New York: Pica Press.

Bailey, Sydney D. 1946. 'Administration in Bengal: The Rowlands Report', *Far Eastern Review*, 15 (6): 90–92.

Bakshi, P.M. 1997. 'Judicial Activism: Some Reflections', *The Administrator*, XLII (2): 5–8.

Basu, Ashok Ranjan. 1990. 'Problem of Coordination and Implementation', in R.D. Sharma (ed.), *District Administration in India: Problems and Prospects.* Delhi: H.K. Publishers.

Beaglehole, T.H. 1977. 'From Rulers to Servants: The ICS and the British Demission of Power in India', *Modern Asian Studies*, 11 (2): 237–55.

Bennis, Warren and Burt Nanus. 1996. *Leaders: The Strategies for Taking Charge.* Cambridge: Harper & Row.

Bhattacharya, G.R. 1977. 'Judicial Activism: Its Message for Administrators', *The Administrator*, XLII (2): 31–42.

Bhattacharya, Mohit. 1975. 'Bureaucratic Response to Emergency: An Empirical Study', *Indian Journal of Public Administration*, XX (4): 846–67.

———. 1987. 'Voluntary Associations, Development and the State', *Indian Journal of Public Administration*, XXXIII (3): 383–94.

———. 1997. 'Rolling Back the State: Public Administration in the Age of Market Supremacy', *Indian Journal of Public Administration*, XLII (3): 245–57.

Bolman, Lee G. and Terrence E. Deal. 2003. *Reframing Organizations: Artistry, Choice, and Leadership.* San Francisco: Jossey-Bass.

Brinkerhoff, Derick W. 1999. 'Exploring State-Civil Society Collaboration: Policy Partnerships in Developing Countries', *Nonprofit and Voluntary Sector Quarterly,* 28 (4): 59–86.

Brown, L. David and Darcy Ashman. 1996. 'Participation, Social Capital and Problem Solving: African and Asian Cases', *World Development,* 24 (9): 1467–79.

Bruner, C. 1991. *Thinking Collaboratively: Ten Questions and Answers to Help Policy Makers Improve Children's Services.* Washington, DC: Education in Human Services Consortium.

Bryson, John M. 1995. *Strategic Planning for Public and Nonprofit organizations.* San Francisco: Jossey-Bass.

Buch, M.N. 1982. 'Who's Afraid of the Big Bad Wolf?', *The Administrator,* XXXVIII (1): 41–48.

Centre for Rural Technology. 1997. 'Social Impact of Technology', in Bhat, Sam and Edwin (eds), *Partners in Progress.* Bangalore: St Paul's Publications.

Chandrashekharan, K.A. 1997. 'What Makes the Best Late 20th Century Public Servant?', *Indian Journal of Public Administration,* XLIII (1): 152–72.

Chatterji, Biswajit and Dilip Kumar Ghosh. 2003. 'Globalization and Decentralized Governance: Reflections of Panchayats in India', *Indian Journal of Public Administration,* XLIX (2): 129–46.

Chatterji, Sushanta. 1997. 'For Public Administration is Judicial Activism Really Deterrent to Legislative Anarchy and Executive Tyranny?', *The Administrator,* XLII (2): 9–24.

Chaturvedi, Anil. 1987. 'Interdependence and Interaction: Inter-organizational Coordination in the District', *Indian Journal of Public Administration,* XX (4): 846–67.

———. 1988. *District Administration: The Dynamics of Discord.* New Delhi: Sage Publications.

Chaturvedi, T.N. 1976. 'Crisis Administration', *Indian Journal of Public Administration,* XXI (1): 172–90.

Child Labor and India. http://www.indianembassy.org/policy/Child_Labor/childlabor.htm. Accessed on 21 March 2006.

Chopra, P.N. (ed.). 1978. *Gazetteer of India: Administration and Public Welfare.* New Delhi: Ministry of Education and Welfare.

Chowdhury, D. Paul. 1987. 'A Critical Appraisal of Voluntary Effort in Social Welfare and Development Since Independence', *Indian Journal of Public Administration*, XXXIII (3): 492–500.

Clark, John. 1995. 'The State, Popular Participation and the Voluntary Sector'. *World Development*, 23 (4): 593–601.

Clayton, Andrew, Peter Oakley and Jon Taylor. 2000. *Civil Society Organizations and Service Provision.* Programme Paper No. 2. Geneva: United Nations Research Institute for Social Development.

Collins, James C. and Jeremy I. Porras. 1997. *Built to Last: Successful Habits of Visionary Companies.* New York: Harper Business.

Comfort, Louise K., Kilkon Ko and Adam Zagorecki. 2004. 'Coordination in Rapidly Evolving Response Systems', *American Behavioral Scientist*, 48 (3): 295–313.

Considine, Mark and Jenny M. Lewis. 2003. 'Bureaucracy, Network or Enterprise? Company Models of Governance in Australia, Britain, the Netherlands, and New Zealand', *Public Administration Review* 63 (2): 131–40.

Constitution of India. Directive Principles of State Policy. http://lawmin. nic.in/ncrwc/finalreport/v1ch3.htm. Accessed on 23 March 2006.

Dasgupta, Subhachari. 1997. 'Government and the People', in Sam Bhat, and Edwin (eds), *Partners in Progress.* Bangalore: St Paul's Publications.

Das, P.K. 2003. 'Development of People's Institutions in Joint Forest Management: Assumptions, Realities, and Opportunities', *Indian Journal of Public Administration*, XLIX (2): 157–70.

Dave, P.K. 1965. 'The Collector, Today and Tomorrow', *Indian Journal of Public Administration*, XI (3): 76–88.

Dayal, Ishwar, Kuldeep Mathur and Mohit Bhattacharya. 1976. *District Administration: A Survey for Reorganization.* Delhi: Macmillan.

Dayal, L. 1988. 'The District Officer in Bihar: Post-Independence Period', in Edwin Eames and Parmatma Saran (eds), *District Administration in India.* New Delhi: Vikas Publications.

D'Cruz, Celine and David Satterthwaite. 2006. 'The Role of Urban Grassroots Organizations and Their National Federations in Reducing Poverty and Achieving the Millennium Development Goals', *Global Urban Development Magazine,* 2 (1), http://www.globalurban.org/GUDMag06Vol2Iss1/d'Cruz%20&%20Satterthwaite.htm. Accessed on 14 September 2006.

Dey, Bata K. 1997. 'Career Management in Government', *Indian Journal of Public Administration,* XLIII (3): 579–95.

Dubashi, P.R. 1965. 'Leadership Role of the Collector', *Indian Journal of Public Administration,* X1 (3): 614–23.

Dwarkadas, R. 1958. *Role of Higher Civil Service in India.* Bombay: Popular Book Depot.

Eames, Edwin and Parmatama Saran. 1989. 'District Officer in India: Agent for Change', *Indian Journal of Public Administration,* XXX (2): 191–206.

Economic Survey of Karnataka. 2002–2003. http://nitpu3.kar.nic.in/planning/ecosur0203/09%20–%20Social%20Infrastructure.pdf.

Edwards, Michael and David Hulme. 1996. 'Too Close for Comfort? The Impact of Official Aid on Nongovernmental Organizations', *World Development,* 24 (1): 961–73.

Farrington, John. 1991. 'Non Governmental Organizations and Government Organizations: Getting Acquainted'. Summary of Main Points. The Asia Regional Workshop on NGOs, Natural Resource Management & Linkages with Public Sector. Hyderabad.

———. 1997. 'The Role of Nongovernmental Organizations in Extension', in Burton E. Swanson, Robert P. Bentz and Andrew J. Sofranko (eds), *Improving Agricultural Extension: A Reference Manual.* Rome: FAO.

Fernando, Jude L. and Alan W. Heston. 1997. 'Introduction: NGOs, between States, Markets, and Civivil Society', *The Annals of the American Academy of Political & Social Science,* 554: 8–20.

Financial Express. 2005. 'Politics and Ballot Boxes Offer Resistance', *Financial Express,* 9 May. Retrieved 18 April 2006 from Lexis-Nexis Data.

312   Public Sector Reforms in India

Financial Times. 2005. 'Rewriting Prescription for Rural Health', *Financial Times*, 1 September. Retrieved 18 April 2006 from Lexis-Nexis Data.

———. 2005. 'Using Mules to Cross the Digital Divide', *Financial Times*, 4 October. Retrieved 18 April 2006 from Lexis-Nexis Data.

Fletcher, A.L. 1965. 'The Collector in the Nineteen Sixties', *Indian Journal of Public Administration*, XI (3): 368–75.

Foresti, Marta, Max Lawson and John Wilkinson. 2002. ' What Role for Civil Society in Monitoring Poverty Reduction Policies?' Discussion Paper Presented at the Round Table 'Role of Civil Society in Monitoring Poverty Reduction Policies, European Evaluation Society Conference, Seville, 9–11 October 2002.

Gandhi, Sailesh. 2005. 'Public Audit Unearths Fraud, Stayed'. *India Together*. http://indiatogether.org/direct/2005/cdr-000075.html, Accessed on 18 February 2006.

Gidron, Benjamin, Ralf M. Kramer and Lester M. Salamon. 1992. *Government & the Third Sector: Emerging Relationships in Welfare States.* San Francisco: Jossey-Bass.

Golman, Daniel. 1998. *Working with Emotional Intelligence.* New York: Bantam Books.

Goold, Michael and Andrew Campbell. 2002. *Designing Effective Organizatioins.* San Francisco: Jossey-Bass.

Government of Gujarat. at http://www.smallindustryindia.com/policies/state/g. Accessed on 21 May 2006.

Gray, Barbara. 1985. 'Conditions Facilitating Inter-organizational Collaboration.' *Human Relations,* 38 (10): 911–36.

Gulick, Luther Halsey and L. Urwick (eds). 1937. *Papers on the Science of Administration.* New York: Institute of Public Administration, Columbia University.

Haldea, Prithwi and Praveen Mohanty. 2003. 'Market-Based Financing for Highways in India'. Working paper 0307. http://www.idfresearch.org/pdf/wp0307.pdf. Accessed on 5 March 2006.

Halpert, Burton P. 1982. 'Antecedents', in David Rogers and David A. Wetten (eds), *Inter Organizational Co-ordination: Theory, Research and Implementation*. Ames: Iowa State University Press.

Haslett, Seth and Michael J. Austin. 1997. 'Service Integration: Something Old and New', in Michael J. Austin (ed.), *Human Services Integration*. New York: The Haworth Press.

Heeks, Richard. 1998. 'Information Age Reform of the Public Sector: The Potential and Problems of IT for India', Working Paper Series on Information Systems for Public Sector Management, Institute for Development Policy and Management, University of Manchester. http://www.man.ac.uk/idpm/idpm_dp.htm#isps_wp.

Heifetz, Ronald A. and Donald L. Laurie. 1997. *Harvard Business Review*, 75 (1): 124–34.

Hindustan Times. 2005. 'Govt. Bid to Privatise Postal Dept. Flayed', *Hindustan Times* (Guwahati), 15 October. Retrieved 18 April 2006 from Lexis-Nexis Data.

———. 2006. 'Successful Partnership in Running of Arunachal PHCs', *Hindustan Times* (Itanagar), 9 April. Retrieved 18 April 2006 from Lexis-Nexis Data.

Hulme, David and Michael Edwards. 1997. 'NGO States and Donors: An Overview', in David Hulme and Michael Edwards (eds), *NGOs, States and Donors: Too Close for Comfort?* New York: St Martins Press.

Huxham Chris and Siv Vangen. 1996. 'Working Together: Key Themes in the Management of Relationships between Public and Non-profit Organizations', *World Development*, 9 (7): 5–17.

Inamdar, N.R. 1987. 'Role of Voluntarism in Development', *Indian Journal of Public Administration*, XXXIII (3): 384–93.

Jaamdar, S.M. 1998. 'Economic Liberalization and the Changing Role of the State in the Context of Relief and Rehabilitation', *The Administrator*, XLVIII (1): 37–51.

Jalan, Bimal. 2005. *The Future of India: Politics, Economics, and Governance*. Delhi: Viking Penguin.

Jennings, Edward, T. Jr. and Drake Krane. 1994. 'Coordination in Welfare Reform: The Quest for the Philosopher's Stone', *Public Administration Review*, 54 (4): 341–48.

Jones, L.R., Fred Thompson and William Zumeta. 2002. 'Public Management in the New Millenium: Developing Relevant and Integrated Professional Curricula'. Accessed on 13 February 2007 at http://verdi.unisg.ch/org/idt/ipmr.nsf/.

Joseph, A. Maurice. 1997. 'State Anti-Poverty Programs: Experiences of an NGO', in Sam Bhat and Edwin (eds), *Partners in Progress*. Bangalore: St Paul's Publications.

Kang, Bhavdeep. 2003. 'Fruits of Dreaming Collectively', *Outlook India. Com*. Accessed on 5 March 2006 at http://www.outlookindia.com/mad.asp?sid=1&fodname=20030922&fname=Making.

Kannan, Ramya. 2004. 'World Bank Approves Rs 502-Crore Loan'. *Financial Times*.

Kapoor, Ilan. 1995. 'Public Sector Management in Development in Developing Countries', Working Paper, Canadian International Development Agency.

Karaborni, Najet. 2005. *NGO/Civil Society Survey Report*. Rome: UNDESA.

Katoch, Rajan. 1995. 'The Impact of Economic Reforms on the Poor in India, in the Context of International Experience, and its Relevance to the Responsibilities of District Officers', *The Administrator*, XL (4): 43–54.

Khera, S.S. 1960. *District Administration in India*. Bombay: Asia Publishing House.

———. 1964. *District Administration in India*. Bombay: Asia Publishing House.

———. 1979. *District Administration in India*. New Delhi: National Publishing House.

Kothari, Rajni. 1987. 'Voluntary Organizations in a Plural Society', *Indian Journal of Public Administration*, XXXIII (3): 433–53.

Kotter, J.P. 1990. 'What Leaders Really Do?', *Harvard Business Review*, 68 (3): 103–11

———. 1996. *Leading Change*. Boston, MA: Harvard Business School Press.

Krishna, Dhirendra. 1988. 'Role of Press in Improving Administration', *Indian Journal of Public Administration*, XXXIV (4): 888–1004.

Krishnamachari, V.T. 1962. *Report on the Indian and State Civil Services and the Problems of District Administation*. New Delhi: Planning Commission of India.

Kudva, Neema. 2005. June. 'Uneasy Relations, the NGOs and the State in Karnataka, India', Paper Presented at the Karnataka Conference, organized by ISEC/Cornell University/ The World Bank, Bangalore, India.

Kumar, Ashok. 2004. 'Computerization of Mandal Revenue Offices in Andhra Pradesh: Integrated Certificate Application'. Accessed on 18 February 2007 at http://unpan1.un.org/intradoc/groups/public/documents/APCITY/UNPAN019009.pdf.

Lawani, B.T. 1999. *Nongovernmental Organizations in Development (Case Study of Solapur District)*. Jaipur: Rawat Publications.

Ledwith, Frank. 1999. 'Policy Contradictions and Collaboration in Community Mental Health Services in Britain', *World Development*, 12 (3): 236–49.

Maheshwari, S.R. 1979. *State Governments in India*. New Delhi: Macmillan.

———. 2000. Public *Administration in India*. New Delhi: Macmillan.

Marshall, P.J. 1997. 'British Society in India under the East India Company', *Modern Asian Studies*, 31 (1): 89–108.

Martens, Kerstin. 2002. 'Mission Impossible? Defining Non-governmental Organization', *International Journal of Voluntary and Nonprofit Organizations*, 13 (3): 271–82.

Marzouk, Mohsen. 1996. 'The Associative Phenomenon in the Arab World: Engine of Democratization or Witness to the Crisis?', in David Hume and Michael Edwards (eds), *NGOs States and Donors: Too Close for Comfort?* New York: St Martin's Press.

Mathur, P.C. 1998. 'Constitutional Panchayats of India: A Radical Innovatory Improvement over the Pre-1993 Developmental PRIs?', in R.P. Joshi (ed.), *Constitutionalization of Panchayat Raj: A Reassessment*. Jaipur: Rawat Publications.

Mencher, Joan. 1999. 'NGOs: Are they a Force of Change', *Economic and Political Weekly,* 24–30 July, 34 (30): 208–86.

Mendiratta, Kavitha and Clay Smith. 2001. 'Advancing Community Organizing Practices: Lessons from Grassroots Organizations in India', Presented as part of the Working Papers series for COMM-ORG: The On-line Conference on Community Organizing and Development, accessed on 23 April 2006 at http://comm-org.wisc.edu/papers2001/mediratta/mediratta.htm.

Menon, N.R. 1997. 'Can Judicial Activism Contribute to a Responsive and Responsible Administration?', *The Administrator*, XLII (2): 25–30.

Milward, H. Brinton, Keith G. Provan and Barbara A. Else. 1993. 'What Does the "Hollow State" Look Like', in Barry Bozeman (ed.), *Public Management: The State of the Art*. San Francisco: Jossey-Bass.

Mintzberg, Henry, Bruce Ahlstrand and Joseph Lampel. 1998. *Strategy Safari: A Guided Tour through the Wilds of Strategic Management*. New York: Free Press.

Mintzberg, Henry. 1983. *Structures in Fives: Designing Effective Organizations*. New York: Prentice-Hall.

Mishra, B.B. 1965. 'The Evolution of the Office of Collector', *Indian Journal of Public Administration*, XI (3): 345–67.

———. 1970. *The Administrative History of India: 1834–1947*. London: Oxford University Press.

Mishra, B.B. 1986. *Government & Bureaucracy in India: 1947–1976*. New Delhi: Oxford University Press.

Mishra, Bimla Kant. 1998. *Indian Administration: An Evolutionary Perspective*. Delhi: Indu Prakashan.

Mishra, Laxmidhar. 1993. 'Role of District Collectors/Deputy Commissioners in Total Literacy Campaign, Management in Government', *Indian Journal of Public Administration*, XXV (2–3): 101–38.

Mohanty, Manoranjan and Anil Kumar Singh. 2001. *Voluntarism and Government: Policy, Programme and Assistance*. New Delhi: VANI.

Mooney, James D. 1953. 'Organization of Public Administration', in Dwight Waldo (ed.), *Ideas and Issues in P.A.: A Book of Readings*. NY: McGraw-Hill.

Moore, M. 1993. 'Good Government? Introduction', *IDS Bulletin*, 24 (1): 1–6.

Mukhopadhyay, Asok. 1983. 'Administrative Accountability: A Conceptual Analysis', *Indian Journal of Public Administration*, XXIX (3): 473–87.

———. 1997. 'Changing Role of the District Magistrate', *Indian Journal of Public Administration*, XLIII (3): 696–702.

Mulford, Charles L. and David L. Rogers. 1982. 'Definition and Models', in David A. Rogers and David A. Whetten (eds), *Interorganizational Coordination, Theory, Research and Implementation*. Ames: Iowa State University Press.

Muttalib, M.A. 1987. 'Voluntarism and Development—Theoretical Perspectives', *Indian Journal of Public Administration*, XXXIII (3): 414–32.

Nanavatty, Meher C. 1996. 'Role of NGOs in the Changing Public Management Scene', *Indian Journal of Public Administration*, XLII (1): 48–52.

'National Training Policy', accessed on 23 April 2006 at http://www.lbsnaa.ernet.in/lbsnaa/research/trdc/NTP/NTP01.htm#preamble.

Nawani, N.P. 2005. *District Administration: Theory & Practice*. New Delhi: Publications Division, GOI.

Nayar, P.K.B. 2003. 'Senior Grassroots Organizations in India', *The Journal of Aging Social Policy*, 15 (2/3): 193–212.

O'Looney, John. 1997. 'Marking Progress towards Service Integration: Learning to Use Evaluation to Overcome Barriers', in Michael J. Austin (ed.), *Human Services Integration*. NewYork: The Haworth Press.

Oyugi, Walter O. 2004. 'The Role of NGOs in Fostering Development and Good Governance in Africa with Focus on Kenya', *African Development*, XXIX (4): 19–55.

Padhi, A.P. 1990. 'District Collector as a Coordinator', in R.D. Sharma (ed.), *District Administration in India: Problems and Prospects*. Delhi: H.K. Publishers.

Pai, M.P. 1962. 'The Emerging Role of the Collector', *Indian Journal of Public Administration*, VII (4): 478–86.

Paul, Samual. 2001. *New Mechanisms for Public Accountability.* Bangalore: Public Affairs Centre.

Peters, B. Guy. 1998. 'Managing Horizontal Governmental: The Politics of Coordination', Research Paper. Canadian Center for Management Development. http://www.myschool-monecole.gc.ca/Research/publications/pdfs/p78.pdf. Accessed on 12 March 2006.

Planning Commission, Government of India. 1984. *Report of the Working Group on District Planning,* Planning Commission.

Pomerol, Jean-Charles and Frederick Adam. 2004. 'Practical Decision-Making—From the Legacy of Herbert Simon to Decision Support Systems', Paper Presented at the IFIP International Conference on Decision Support in an Uncertain and Complex World, accessed on 29 March 2006 at http://dsslab.infotech.monash.edu.au/dss2004/proceedings/pdf/64_Pomerol_Adam.pdf.

Potter, David. 1986. *India's Political Administrators: From ICS to IAS 1919–1983.* New Delhi: Oxford University Press.

PRADAN. 1997. 'Overview of Tank Rehabilitation Program', in Bhat, Sam and Edwin (eds), *Partners in Progress.* Bangalore: St Paul's Publications.

Pradhan, Bimbadhar. 2002. Marketing in the District Administration. Master's Dissertation Submitted at School of Public Policy, IDD, University of Birmingham. http://www.idd.bham.ac.uk/research/dissertations/2001–2002/B%20Pradhan.pdf. Accessed on 21 February 2006.

Pradhan, Gireesh. 2001. 'Civil Service Reform in Independent India: An Overview', *Indian Journal of Public Administration,* XLVII (4): 726–51.

Prime Minister's Speech. 1964. *Indian Journal of Public Administration,* X (4): 595–96.

Prime Minister's Speech. 2005. National Collectors' Conference. 20 May 2005. http://pmindia.nic.in/speech/content.asp?id=130. Accessed on 23 February 2006.

Provan, Keith G. and H. Brinton Milward. 2001. *Public Administration Review,* 61 (4): 414–23.

Purushottam, P.W. 1996. 'New Challenges and Changing Approaches in District Adminsitration: A Fresh Perspective on Concept,' in D. Sundar Ram (ed.), *Dynamics of District Administration: A New Perspective*. New Delhi: Kanishka Publishers.

Quinn, Robert E., Sue R. Faerman, Michael P. Thompson and Michael R. McGrath. 2003. *Becoming a Master Manager: A Competency Framework*. New York: Wiley & Sons.

Radha. 1997. 'Leading Where Angels Fear to Tread', in Sam, Bhat and Edwin (eds), *Partners in Progress*. Bangalore: St Paul's Publications.

Raghavan, P. 1982. 'Camp Approach in District Administration', *The Administrator*, XXVIII (2): 251–66.

Rai, Haridwar and Awadhesh Prasad. 1983. 'Restructuring District Administration in Bihar: Restoration of the Cambellian Idea', *Indian Journal of Public Administration*, XXIX (1): 53–67.

Rai, Haridwar. 1965. 'The Changing Role of the District officer', *Indian Journal of Public Administration*, XI (3): 376–88.

Rajan, M.A.S. 1990. 'District Plans Monitoring and the Poor—An Administrator's Viewpoint', *Indian Journal of Public Administration*, XXXVI (1): 209–27.

Ramachandran, Padma. 1996. *Public Administration in India*. New Delhi: National Book Trust.

Rao, C. Arjuna. 1981. 'Challenges to District Administration in 1970s', *The Administrator*, XXVI (1): 27–40.

Ray, Jacob D. and Daisy Dharmaraj. 1997. 'A Movement against Shrimp Industry', in Sam, Bhat and Edwin (eds), *Partners in Progress*. Bangalore: St Paul's Publications.

Reddy, Y. Venugopal. 1988. 'Decentralizing Administrative Machinery for Development Needs: A Case Study of Andhra Pradesh', *Indian Journal of Public Administration*, XXXIV (1): 34–35.

Report of the Expenditure Reforms Commission. 2000. New Delhi: Ministry of Finance, Government of India.

Riggs, Fred. 1980. 'The Ecology and Context of Public Administration: A Comparative Perspective', *Public Administration Review*, 40 (2): 107–15.

Robinson, Mark. 1992. 'Privatising the Voluntary Sector: NGOs as Public Sector Contractors?', in David Hume and Michael Edwards (eds), *NGOs States and Donors: Too Close for Comfort?* New York: St Martin's Press.

Rossi, Robert J., Kevin J. Gilmartin and Charles W. Dayton. 1982. *Agencies Working Together.* London: Sage Publications.

Roy, Sanjit (Bunker). 1987. 'Voluntary Agencies in Development', *Indian Journal of Public Administration*, XXXIII (3): 454–81.

Sadasivan, S.N. 1968. 'The Problem of District Level Coordination in Madras', *The Administrator*, XIII (2): 116–38.

———. 1979. *Aspects of Kerala's Administration.* Trivandrum: IIPA, Kerala Regional Branch.

———. 1985. 'Towards a Theory of District Administration', *Indian Journal of Public Administration*, XXXI (3): 729–44.

———. 1988. 'District Level Coordination in India', in S.N. Sadasivan (ed.), *District Administration (A National Perspective).* New Delhi: IIPA.

Saigal, K. 1977. 'Management of Rural Development Programmes at the District Level', *Management in Government*, IX (3): 2703–16.

Sanjay, Alok Kumar and Vivek Gupta. 2003. 'Gyandoot: Trying to Improve Government Services for Rural Citizens in India', http://www.egov4dev.org/gyandoot.htm. Accessed on 9 April 2006.

Sanyal, Biswapriya. 1991. 'Antagonistic Cooperation: A Case Study of NGOs, Government and Donor Relationships in Income Generating Projects in Bangladesh', *World Development*, 19 (10): 1367–80.

Sarason, Seymour B. and Elizabeth M. Lorentz. 1998. *Crossing Boundaries: Collaboration, Coordination and the Redefinition of Resources.* San Francisco: Jossey-Bass.

Saxena, K.B.C. 2005 . 'Towards Excellence in E-governance', *International Journal of Public Sector Management,* 18 (6): 498–513.

Saxena, Naresh C. 2004. 'Improving Delivery of Programmes through Administrative Reforms', Paper prepared for the National Advisory Council.

Saxena, P.K. 2003. 'Civil Service Reforms in India', Paper presented at the EUROPA Conference in Delhi. UNPAN021217.pdf.

Sen, Siddharta. 1998. 'The Nonprofit Sector in India', in Helmut K. Anheier and Lester M. Salamon (eds), *The Nonprofit Sector in the Developing World: A Comparative Analysis*. Manchester: Manchester University Press.

Senge, Peter M. 2000. *The Fifth Discipline: The Art & Practice of the Leadership Organization*. New York: Currency Doubleday.

Seth, J.L. 1990. 'District Administration in Uttar Pradesh', in R.D. Sharma (ed.), *District Administration in India: Problems and Prospects*. Delhi: H.K. Publishers.

Shafritz, Jay M. and Albert C. Hyde. 1987. *Classics of Public Administration*. Chicago: The Dorsey Press.

Sharma, B.B.L. and A.D. Tripathi. 1989. 'District Collector and Decentralized Health Planning', *Indian Journal of Public Administration*, XXXV (4): 887–903.

Sharma, Sudesh Kumar. 1985. 'Revisitation of Panchayti Raj', *Indian Journal of Public Administration*, XXXI (3): 745–54.

Simon, Herbert A., Donald W. Smithburg and Victor A. Thompson. 1961. *Public Administration*. New York: Alfred A. Knopf.

Singh, Abhimanyu. 1986. 'Changing Role of the District Officer', *Indian Journal of Public Administration*, XXXII (2): 251–67.

Singh, Akhileshwar Prasad. 1994. 'The Changing Role of Collector and D.M.', *Indian Journal of Political Science*, 55 (2): 166–72.

Singh, Bhupinder. 1985. 'Tribal Administration: A Critique', *Indian Journal of Public Administration*, XXXI (3): 878–901.

Singh, Mohinder. 2003. 'Transparency in Function: Vital for Gram Panchayats', *Indian Journal of Public Administration*, XLIX (2): 767–72.

Singh, Montek. 2005. 'Organizations should be Involved in Quality Testing', *The Hindustan Times*, 23 December. Accessed on 18 April 2006 from Lexis-Nexis Data.

Singhvi, G.C. 1983. 'District and State Administration: A New Leadership Role of the IAS', *Indian Journal of Public Administration*, XXIX (4): 808–20.

Sinha, B.K. 1998. 'How Not to Implement a Rehabilitation Project—Prescriptions from Koel Karo', *The Administrator*, XLIII (1): 105–30.

Sivaraman, B. 1962. 'The Collector and Panchayati Raj', *Indian Journal of Public Administration,* VIII (4): 489–99.

———. 1965. 'The Collector of the Seventies', *Indian Journal of Public Administration,* XI (3): 624–36.

Sooryamoorthy, R. 2002. 'The NGO Sector: Lessons From Kerala', *Indian Journal of Public Administration,* XLVIII (2): 165–82.

Srivastava, D.C. 1989. 'Minimum Wages in Agriculture—A Critique', *The Administrator,* XXXIV (2): 1–20.

Streeten, Paul. 1997. 'Non-governmental Organizations & Development', *The Annals of the American Academy of Political & Social Science,* 554: 193–210.

Sudan, M.L. 1985. 'Administrative Reforms Required at the Block and District Levels in the Context of Rural Development', *Indian Journal of Public Administration,* XXXI (3): 755–76.

Sudan, Randeep. 1993. 'Proposals to Confer Magisterial Powers on Police Officers in Andhra Pradesh: A Critical Appraisal', *The Administrator,* XXXVIII (3): 89–110.

Sundaram, P.S.A. 1997. 'Recent Initiatives for Administrative Reforms in India', *Indian Journal of Public Administration,* XLIII (3): 553–59.

Teisman, Cicert R. and Erik-Hans Klijn. 2002. 'Partnership Arrangements: Governmental Rhetoric or Governance Scheme?', *Public Administration Review,* 62 (2): 194.

The Economic Times. 2002. 'Staff Crunch Hits Fire Service Department', *The Economic Times* (Hyderabad), 27 October. Retrieved 18 April 2006 from Lexis-Nexis Data.

———. 2002. 'They Cleared the Red Tape to Make the System Work', *The Economic Times,* 31 December. Retrieved 18 April 2006 from Lexis-Nexis Data.

———. 2003. 'State Lifts Ban on Recruitment in Prison Dept', *The Economic Times* (Pune), 27 August. Retrieved 18 April 2006 from Lexis-Nexis Data.

The Hindu. 2001. 'Govt. "Helpless", Commuters Disappointed', *The Hindu* (Chennai), 17 November 2001. Retrieved 18 April 2006 from Lexis-Nexis Data.

The Hindu. 2003. 'Kerala Govt. Abolishes 3,510 Posts', *The Hindu* (Thiruvanantapuram), 23 November 2003. Retrieved 18 April 2006 from Lexis-Nexis Data.

———. 2004. 'More Tourism Projects for City', 10 August 2004. *The Hindu,* Retrieved 18 April 2006 from Lexis-Nexis Data.

———. 2005. 'E-Governance Reaches Five Villages in Kundagol District', *The Hindu*, 23 November 2005. http://www.hindu.com/2005/11/23/stories/2005112312180300.htm. Accessed on 7 March 2006.

———. 2005. 'Govt. Staff Planning Signature Campaign', *The Hindu*, 13 November. Retrieved 18 April 2006 from Lexis-Nexis Data.

———. 2005. 'Hike in Water, Sewerage Charges Mooted', *The Hindu*, 14 March 2005. Retrieved 18 April 2006 from Lexis-Nexis Data.

———. 2005. 'Panchayats Told to Finish Works Under Swachacha Grama Scheme', *The Hindu* (Bangalore), 11 August 2005. Retrieved 18 April 2006 from Lexis-Nexis Data.

———. 2005. 'Plea to Lift Ban on Recruitment', *The Hindu* (Chennai), 23 May. Retrieved 18 April 2006 from Lexis-Nexis Data.

———. 2005. 'Research Not Benefiting Farmers: Panel 2005', *The Hindu* (Bangalore), 4 October. Retrieved 18 April 2006 from Lexis-Nexis Data.

The President's Address. 1964. *Indian Journal of Public Administration,* X (4): 595–96.

The Statesman. 2003. 'Govt. to Redeploy Staff in Excise', *The Statesman*, 29 July 2003. Retrieved 18 April 2006 from Lexis-Nexis Data.

The Times of India. 2002. 'Health Policy Pops Privatization Pill', *The Times of India* (New Delhi), 8 May. Retrieved 18 April 2006 from Lexis-Nexis Data.

———. 2003. 'Entry Fees for State Parks', *The Times of India* (Kolkata), 18 March. Retrieved 18 April 2006 from Lexis-Nexis Data.

Tiwary, Manish. 2003. 'NGOs in Joint Forest Mangement and Rural Development', *Economic and Political Weekly*, 38 (51–52): 5382–90.

Toulmin, Stephen. 1994. 'The Role of Transnational NGOs in Global Affairs', Global Policy Forum: OECD. http://www.globalpolicy.org/ngos/role/globalact/state/2000/1122.htm. Accessed on 21 March 2006.

Tremblay, Reeta C. 2001. 'Globalization of Indian Federalism', *Indian Journal of Public Administration*, XLVII (2): 208–21.

Uvin, Peter, Pankaj S. Jain and L. David Brown. 2000. 'Think Large and Act Small: Towards a New Paradigm for NGO Scaling Up', *World Development*, 28 (8): 1409–20.

Valsan, E.H. 2005. 'Leadership in Public Administration for Poverty Alleviation Programmes: A Conceptual Approach'. http://www.adb.org/Documents/Books/Role-of-Public-Administration/session1.pdf. Accessed on 13 February 2007.

Vayunandan, E. and Dolly Matthew. 2001. Organisational Permeability with Information and Communication Technology: Opportunities and Challenges. unpan1.un.org/intradoc/groups/public/documents/EROPA/UNPAN014262.pdf. Accessed on 18 April 2006.

Venkataraman, R. 1986. 'The Role of Bureaucracy in Development Administration in India', *Management in Government*, XVIII (1): 273–80.

Vicki, Eaton Baicr, James G. March and Harald Sautren. 1994. 'Implementation and Ambiguity', in David McKevitt and Alan Lawton (eds), *Public Sector Management: Theory, Critique and Practice*. London: Sage Publications.

Vigoda, Evan. 2002. 'From Responsiveness to Collaboration: Governance, Citizens and the Next Generation of Public Administration', *Public Administration Review*, 62 (5): 528–37.

Wils, Frits. 1996. 'Scaling up, Mainstreaming and Accountability: The Challenge for NGOs', in Michael Edwards and David Hume (eds), *Beyond the Magic Bullet:Ngo Performance and Accountability in the Post-Cold War World*. New York: St. Martin's Press.

Wise, Charles R. 1990. 'Public Service Configurations and Public Organization Design in the Post Privatization Era', *Public Administration Review*, 50 (2): 141–55.

Woodruff, Philip. 1954. *The Men Who Ruled India: The Guardians*. London: Vintage/Ebury.

Index

About the Author

Chandan Sinha is currently serving as Project Director and ex-officio Special Secretary with the Department of Health and Family Welfare, Government of West Bengal, India. A member of the Indian Administrative Service (IAS), he studied English Literature at St Stephen's College, Delhi, and Public Administration and International Management at the University of South Carolina and the Maxwell School of Citizenship and Public Affairs, Syracuse University. An astute analyst of public management in India, Sinha has published papers in peer-reviewed journals and books. He has also conducted a survey of training programmes and courses in the areas of Public Administration and Public Policy in some of the leading universities in the United States including Syracuse, Harvard, Princeton, Duke and Columbia.

The author may be contacted at sinhamailbox@gmail.com